Gospel Light's

REALLY BIG BOOK
OF BIBLE GAMES

More Than 250 Fun Games for Ages 6 to 12

CD-ROM INCLUDED

- Bible learning, life application and recreational games
- Outdoor, indoor, water and large-group games
- Discussion questions

Reproducible!

D1613999

Gospel Light

HOW TO MAKE CLEAN COPIES FROM THIS BOOK

You may make copies of portions of this book with a clean conscience if

- you (or someone in your organization) are the original purchaser;
- you are using the copies you make for a non-commercial purpose (such as teaching or promoting your ministry) within your church or organization;
- you follow the instructions provided in this book.

However, it is ILLEGAL for you to make copies if

- you are using the material to promote, advertise or sell a product or service other than for ministry fund-raising;
- you are using the material in or on a product for sale; or
- you or your organization are not the original purchaser of this book.

By following these guidelines you help us keep our products affordable.

Thank you,

Gospel Light

Editorial Staff

Founder, Dr. Henrietta Mears • **Publisher Emeritus,** William T. Greig • **Publisher, Children's Curriculum and Resources,** Bill Greig III • **Senior Consulting Publisher,** Dr. Elmer L. Towns • **Senior Managing Editor,** Sheryl Haystead • **Senior Consulting Editor,** Wesley Haystead, M.S.Ed. • **Senior Editor, Biblical and Theological Issues,** Bayard Taylor, M.Div. • **Editor,** Jim Hawley • **Art Directors,** Lenndy McCullough, Christina Renée Sharp, Samantha A. Hsu • **Designer,** Christina Renée Sharp

Some of these games originally published in *The Big Book of Bible Games* (Ventura, CA: Gospel Light, 1996), *The Big Book of Bible Games #2* (Ventura, CA: Gospel Light, 2002) and *The Big Book of Bible Skills* (Ventura, CA: Gospel Light, 1999).

Scripture quotations are taken from the *Holy Bible, New International Version®*. Copyright © 1973, 1978, 1984 by International Bible Society. Used by permission of Zondervan Publishing House. All rights reserved.

© 2006 Gospel Light, Ventura, CA 93006. All rights reserved. Printed in the U.S.A.

How to Use This Book

If you are a teacher or small-group leader in any children's program (Sunday School, second hour, midweek, etc.),

1. Read "Games Overview" (p. 8) and "Game Leader Ideas" (p. 9) to get an understanding of the purpose and goals of *The Really Big Book of Bible Games.*

2. Look at the Contents and then skim through this book to get an idea of the kinds of games that are provided.

3. As you prepare a lesson for the program in which you serve, use the Contents and the Indices to choose games in this book that will complement your students' understanding of the lesson. Photocopy game pages for your own ease of use in leading games.

If you are the children's pastor,

1. Follow the directions in numbers one and two above.

2. At the beginning of each teaching term, refer to the scope and sequence of the curriculum being used in your children's program and use the Contents and the Indices to locate games in this book that will enrich students' understanding of the lessons. Photocopy the needed pages and provide them to teachers and small-group leaders at least one week prior to the lesson.

3. Consider providing a copy of *The Really Big Book of Bible Games* for each classroom for students to use as a general Bible study resource.

The Really Big Book of Bible Games

Contents

Recreational Games

Indices

Games Overview

Games are a great way for children to have fun—and learn! *The Really Big Book of Bible Games* is your one-stop resource for all the games you'll likely ever need for elementary children, grades 1 thorough 6. Here's a quick overview of the book's three sections:

1. Bible Learning Games

There are three types of games in this section. The first, Bible Skills, are games and activities that help children learn basic Bible skills, such as locating Bible references, listing Bible books in order, or identifying Bible divisions. Next, Bible Story Review games are fun games that can be used with any Bible story. These games help children remember important facts or concepts of any story. Lastly, Bible Verse Memory games also may be used with any Scripture passage. These easy-to-play games can be used anytime to help children remember life-changing Bible truths.

2. Life Application Games

The second section has more than 175 games organized under 17 topics designed to give quick game options for many Bible lessons. Scripture passages are included with each game, and discussion questions with familiar practical tie-ins to children's lives. Many games include options for adapting for younger or older children, a fresh twist on a familiar game, or how to play an indoor game outside.

3. Recreational Games

Sometimes you just want to have fun! We've got you covered with more than 35 games indoor, outdoor, large group, water just about any game you might need for special events, camps, sleepovers, or any fun-filled event. Let the fun begin!

Leading Games Step-by-Step:

1. Energy-level indicator:

Low: Mostly staying in seats with little movement
Medium: Some walking or movement
High: Lots of running, movement and noise

2. Location indicator:

In: Games that need walls, electricity, or furnishing
Out: Games that need outdoor settings, such as water games, or larger area
In/Out: Games that could work either way; Options or Game Tips give info for making the switch from one to the other.

3. Materials

Common supplies are listed without quantity needed, but unique or specific items do include number you'll need. Just so you know, Optional activity materials are not listed here.

4. Preparation

What you'll need to do before kids arrive, if anything. Prep time of a minute or less are not included here. Measuring playing areas, setting up obstacle courses or writing index cards are examples of preparation that may be needed. Sketches of game layouts are provided to make your game prep quick and easy.

5. Lead the Game

Numbered steps allow you to lead the game with ease! Bold print are used with statements or questions you impart to kids. Sketches show what the game looks like with kids.

6. Options and Game Tips

Many games have options for adapting the game for a variety of situations. But if you don't see an option, be creative and try your own idea! Game Tips are helps for handling situations that may come up while playing games—ways to help you become a better Game Leader Person.

7. Discussion Questions

See Leading a Good Discussion on page 10 for tips on asking the Discussion Questions included with the Life Application Games in this book.

Game Leader Ideas

Here are some additional tips to help you become a better game leader!

Creating a Playing Area

Before leading a game, give yourself ample time to set up the game area. You may have little space in your classroom for a game area, so consider alternatives: outdoors, a gymnasium or a vacant area of the church from which sound will not carry to disturb other programs. **Once you have chosen the area, plan what you will need:**

- Will you need to move furniture?

- Will you need to mark boundaries? Use chalk or rope outdoors; yarn or masking tape works indoors. (Remove masking tape from carpets after each session.)

- How much space will you need? Carefully review the game procedures to plan what amount and shape of space will be needed.

From time to time, take stock of your classroom area. Is it time to remove that large table or unused bookshelf? Should the chairs be rearranged or the rug put in a different place? Small changes in arrangement can result in more usable space!

Forming Groups or Teams

To keep students' interest high and to keep cliques from forming, use a variety of ways to determine teams or groups:

- Group teams by clothing color or other clothing features (wearing a sweater, wearing tennis shoes, etc.).

- Place equal numbers of two colors of paper squares in a bag. Students shake the bag and draw out a square to determine teams.

- Group teams by birthday month (for two teams, January through June and July through December); adjust as needed to make numbers even.

- Group teams by the alphabetical order of their first or last names.

- Group teams by telling them to stand on one foot: those standing on a right foot form one team; those standing on a left foot form the other team.

After playing a round or two of a game, announce that the person on each team who is wearing the most (red) should rotate to another team. Then play the game again. As you repeat this rotation process, vary the method of rotation so that students play with several different students each time.

Leading the Game

Explain rules clearly and simply. It's helpful to write out the rules to the game. Make sure you explain rules step-by-step.

Offer a practice round. When playing a game for the first time with your group, play it a few times just for practice. Students will learn the game's structure and rules best by actually playing the game.

Dealing with Competition

For younger children (and for some older ones) competition can make a game uncomfortable—especially for the losers. If your group is made up primarily of younger children, consider making a game more cooperative than competitive: give a special job (calling time, operating the CD player) to a child who is out; have the winning team serve a snack to the losing team; rotate players so that no one remains on the winning or losing team.

Guiding Conversation

Using guided conversation turns a game activity into discovery learning! Make use of the discussion questions provided in the curriculum throughout game time. You might ask a game's winners to answer questions or to consult with each other and answer as a group. You might discuss three questions between the rounds of a game or ask a question at the beginning of the round, inviting answers when the round is over.

Walk straight and then turn left.

Leading a Good Discussion

A good discussion requires leaders to listen as much as—or more than—they speak. However, encouraging others to speak up can be difficult. The following questions are commonly asked about making a discussion truly productive, and not an unfocused, rambling monologue.

How do I keep the discussion on track?

Use the discussion questions provided with the Life Application Games to focus on children's personal experiences. When Bible truths relate to daily life, interest in the discussion will grow.

How do I get the discussion back on track if a digression occurs?

If significant interest is shown in the new topic and it has real value and if you feel able to guide this new topic for discussion, then you may decide to stay with the new issue. Otherwise, use questions to bring attention back to the original topic. Move on to a new question, restate your question or rephrase it if the group did not understand what you asked.

If an outside interruption catches the group's attention, acknowledge it as matter-of-factly as possible, and then restate the question being discussed. You may also want to summarize some of the key points already made in the discussion.

What do I do when no one says anything or when kids are giving "pat" answers?

If you've asked a thought-provoking question, assume that kids need at least a few moments to think. Be silent for a bit (no more than 20-30 seconds), and repeat or rephrase the question. If you still get no response, give your own answer to the question and move on.

If silence is a recurring problem, evaluate the questions you ask. Are they too vague? Threatening? Do they require knowledge the kids do not have? Are the answers too obvious?

If the questions are fine, evaluate your response to what the group says. Are you unwilling to accept answers if they differ from what you consider to be the correct responses? Do you tend to always improve the students' answers? Work to create a climate of openness and trust.

Finally, add some variety to your approach in asking questions:
• Have students write their answers on paper. This allows them time to organize their thoughts. Then invite them to read what they wrote.

• Divide the class into smaller groups. You may ask all groups the same questions, or assign different questions to each group. Invite volunteers to share the answers for their groups.

The same suggestions apply when students are giving only "pat" answers. The root problem is often the same in either case: The discussion participants do not feel secure sharing what they really think.

Leading a Child to Christ

One of the greatest privileges of serving in children's ministry is to help children become members of God's family. Pray for the children you know. Ask God to prepare them to understand and receive the good news about Jesus and to give you the sensitivity and wisdom to communicate effectively and to be aware as opportunities occur.

Because children are easily influenced to follow the group, be cautious about asking for group decisions. Instead, offer opportunities to talk and pray individually with any child who expresses interest in becoming a member of God's family—but without pressure. A good way to guard against coercing a child to respond is to simply ask, "Would you like to hear more about this now or at another time?"

When talking about salvation with children, use words and phrases they understand; never assume they understand a concept just because they can repeat certain words. Avoid symbolic terms that will confuse these literal-minded thinkers. Here is a simple guideline:

1. God wants you to become His child. Why do you think He wants you in His family? (See 1 John 3:1.)

2. Every person in the world has done wrong things. The Bible word for doing wrong is "sin." What do you think should happen to us when we sin? (See Romans 6:23.)

3. God loves you so much that He sent His Son to die on the cross to take the punishment for your sin. Because Jesus never sinned, He is the only One who can take the punishment for your sin. (See 1 Corinthians 15:3; 1 John 4:14.)

4. Are you sorry for your sin? Tell God that you are. Do you believe Jesus died for your sin and then rose again? Tell Him that, too. If you tell God you are sorry for your sin and believe that Jesus died to take your sin away, God forgives you. (See 1 John 1:9.)

5. The Bible says that when you believe Jesus is God's Son and is alive today, you receive God's gift of eternal life. This gift makes you a child of God. (See John 3:16.) This means God is with you now and forever.

There is great value in encouraging a child to think and pray about what you have said before responding. Encourage the child who makes a decision to become a Christian to tell his or her parents. Give your pastor and the child's Sunday School teacher(s) his or her name. A child's initial response to Jesus is just the beginning of a lifelong process of growing in the faith, so children who make decisions need to be followed up to help them grow.

Bible Learning Games

Bible Skills

Bible Ball Toss

Bible Skill ▸ Put Bible Books in Order

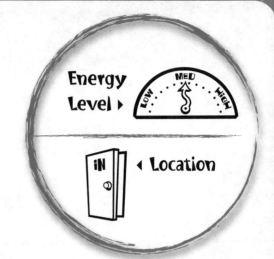

Energy Level ▸ LOW MED HIGH

iN ◂ Location

Materials
Bibles, ball.

Preparation
Make copies of the contents page in a Bible.

Lead the Game

1. **It is easier to find places in the Bible when we know the order of the books. Let's practice saying the books of the Bible in order:**

2. Distribute copies of the Bible contents page for students to review.

3. Students stand in a circle. Toss a ball to a student and say "Genesis." Student who catches the ball says, "Exodus" and tosses the ball to another student. Continue tossing the ball and saying the names of the books of the Bible in order until all the books have been named. Repeat game as time permits.

Options

1. For younger students, limit the number of books named, gradually adding more books as students are able to recall them.

2. For older students, form more than one circle and have circles compete to see which circle can say the names of Bible books in a specific division of the Bible, such as minor prophets.

Game Tip
If students are unfamiliar with books of the Bible, ask students to read aloud the names, referring to Bible contents pages. As students say names, print names of books in order on large sheet of paper. Display paper where all students can see it. Each student chooses a book to find in his or her Bible. After playing several rounds of the game, remove the paper.

Book Guess

Bible Skill ▸ Identify and Spell Books

Materials

Bibles, chalkboard and chalk or large sheet of paper and marker.

Energy Level ▸ LOW MED HIGH

iN ◂ Location

Lead the Game

1. Lead students to play a game similar to Hangman. On chalkboard or a large sheet of paper draw blank lines for each letter of a Bible book.

2. Students guess letters of the alphabet. Print correct letters on the appropriate blank lines. Print an incorrect letter to the side of the blank lines and print one letter of the word "Bible." Students try to guess and find the correct book in their Bibles before the word "Bible" is completed. Student who correctly guesses the word secretly chooses a different book of the Bible and draws lines for other students to guess. Continue as time permits.

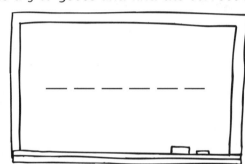

Game Tips

1. This game will help students begin to recognize and spell the names of Bible books so they will become confident when reading these names, and will help them to recognize and find books in their Bibles.

2. If playing this game with only a specific section of the Bible, introduce the game by making a comment such as, **Today we are going to play a game to find out more about the second group of books in the Bible. These books are called the books of History because they tell the story of how God brought Abram's descendants back to their homeland many years after Abram died. The books also tell about how the people sometimes obeyed God, but more often did not obey God.** Referring to contents page in their Bibles, students take turns reading aloud the names of books of History (Joshua, Judges, Ruth, 1 Samuel, 2 Samuel, 1 Kings, 2 Kings, 1 Chronicles, 2 Chronicles, Ezra, Nehemiah, Esther). Students may also locate each book.

Gospel Puzzles

Bible Skill ▸ Locate References: New Testament

Energy Level ▸ LOW MED HIGH

◂ Location — IN

Materials

Bibles; index cards; blue, red, purple and green markers; scissors.

Preparation

Print in the colors indicated the following references on separate index cards: blue—Matthew 21:1-3; Mark 11:1-3; Luke 19:28-31; red—Mark 11:4-6; Luke 19:32-34; purple—Matthew 21:9; Mark 11:9-10; Luke 19:38; John 12:13; green—Matthew 21:15,16; Mark 11:18; Luke 19:39-40. Cut each card into two puzzle pieces as shown in sketch.

Lead the Game

1. Count the number of students present. Ask students to close eyes while you hide puzzle pieces, making sure to hide one piece for each student. (Use all the cards of one color before using another color.) Participate in this activity yourself if needed to create an even number of players. Each student finds a hidden puzzle piece and then finds the student holding the matching puzzle piece. Students read the Bible passage in their Bibles.

2. Invite students to read their Bible passages aloud. **In what section of the Bible are these verses found?** (The Gospels.) **What is similar about all the (blue) passages?** (They tell what Jesus told His disciples to do.) **How are the (blue) passages different from each other? Each of the Gospels tells the story of Jesus' life in a slightly different way. The people who wrote these books included different information about the same events. When we read the different accounts of each event, we get a better idea of everything that happened.**

3. Repeat activity as time permits, hiding different puzzle pieces or hiding the same pieces again.

Mark 11:4-6

Mixed-Up Books

Bible Skill ▸ Identify Bible Divisions: New Testament

Energy Level ▸

iN ◂ Location

Materials

Bibles, index cards, marker, masking tape.

Preparation

Print names of the books of the New Testament on index cards, one name on each card. On separate cards print the names of the main divisions of New Testament books (Gospels, History, Letters, Prophecy). Make at least two sets of cards or one set of book and main division cards for every 10 students. Tear masking tape into 3-inch (7.5-cm) strips, making at least 56 strips of tape. Place strips on a table or chair where they can easily be reached and removed by students.

Lead the Game

1. Mix up the book cards you prepared. One at a time, hold up the cards. Students tell which division each book is   part of. **All the stories in the Bible—from Adam and Eve to the very end—fit together to show us God's great plan for our world and for our own lives. In the New Testament part of the Bible we read about the coming of the King and Savior God promised to send and all the great things that happened after God kept His promise.**

2. Divide class into at least two teams of no more than 10 students each. Teams line up in single-file lines at opposite side of classroom from where the masking-tape strips have been placed. Place a set of mixed-up book cards facedown in a pile on the floor next to the first student on each team. Tape a set of main division cards on the wall across from each team near the masking-tape strips. Leave room under each card for book cards to be taped.

3. At your signal, the first student in each line takes a book card, runs to the division cards, grabs a piece of tape and tapes the book card to the wall, below the correct division card. Student returns to his or her team and tags the next student in line. Play continues until all the cards are taped onto the wall under the correct category.

Game Tip

If your students are not familiar with the New Testament divisions, give each team a copy of the contents page from a Bible.

People Scrabble

Bible Skill ▸ Locate References: New Testament

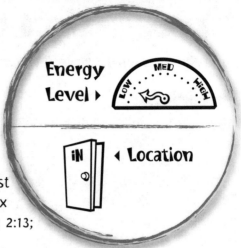

Energy Level ▸

iN ◀ Location

Materials

Bibles, graph paper, pencils, index cards.

Preparation

On a sheet of graph paper, outline a grid with at least 20 vertical and horizontal columns. On separate index cards, print these Bible references: Matthew 1:18; 2:1; 2:13; Luke 1:5; Luke 1:19; 1:26-27; Luke 2:1; 2:8; 2:10; 2:46.

Lead the Game

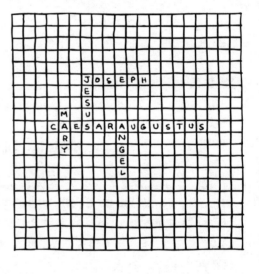

1. **What do you think are some of the most famous stories in the Bible?** Volunteers tell opinions (stories of creation, Noah's ark, David and Goliath, Jesus' miracles, etc.). **Why are these stories so famous?** (People like hearing them. The stories are exciting. They tell about important things.) **Some stories in the Bible are so important they are written about more than once. The events that happened during the time when Jesus was born and grew as a child are described in several different books of the Bible. What are the books called which tell the stories of Jesus' life?** (The Gospels: Matthew, Mark, Luke and John.) **Let's practice finding references in these books.**

2. Group students into pairs or trios. Place index cards facedown near grid. At your signal each group chooses an index card and finds the Bible reference printed on the card. First group to find reference reads verses to discover one or more names of people. Group prints name(s) of person on graph paper, trying to connect the names together as in Scrabble (see sketch).

3. If a group is unable to connect a name, group selects another Bible reference, trying to add the first name to the grid later on. Groups continue taking turns until all references have been read or until there is no more space to add names onto the grid. (Names may be written more than once.) **What are some of the events these names remind you of?** Volunteers answer.

Game Tip

If you do not have any graph paper, draw grid on large sheet of paper.

Promise Search

Bible Skill ▸ Locate References: Old Testament

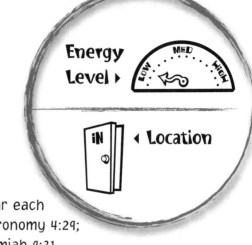

Energy Level ▸

iN ◀ Location

Materials

Bibles, large sheet of paper and markers or chalkboard and chalk.

Preparation

Print these Bible references on paper or chalkboard in random order, leaving room to write near each reference: Genesis 8:22; Exodus 15:13; 20:12; Deuteronomy 4:29; Joshua 1:9; 1 Samuel 26:23; 2 Chronicles 7:14; Nehemiah 9:31.

Lead the Game

1. **God's promises are written about in the Bible.** Show paper you prepared. **Each of these Bible verses tells about a promise God makes or something we can depend on God to do. The verses are all in the first two sections of the Bible. What are these sections called?** (The books of Law and History.)

2. Group students in pairs or trios. Assign each pair or trio a Bible reference you prepared. Group finds and reads assigned verse, choosing a key word from the promise described in the verse. To help groups choose key words ask, **Which word is most important in this verse? Why? Which word helps you understand the main idea of the verse?**

Joshua 1:9

3. Volunteer from each group takes a turn to say a word that rhymes with the key word. Other students try to guess the key word. Volunteer says additional rhyming words as needed. When the key word has been identified, group reads verse from Bible and writes key word near the correct reference.

Game Tip

Repeat the books of Law and History (Genesis through Esther) with students before dividing class into pairs or trios. You may also suggest students refer to contents page in front of Bibles if they need help locating a specific Bible book.

Prophet Talk

Bible Skill ▸ Identify Bible Divisions:
Old Testament—Prophecy

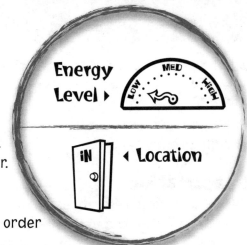

Energy Level ▸ LOW MED HIGH

iN ◂ Location

Materials

Bibles, chalkboard, chalk and eraser or large sheet of paper and marker, children's music CD and player.

Preparation

Print the books of the Major and Minor Prophets in order on large sheet of paper or chalkboard.

Lead the Game

1. Students sit on the floor in a circle. Volunteer reads book names aloud from chalkboard or paper. **God sent many messengers, called prophets, to His people. These prophets spoke or wrote what God wanted His people to know. They gave many warnings to obey God and many promises about the great King and Savior who was coming! We can read these messages in the books of Prophecy. The first five books of prophecy are called the "Major Prophets" because these books are longer than the "Minor Prophets," 12 smaller books that complete the Old Testament.**

2. Students play a game of Hot Potato, passing the eraser or marker while music plays. When music stops, say either "Major Prophets" or "Minor Prophets." Student with eraser erases a book of division you name (if using marker, student completely marks out the name).

3. Students repeat books of Major and Minor Prophets together, reciting erased or marked out books from memory. Continue playing until all books are erased or marked out and students can repeat all the books in each division from memory.

Game Tips

1. If you have a student who is reluctant to play the game, invite him or her to start and stop the music and name the division.

2. Sit in the circle with the students. Students enjoy getting to know their teachers while playing games together.

Walk and Talk

Bible Skill ▸ Identify Bible Divisions: New Testament

Energy Level ▸ LOW MED HIGH

iN ◂ Location

Materials

Bibles, butcher paper, tape, markers, children's music CD and player.

Preparation

Cover tabletop with butcher paper. Draw lines to divide the paper into sections, one section for each student. Print names of divisions of the New Testament in separate sections, repeating divisions as needed ("Gospels," "History," "Letters," "Prophecy").

Lead the Game

1. **The New Testament tells about how God's promise to send a Savior came true and how God's keeping of His promise makes a difference in our world.**

2. Students walk around table holding Bibles while you play music. When you stop the music, each student puts a hand on one section on the paper and then refers to the contents page in his or her Bible to find a book in the New Testament from the division named in the section. After all students have found books in their Bibles, each student says the division and book names aloud. Repeat as time permits.

3. Turn over the butcher paper and tape it to tabletop. Students walk around table while you play song. When you stop the music, call out a New Testament division. Each student writes the name of a book in the division. Play several rounds of the game.

Game Tips

1. Introduce the New Testament sections by explaining, **The word "gospel" means "good news." The four Gospels tell the good news about Jesus. The History book, Acts, tells what God's Holy Spirit did through people who told the good news about Jesus to the rest of the world. The next section of the New Testament is Letters. The Letters were written to encourage people to live as Christians. The last section is Prophecy. This book, Revelation, tells about the future time when Jesus will come back to Earth, and everyone will know He really is the King of kings.**

2. Give each student a copy of a contents page from a Bible to use in playing this game.

Who's Got the Beans?

Bible Skill ▸ Identify Bible Divisions:
Old Testament—Law, History, Poetry

Energy Level ▸ LOW MED HIGH

iN ◂ Location

Materials

Bibles, 10 beans or other small objects for each student, children's music CD and player.

Lead the Game

1. Ask students to open their Bibles to the contents page. **Which books are in the Law division of the Old Testament?** (Genesis through Deuteronomy.) Volunteer reads names of the books of Law aloud. Identify the books of History and Poetry in the same way.

2. Give each student 10 beans. Group students into two equal teams: A and B. (Participate in this activity yourself if needed to balance teams.) As you play music, students move randomly around the room. When you stop the music, each student finds a partner from the opposite team. Call out either A or B. Each student in the named group says the name of a book in one of the first three divisions of the Old Testament (Law, History, Poetry). Student's partner responds by saying the name of the correct division and names another book in the division. (Optional: If students are unfamiliar with books of the Bible, invite them to use contents page in Bibles to find book names.) If division named is correct, first student gives his or her partner a bean. If division named is incorrect, partner gives the first student a bean. Repeat activity as time permits. The object of the game is to have the most beans at the end of the playing period.

Game Tips

1. Coins or uncooked pasta shapes may be used instead of beans.

2. Before playing, briefly review the first three divisions of the Old Testament: **The books of Law tell about the beginning of the world and record God's instructions to His people. The books of History tell how God led His people to a new land and give us stories about their leaders. The books of Poetry are stories, songs, sayings and poems about how great and wonderful God is and how we can live in ways that please Him.** (Optional: Distribute a copy of the contents page from a Bible to each student.)

3. Play several practice rounds to help students become familiar with game procedures.

Bible Learning Games

Bible Story Review

Chair Scramble

Bible Skill ▸ Bible Story Review

Materials

Bibles, paper, markers, large index cards, tape, chairs.

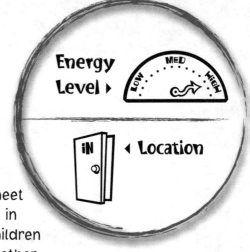

Energy Level ▸ LOW MED HIGH

iN ◂ Location

Preparation

Choose a Bible story students have studied. On a sheet of paper, list true or false statements about events in the Bible story. List one statement for every two children in your group. Letter one index card "True" and another "False." Tape labeled index cards to chairs (sketch a).

Lead the Game

1. Divide class into two equal teams. (If you have an extra student, he or she may read aloud the true or false statements.) Teams sit on floor as shown in sketch. Assign each child a number (sketch b).

2. After teams are seated, leader reads aloud a statement about the Bible story and then calls out a number. The students from each team with that number jump up and run to sit in their team's "true" or "false" chair. The student who sits in the correct chair first scores a point for his or her team. In case of a tie, each team scores a point. Repeat process until all true or false statements have been read. Pause to allow students to correct each false statement.

3. Repeat game as time permits. Ask, **What did you learn about the story?**

a.

True   False

b.

chairs for team 1

team 2   team 1

chairs for team 2

Chopstick Relay

Bible Skill ▸ Bible Story Review

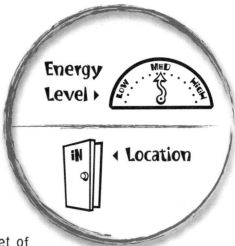

Energy Level ▸

Location ▸ IN

Materials

Bibles, paper, marker, two large bowls, three Chinese take-out food containers, marker, chalkboard and chalk or butcher paper. For each player: Ping-Pong ball or large marshmallow, set of chopsticks.

Preparation

Choose a Bible story students have studied. On a sheet of paper, list true or false statements about events in the Bible story—one statement for every two students. Include several statements which do not relate to the story. (Examples: Ruth was Naomi's daughter-in-law [true]; Ruth and Naomi moved to Egypt [false]; Naomi loved to sew [not in story]). Letter one container "True," one "False," and one "Not in Story" (sketch a). Place an even amount of balls or marshmallows in each bowl. Place containers on table at one side of room and place bowls on the floor across the room.

Lead the Game

1. Divide class into two equal teams. (If you have an extra student, he or she may read aloud the true or false statements and keep score.) Teams line up between bowls and containers as shown in sketch b. Give each player a set of chopsticks.

2. Read aloud a statement about the Bible story and say, "Go!" First player in line uses chopsticks to pick up a ball or marshmallow. He or she then passes ball or marshmallow to next player with chopsticks. Ball is passed most effectively if it rests on top of chopsticks (sketch c). Procedure continues until ball or marshmallow reaches the end of the line. The last player carries the ball or marshmallow with the chopsticks and drops it into the appropriate food container. Player then goes to the front of the line. The first student to put the ball or marshmallow in the correct container scores a point for his or her team. In case of a tie, each team scores a point.

3. Repeat process until all players have had a turn. Record each team's score on chalkboard or large sheet of paper. Ask, **What part of this story is the most important? Why? What did you learn from this story?**

Community Chaos

Bible Skill ▸ Bible Story Review

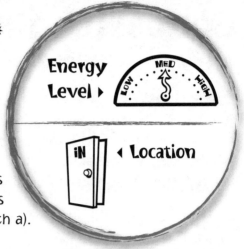

Energy Level ▸

iN ◂ Location

Materials

Bibles, 20 large index cards, marker.

Preparation

Choose a Bible story or Bible memory verse students have studied. List 10 events from the story (or words from verse)—one event (or word) on each card (sketch a). Make two identical sets of cards.

Lead the Game

1. Divide class into two teams. Teams line up as in sketch b. Shuffle both sets of cards together and spread all cards facedown on the floor between teams.

2. Assign each child on one team a city occupation (bus driver, firefighter, police officer, librarian, doctor, barber, teacher, hairstylist, baker, crossing guard, etc.). Assign players on other team the same occupations. To begin play, call out a job description such as "I drive people from one place to another." Each of the two children who have that occupation quickly choose any one of the cards on the floor and brings it back to his or her team. Repeat process by calling out another job description. As children bring cards to their teams, team members try to place their cards in the correct story sequence or word order. If a child brings a duplicate card, player who is called next returns card to pile before choosing a new card. Team which first places all the cards in the correct order wins.

a.

Jesus visited Mary and Martha.	Martha cleaned the house.	Mary talked to Jesus.
Martha became angry.	Jesus loves both Mary and Martha.	Jesus was arrested and crucified.
Mary and Martha were sad and cried.	Jesus rose from the dead.	Jesus died so we could be forgiven

Each person has a special place in God's family.

b.

bus driver
Police officer
barber
grocer
baker

baker
grocer
barber
police officer
bus driver

3. Discuss the Bible story by asking questions such as, **Which of these events was the most important? Why? What did the characters from this story demonstrate? How? What did you learn from this Scripture passage?**

Count Your Cards!

Bible Skill ▸ Bible Story Review

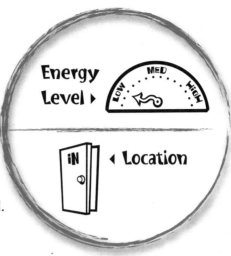

Energy Level ▸ LOW MED HIGH

iN ◂ Location

Materials

Bibles, 30 large index cards, pen, number cube.

Preparation

On each index card, write a true or false statement about one or more Bible stories children have studied.

Lead the Game

1. Place cards facedown in five rows with six cards to a row. Divide group into two teams. Player from first team rolls number cube. He or she counts that number from the top left card across row to the right. Player turns over card (see sketch) and reads statement aloud.

2. Player's team identifies the statements as true or false. If correct response is given, team keeps the card. If incorrect response is given, player replaces the card facedown. (If the statement is false, team must correct the statement in order to gain the card.) Player from second team repeats process, counting from the card which was turned over. Play continues in this manner. When all cards have been collected or time is up, team with most cards wins the game.

Luke preached to the crowd on Pentecost.

Friendly Feud

Bible Skill ▸ Bible Story Review

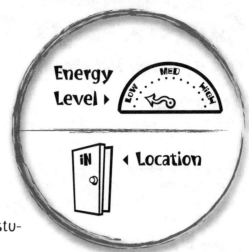

Energy Level ▸

iN ◂ Location

Materials

Bibles, index cards, pen, game bell or noise-maker, whiteboard and marker or butcher paper and marker.

Preparation

On index cards write questions about Bible stories students have studied.

Lead the Game

1. Divide class into two teams. Have them sit in rows or chairs facing each other. Place the game bell on a table between the two rows.

2. First player from each team comes to the table and stands with one hand on the table and one hand behind his or her back. Read aloud the question on the first card. The first person to ring the bell may answer the question for 10 points. If answer is incorrect, the other contestant may give answer, winning five points for his or her team if the answer is correct. If neither contestant gives the correct answer, place card at the bottom of the pile to be asked later. Repeat procedure until all players have had several turns. Keep score on the whiteboard or paper.

3. When game is over ask, **What is the most important thing to remember from this Bible story? Why?**

Fruit Pop

Bible Skill ▸ Bible Story Review

Materials

Bibles, small paper strips, pen, balloons in a variety of colors, large plastic bags.

Preparation

Choose a Bible story students have studied. List 10 events from the story, one event on each strip of paper (see sketch). Roll strips and insert into a balloon. Inflate balloons and tie. Put balloons into a large plastic bag. Make an identical set of balloons for each team of six to eight students. (Optional: Make one set of all orange balloons and label bag "oranges." Make another set of purple balloons and label bag "grapes," etc.)

Lead the Game

1. Divide class into teams of six to eight students each. Give each team a plastic bag with balloons. At your signal, students remove balloons from bag, pop them and put the Bible story events in the correct sequence. (If a child has a negative reaction to popping balloons, allow him or her the choice of not participating, or helping only with the sequencing.)

2. After all teams have put their strips in order, discuss the Bible story by asking questions such as, **Which of these events was the most important? Why? What do you learn about God from this story? Which character showed (kindness)? How?**

Energy Level ▸

iN ◂ Location

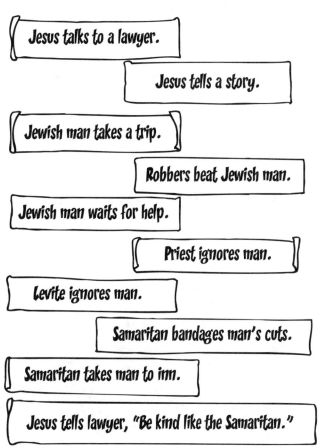

Jesus talks to a lawyer.

Jesus tells a story.

Jewish man takes a trip.

Robbers beat Jewish man.

Jewish man waits for help.

Priest ignores man.

Levite ignores man.

Samaritan bandages man's cuts.

Samaritan takes man to inn.

Jesus tells lawyer, "Be kind like the Samaritan."

Hit or Miss

Bible Skill ▸ Bible Story Review

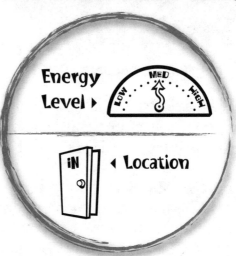

Energy Level ▸ LOW MED HIGH

◂ Location iN

Materials

Bibles, large paper sheet, marker, masking tape, blindfold.

Preparation

Write on the paper 10-15 words that were mentioned in a Bible story studied by the children. Add some words that have nothing at all to do with the story. (See sketch.) Attach paper to wall or bulletin board at children's eye level.

Lead the Game

1. Blindfold a volunteer. At a distance of about 5 feet (1.5 m) turn volunteer around three times and direct him or her toward the paper. Volunteer touches paper with index finger. Remove blindfold. If volunteer "hits" a word by touching it, he or she tells if the word belongs in the Bible story. If the word belongs, volunteer (or class-mate chosen by volunteer) uses the word in a sentence telling information from the Bible story.

2. Repeat process with additional volunteers until all words have been used. Ask, **What is one thing you need to remember about this Bible story or passage? Why?**

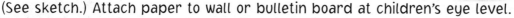

Cornelius prison tree Joppa Gentile Caesarea dream dinner animals soldiers unclean bread sheet Peter angel salvation robbers Jewish

Question Cube

Bible Skill ▸ Bible Story Review

Energy Level ▸ LOW MED HIGH

◂ Location iN

Materials

Bibles, square-shaped box (6x6 inches [15x15 cm] or larger), markers, butcher paper, scissors, whiteboard and marker, tape, glue.

Preparation

If necessary, cover the box with butcher paper. On the sides of the box, letter each of the following words—a different word on each side: "Who?", "What?", "Where?", "When?", "Why?", "Free points!"

Lead the Game

1. Divide class into two teams. Play begins as a volunteer from Team A rolls the question cube. If the word "Why?" lands face up the volunteer must use the word "Why?" in a question about the story. For example, in the story of the Prodigal Son, a question might be "Why did the son want to leave his father's home?"

2. Players on Team B who want to answer the question stand up quickly. The first player who stands may answer. Continue play, alternating which team rolls the cube. For each correct answer, the team is given 10 points. Keep score on a whiteboard. When the game is over say, **You remembered a lot of facts from our story today! What do you learn from this story about a way to love and obey God?**

Game Tip

For younger students or if you think your students will have difficulty coming up with questions, you may want to have a list of questions prepared that can be read by the students.

Quick Draw

Bible Skill ▸ Bible Story Review

Materials

Bibles, slips of paper, pen, box, whiteboard and marker or butcher paper taped to wall and markers.

Energy Level ▸ LOW MED HIGH

iN ◂ Location

Preparation

On separate slips of paper write 10 or more words or phrases from a Bible story students have studied. (Example: Jesus, lawyer, rocks and hills, money, robbers, bruises and cuts, priest, donkey's hooves, Samaritan, inn.)

Lead the Game

1. Divide class into two teams and have each team sit on the floor as far away from each other as possible. Teams each choose one artist and one runner. Place chair between teams (see sketch). Leader stands in front near whiteboard or paper. At your signal, artist from each team runs to the leader, reads word or phrase on a slip of paper that leader is holding and returns to his or her team. Artists quickly draw a picture of the word or phrase, without speaking or drawing letters or words. Teams try to guess the correct word or phrase. When a team has the correct answer, team runner quickly runs and sits in the chair and calls out word or phrase. Team gets one point and play starts over again.

2. Teams choose a different artist and runner for each round. When all words have been drawn, team with the most points wins. At end of game ask questions such as, **What did you learn about God from this story? Which character showed (kindness)? How?**

Game Tip

For younger students, whisper words or phrases instead of writing them on slips of paper.

Sentence Connect

Bible Skill ▸ Bible Story Review

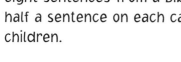

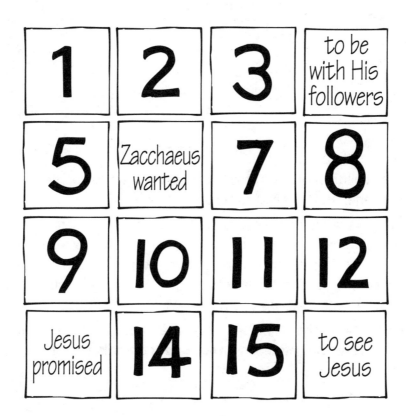

Energy Level ▸ LOW · MED · HIGH

iN ◂ Location

Materials
Bibles, posterboard, scissors, marker.

Preparation
Cut posterboard into 16 4-inch (10-cm) squares to make gamecards. With marker, number the cards 1 through 16. On the opposite side of cards, write eight sentences from a Bible story students have studied— half a sentence on each card (see sketch). Make one set of game cards for every four children.

Lead the Game

1. Lay cards, with numbered sides up, on floor or table. Children take turns turning over two cards at a time. If the two cards chosen make a complete sentence, the child may keep the cards and take another turn.

2. When all cards have been matched, have children read the sentences in the correct order to review the Bible story. Ask, **What is something new you learned from this Bible story or study?**

1	2	3	to be with His followers
5	Zacchaeus wanted	7	8
9	10	11	12
Jesus promised	14	15	to see Jesus

Street Corners

Bible Skill ▸ Bible Story Review

Materials

Bibles, scissors, poster board, marker, tape, red and green construction paper, two rulers, paper.

Preparation

To make street signs, cut and letter poster board as shown in sketch a. Tape street signs in four different corners of your classroom. Cut red and green construction paper into matching octagon shapes. Letter "Stop" on red paper and "Go" on green paper. Tape a ruler onto each octagon to make "Stop" and "Go" signs (sketch b). On a sheet of paper, list several "what, where, why and who" questions about the session's Bible story (sketch c). Make an even amount of each type of question.

a.

WHAT ST.

WHERE AVE.

WHY RD.

WHO DR.

b. STOP GO

ruler

c.
What did Jonathan and David do when they said good-bye?
Where did David hide from Saul?
Who did David marry?
Why did Saul want to kill David?

Lead the Game

1. Divide class into four teams. Stand in center of room and hold up "Go" sign while teams walk around perimeter of room. After 5 to 10 seconds, hold up "Stop" sign. As soon as children notice "Stop" sign, teams run to the nearest corner and sit down. (Each team must be in a different corner.)

2. The first team to have all its members seated at the same corner receives one point. Once all the teams are seated, the teacher asks each team a question that corresponds with its street sign. If the team answers correctly, it gets one point. If answer is incorrect, second team gets a chance to answer question. Play resumes when "Go" sign is held up again.

3. Game continues until all the questions have been answered. Team with the most points wins. Ask, **What do you learn about God from this story?**

That's the Way It Was

Bible Skill ▸ Bible Story Review

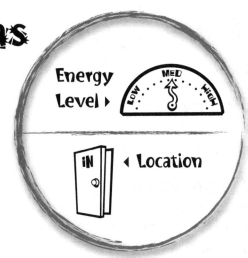

Energy Level ▸

iN ◀ Location

Materials

Bibles, slips of paper.

Preparation

For each child, except one, choose a word that is repeated several times in a Bible story children have studied. Write the words on slips of paper—one word on each slip. Place chairs in a circle.

Lead the Game

1. Children sit on chairs. One child stands in the middle of the circle. Give one slip of paper to each seated child. Read or tell the Bible story with expression. Each time you say a word that is on a slip of paper, the child holding that paper must stand, turn around and sit down again in the same chair. Meanwhile, the player in the middle tries to sit on the chair before the child sits down. If the player in the middle succeeds, the child now without a seat becomes the player in the middle and gives his or her slip to the child now seated.

2. Continue telling the story at a pace that is comfortable for your students. Ask, **How can what you've learned about this story help you follow Jesus more?**

Option

For an added challenge, insert the phrase "That's the way it was!" at various times during the story. Whenever you say this phrase, all children must stand and find a new seat. The player in the middle can use this opportunity to find a seat. The child left without a seat after the scramble will be the player in the middle as you continue to read the story.

Toss 'n Tell

Bible Skill ▸ Bible Story Review

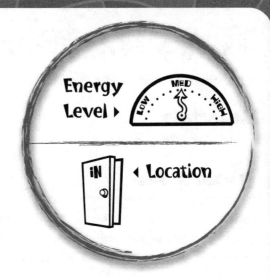

Energy Level ▸ LOW MED HIGH

iN ◂ Location

Materials

Bibles, large sheet of newsprint, markers, measuring stick, several beanbags.

Preparation

Divide paper into nine sections. Letter the words "Who?", "What?", "When?", "Where?" and "Why?" and four Xs on paper as in sketch.

Lead the Game

1. Place paper on floor in open area of room. Children stand at least four feet (1.2 m) from paper. Each child takes a turn to toss a beanbag onto the paper. Child then reviews the Bible story by answering the question on which the beanbag landed. (Example: Who? Abraham and Sarah; What? God promised Abraham a child; When? In Old Testament times; Where? In the Promised Land—Canaan; Why? Because God wanted to make a great nation out of Abraham's descendants. Children may think of many answers to the same questions.)

2. If the beanbag lands on an X, the child tosses the beanbag again—until the beanbag lands on a question. Ask, **What is the most important thing you've learned about God from this story?**

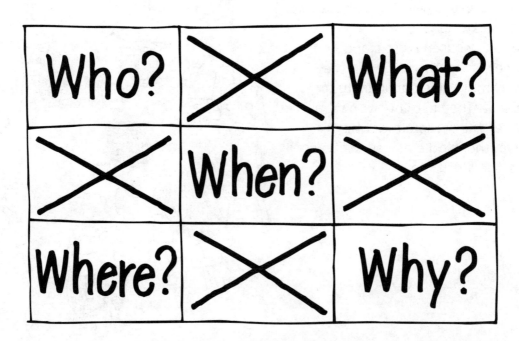

We Got It!

Bible Skill ▸ Bible Story Review

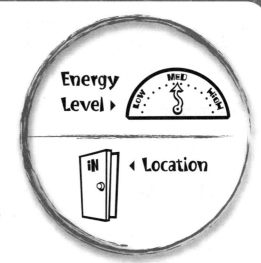

Energy Level ▸

iN ◂ Location

Materials

Bibles, large index cards, marker.

Preparation

Letter the alphabet on index cards—one letter on each card. Omit the letters Q and X. Make two sets of alphabet cards.

Lead the Game

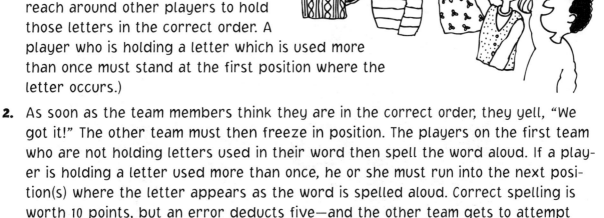

1. Divide the group into two teams. Give each team a set of alphabet cards to be divided as evenly as possible among team members. Then call out a word or name from a Bible story students have studied. The players with those letters must arrange themselves to correctly spell the word. (A player who is holding two or more letters used in the word must reach around other players to hold those letters in the correct order. A player who is holding a letter which is used more than once must stand at the first position where the letter occurs.)

2. As soon as the team members think they are in the correct order, they yell, "We got it!" The other team must then freeze in position. The players on the first team who are not holding letters used in their word then spell the word aloud. If a player is holding a letter used more than once, he or she must run into the next position(s) where the letter appears as the word is spelled aloud. Correct spelling is worth 10 points, but an error deducts five—and the other team gets to attempt the correct spelling.

3. When word has been spelled correctly, have a player tell its meaning or explain how the word was used in the Bible story. Ask, **How can knowing this story help you love Jesus more?**

Game Tip

Play a practice round before you begin keeping score.

Who Said That?

Bible Skill ▸ Bible Story Review

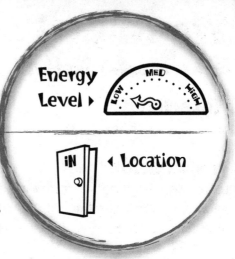

Energy Level ▸

iN ◂ Location

Materials

Bibles, video recorder and blank tape, whiteboard and marker.

Preparation

Tape various phrases that were spoken by characters in one or more Bible stories students have studied. You may want to use a different voice for each phrase.

Lead the Game

1. Divide group into two teams. Show first recorded phrase from Bible story. Then ask, **"Who said it?"** The first person to stand may answer to gain 100 points for his or her team. Next ask, **"Why did he (or she) say it?"** Again, the first person to stand may answer the question to gain points for his or her team. Then ask, **"What happened next?"** Record points on whiteboard.

2. Continue until all phrases have been identified. Ask, **What did you learn that can help you please God more?**

Bible Learning Games

Bible Verse Memory

Around the Verse

Bible Skill ▸ Bible Verse Memory

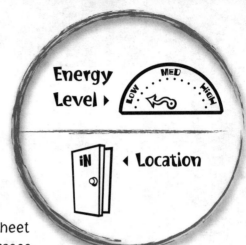

Energy Level ▸

iN ◂ Location

Materials

Bible, large sheet of paper, marker, small unbreakable object, children's music CD and player, individually wrapped candy.

Preparation

Print the words of a Bible memory verse on large sheet of paper, dividing the verse into seven or eight phrases.

Lead the Game

1. Students sit in a circle around large sheet of paper you prepared. Students play a game similar to Hot Potato. As you play music, students pass object around the circle. When the music stops, the student holding the object says the first phrase of the verse (see sketch). Student on his or her right says the next phrase of the verse.

2. Continue around the circle until the entire verse has been quoted. Last student places a piece of candy on a word on the paper. Repeat activity until all the words are covered or as time permits.

3. Eat candy together, making sure that students have equal amounts of candy. Ask, **How can this verse help you live?**

Game Tip

If you have students who cannot eat candy, be sure to provide other snacks or treats such as crackers, raisins, stickers, etc.

Balloon Bop

Bible Skill ▸ Bible Verse Memory

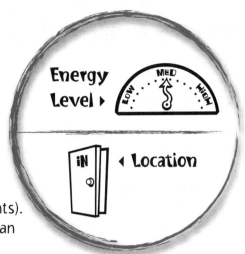

Energy Level ▸ LOW MED HIGH

iN ◂ Location

Materials

Bibles, balloons, masking tape, large sheet of paper, permanent markers.

Preparation

Blow up and tie balloons (one for each pair of students). Use masking tape to make a long line on the floor in an open area. Print verse on large sheet of paper.

Lead the Game

Divide class into pairs. Pairs stand on opposite sides of the masking-tape line. Give one student in each pair an inflated balloon. Pairs attempt to tap the balloon back and forth across the line to each other, repeating the words of the Bible memory verse in order.

Options

1. Students stand in a circle and attempt to tap the balloon around the circle, repeating the words of the verse in order.

2. Instead of tapping balloons back and forth, students in each pair sit on opposite sides of a table and slide coins across table to each other. Ask, **What part of this verse do you need to hear?**

Burst Your Bubble

Bible Skill ▸ Bible Verse Memory

Energy Level ▸ LOW · MED · HIGH

iN ◂ Location

Materials
Bibles, slips of paper, marker, balloons, garbage bag.

Preparation
Print one to three words of a Bible memory verse on separate slips of paper, making one paper for each student. (Repeat key words of verse if needed.) Blow up balloons, inserting one rolled slip of paper into each balloon before tying. Put balloons in garbage bag to bring to class.

Lead the Game
1. Students choose balloons, pop them and find papers inside.
2. Students read the verse in their Bibles and arrange slips of paper in verse order. Ask, **How will following the truths of this verse help you love God more?**

Fill-in-the-Blanks

Bible Skill ▸ Bible Verse Memory

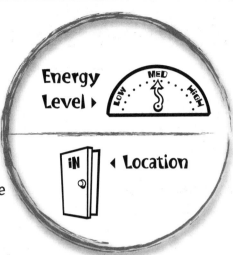

Energy Level ▸ LOW MED HIGH

iN ◂ Location

Materials

Bibles, index cards, marker, pencils, paper.

Preparation

Print each word of a Bible memory verse on a separate index card. Number the cards in verse order, writing numbers on the backs of the cards.

Lead the Game

1. Give each student a sheet of paper and pencil. Tell students the number of words in the verse. Students draw horizontal lines on their papers and number the lines in order, making a line for each word in the verse and leaving enough room to write a word on each line. Pass out index cards. Depending on the number of students in your group, some students may have more than one card.

2. Students move around the room asking other students what numbers and words are on their cards and recording words on the numbered lines on their papers. When finished, students read verse aloud together. Ask, **What is the most important part of this verse to you?**

Hidden Words

Bible Skill ▶ Bible Verse Memory

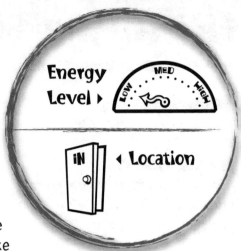

Energy Level ▶ LOW MED HIGH

IN ◀ Location

Materials

Bibles, index cards in a variety of colors, marker, scissors.

Preparation

Print the words of a Bible memory verse on index cards, one word on each card. Cut cards in half. Hide the pieces in the classroom for students to find. Make a set of same-colored cards for each small group of students.

Lead the Game

1. Students divide into as many groups as card sets you made. Invite the groups to search for pieces of the verse cards. Once a student finds the first card, his or her group keeps looking for the same-colored cards.

2. Students place cards together to find the words of the verse. Students find verse in their Bibles and put cards in order. Students read verse together. Ask, **How can you remember the words of this verse?**

Listen Up!

Bible Skill ▸ Bible Verse Memory

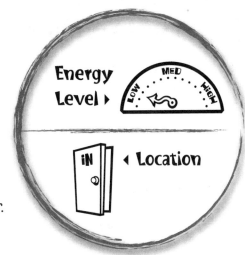

Energy Level ▸ LOW MED HIGH

iN ◂ Location

Materials

Bible, two sheets of paper, marker, blindfold.

Preparation

Divide the words of a Bible memory verse into two parts. Print each part on a separate sheet of paper.

Lead the Game

1. Play a game like Marco Polo. Ask a volunteer to stand on one side of the room. Blindfold the volunteer. Remaining students stand on other side of classroom. Give the papers you prepared to two students who quietly position themselves at random in the room.

2. At your signal, student with the first part of the verse calls out the words several times, pausing between each repetition. Blindfolded volunteer moves toward the student by listening to his or her voice. After finding first student, volunteer repeats the process to find the second student.

3. Continue with other volunteers and students as time permits. Ask, **How can this verse help you live?**

Option

Print verse on cards, one word on each card. Spread out cards on table in mixed-up order. Blindfolded student puts verse cards in order, listening to instructions from other students.

Missing Words

Bible Skill ▸ Bible Verse Memory

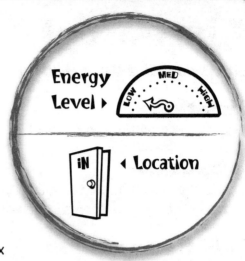

Energy Level ▸ LOW MED HIGH

iN ◂ Location

Materials

Bibles, marker, large sheet of paper, index cards, tape.

Preparation

Print the words of a Bible memory verse on large sheet of paper, drawing blank lines for six to eight key words. Write each key word on a separate index card.

Lead the Game

1. Place index cards and paper you prepared face up on table or floor. Students take turns choosing index cards to place in blanks on large sheet of paper. When taking his or her turn, student may ask classmates if they agree or disagree with the placement of a card by a previous student. Student may switch or remove cards only if a majority of the class disagrees.

2. After students think they have correctly completed the verse, students check verse in Bibles and correct placement of cards as needed. Students tape cards in place. Ask, **How will following the truths of this verse help you love God more?**

Puzzling Words

Bible Skill ▸ Bible Verse Memory

Energy Level ▸ LOW · MED · HIGH

Location ▸ in

Materials

Bibles, large index cards, red and green markers, scissors, tape.

Preparation

Using a green marker, print the words of a Bible memory verse on large index cards, two or three words on each card. Using a red marker, print definitions of several key words in the verse on the backs of the corresponding cards. Cut cards into puzzle pieces and hide pieces around the room.

Lead the Game

1. Invite students to find puzzle pieces hidden in the room. Referring to green letters, students put pieces together. Students then tape pieces in place and put cards in verse order, referring to verse in their Bibles as needed.

2. Volunteers take turns reading definitions of words written on the backs of cards. Ask, **What is the most important part of this verse to you?**

Rearranged Verse

Bible Skill ▸ Bible Verse Memory

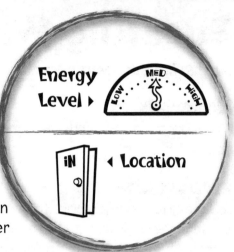

Energy Level ▸ LOW MED HIGH

iN ◂ Location

Materials

Bibles, small sheets of construction paper or large index cards, marker.

Preparation

Print the words of a Bible memory verse on construction paper or index cards, one or two words on each paper or card.

Lead the Game

1. Divide class into two groups. One group stands in front of the class holding verse papers or cards you prepared in a mixed-up order. Second group finds verse in their Bibles and takes turns giving instructions for first group to rearrange themselves in verse order ("Nathan, take two steps to your right"). If there are more papers or cards than students, arrange words of one phrase at a time.

2. Students read completed verse aloud together. Ask, **How can you remember the words of this verse?**

Secret Pass

Bible Skill ▸ Bible Verse Memory

Materials

Bibles, index card, marker, children's music CD and player.

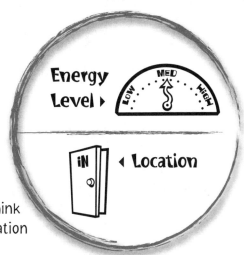

Energy Level ▸

iN ◂ Location

Preparation

Print the words of a verse on a small index card. Think of a question which can be answered by the information given in the verse.

Lead the Game

1. Students stand in a circle (shoulder-to-shoulder if possible) to play a game similar to "Button, button, who's got the button?" Choose one student to be "It." "It" stands in the middle of the circle and closes eyes. Give the verse card to a student in the circle. (Optional: If you have a large group of students, make more than one verse card for students to pass.) "It" opens eyes.

2. As you play music, students pass card around the circle behind their backs, trying to keep "It" from seeing who has the card. When you stop the music, "It" tries to identify who has the card by asking a student the question you prepared. If the student does not have the card he or she answers, "Keep searching," and "It" asks another student. If the student does have the card, he or she answers by reading the verse from a Bible. Student with the card becomes "It." Continue game as time permits. Ask, **How will following the truths of this verse help you love God more?**

Sticky Verses

Bible Skill ▸ Bible Verse Memory

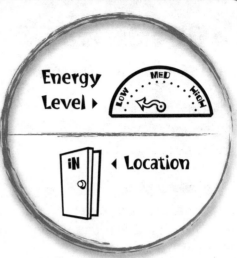

Energy Level ▸

Location

Materials
Bibles, craft sticks, markers.

Preparation
Print the words of a Bible memory verse on craft sticks, two or three words on each stick (see sketch). Make several sets of sticks, one for each group of three or four students.

Lead the Game

1. Divide class into three groups. Groups gather in a circle. Mix and distribute all the sticks so that each group has an equal amount.

2. Students find and read verse in their Bibles. Groups arrange sticks in verse order. The first group decides on a stick it doesn't need (a duplicate if possible), and then passes the stick to the group on its right. The second group passes a stick it doesn't need to the right. Play continues until a group has the entire verse in order. Read verse aloud. Ask, **How can you remember the words of this verse?**

" FOR GOD

SO LOVED

THE WORLD

THAT HE GAVE

Tape Time

Bible Skill ▸ Bible Verse Memory

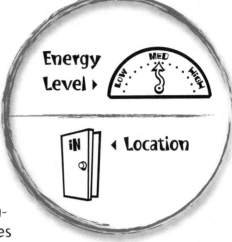

Energy Level ▸ LOW MED HIGH

iN ◂ Location

Materials

Bibles, masking tape, marker.

Preparation

Print the words of a Bible memory verse on masking tape with enough space between the words to tear them into separate pieces. (If you have a smaller number of students than words in the verse, print phrases instead of words.) Lightly place the separate pieces of tape on the underside of chairs or tables or on the walls around your classroom. In the same manner, print a paraphrase of the verse on masking tape, but do not distribute pieces.

Lead the Game

1. Students find the words you've hidden around the classroom. After all words have been found, students find the verse in their Bibles and put the pieces in order, taping them to table or floor. While students complete this task, put the paraphrase pieces around the classroom.

2. **Now find some tape pieces which say this verse in a way which helps us understand it better.** Students find paraphrase pieces, put in order and compare to verse. Students read both the verse and its paraphrase aloud. Ask, **What is the most important part of this verse to you?**

Verse Circles

Bible Skill ▸ Bible Verse Memory

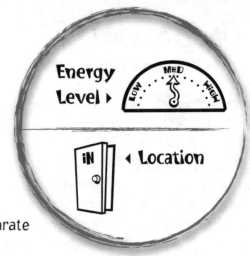

Energy Level ▸

iN ◂ Location

Materials

Bibles, index cards, marker, carpet square (or sheet of construction paper), children's music CD and player.

Preparation

Print each word of a Bible memory verse on a separate index card.

Lead the Game

1. Students form a circle. Place carpet square or sheet of paper between two students so that it forms a part of the circle. Distribute index cards in a mixed-up order.

2. As you play music, students walk around the circle, stepping on the carpet square as they come to it. When you stop the music, student standing on or near the carpet square places his or her card on floor in the middle of the circle. Students holding words before and after put their cards in the correct places.

3. Continue until all cards have been arranged, referring to Bibles for help. Read completed verse in order. Ask, **How will following the truths of this verse help you love God more?**

Verse Walk

Bible Skill ▸ Bible Verse Memory

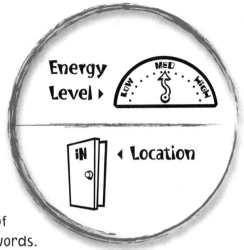

Energy Level ▸ LOW MED HIGH

iN ◂ Location

Materials

Bibles, large sheets of paper, marker, Post-it Notes, tape, children's music CD and player.

Preparation

Print the words of a Bible memory verse on large sheets of paper, two or three words on each sheet of paper. Place a Post-it Note on each paper near the words. Number phrases in verse order, writing numbers on the Post-it Notes. Tape papers randomly to classroom walls.

Lead the Game

1. As you play music, students walk around the room. When music stops, each student places his or her hand on the nearest paper. More than one student may touch each paper.

2. Students touching paper with first phrase read phrase aloud. Then group touching the second phrase reads second phrase. Continue until entire verse has been read in the correct order.

3. Repeat activity. After several rounds, remove Post-it Notes to see if students can remember the order of the words. Ask, **How can you remember the words of this verse?**

Writing Relay

Bible Skill ▸ Bible Verse Memory

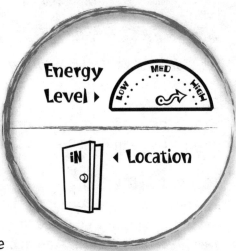

Energy Level ▸

◂ Location

Materials

Bibles, large sheets of paper, markers, small prizes such as candy or stickers; optional—two stopwatches.

Preparation

Print the reference for a Bible memory verse at the top of a large sheet of paper—one paper for each group of up to six students. Place papers on one side of the room. Place a marker and a Bible open to the verse next to each paper.

Lead the Game

1. Divide class into teams of up to six students. Students line up on the side of the room opposite from papers. At your signal, first student in each line runs to nearest paper, reads the verse and writes first word of the verse on the paper. Student leaves Bible open and returns to tag the next person in line. Second student then runs to find and write second word of the verse. Play continues until one team completes the entire verse. (Optional: Groups use stopwatches to time themselves racing to complete the verse.)

2. When all teams have completed the relay, read the verse aloud together. Ask, **How will following the truths of this verse help you love God more?**

Life Application Games
Faith in God

Faith Encouragers

Bible Focus ▸ 1 Thessalonians 5:11

Energy Level ▸ LOW MED HIGH

iN ◂ Location

Materials

Bibles, posterboard, marker, masking tape, measuring stick; for each team of six to seven players: 16 index cards of the same color.

Preparation

Write the words of 1 Thessalonians 5:11 on poster board. On the floor, use masking tape to mark off a 3-foot (.9-m) square for each team (see sketch). On one team's index cards, print 1 Thessalonians 5:11, one word or the reference on each card. Use a different color of cards to make an identical set for each team.

Lead the Game

1. **We're going to play a game where you help each other get an encouraging message.** Indicate masking-tape squares on the floor. **These squares are your houses. To play this game, your team needs to collect all its cards and put the verse in order. You can leave your house, but only if you stay connected to someone! Everyone outside of the box has to be connected to someone who is inside the box.**

2. Divide class into teams. Each team stands inside a House. Assign each team one color of index cards. Scatter index cards on the floor at varying distances from the boxes. At your signal, teams collect their index cards by forming an unbroken chain with at least one team member remaining in the House (see sketch). As cards are gathered, they are passed back to the House with team members remaining connected. When all cards have been gathered, the team places the cards on the floor of the House in correct verse order. They may refer to the memory verse poster you created or their Bibles. The first team to have their complete verse in order wins. **In this game, could one person have gathered all the cards alone? Why not?** Volunteers respond.

3. Ask winning team to say verse aloud, and then ask all students to say verse aloud together. Ask the Discussion Questions.

Discussion Questions

1. **What does it mean to build each other up?** (It means to encourage them to do something.)

2. **When are times you know a good thing to do, but it's hard to do?**

3. **What are some things you can do to encourage your friends?** (Pray for them. Offer to help. Help them learn what the Bible says to do.)

Faithful Pitch

Bible Focus ▸ Luke 21:1-4

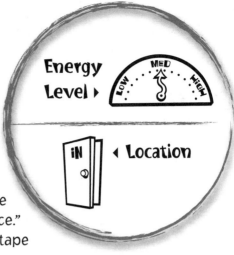

Energy Level ▸ LOW MED HIGH

iN ◂ Location

Materials

Bibles, paper, marker, four metal bowls or pie tins, masking tape, coins.

Preparation

Print the following words on four sheets of paper, one word per paper: "time," "money," objects," "obedience." Arrange bowls and papers as shown. Lay a masking-tape line about 3 feet (.9 m) from the bowls.

Lead the Game

1. **The poor widow showed her faith in God by giving her last coins to God. Let's play a game to show the different things we can give to God to show our faith in Him.**

3 feet (.9m)

2. Show papers you prepared. **These are different kinds of gifts people give. How can we give these kinds of gifts to God?** (Giving time to God by reading the Bible or praying. Giving money to the church or to people who need it. Giving objects by sharing what we have with others who don't have as much. Giving obedience to God by acting in kind ways.)

3. Give each student several coins. Students stand behind masking-tape line and take turns tossing the coins into the bowls. When a coin lands in a bowl, student tells a way he or she could give to God the kind of gift described on the paper next to the bowl.

4. Continue as time permits. Tell students a way you plan to show your faith in God during the week. Invite students to tell ways they will show their faith in God, using the Discussion Questions as encouragement.

Discussion Questions

1. **How can you show your faith in God?** (Read about God in His Word. Pray to God. Thank God for the good things He gives.)

2. **What are some times you have seen other people show their faith in God?** Briefly share your own answer before you ask for responses from students.

3. **How can you show faith in God when you are with your friends?**

Promise Seekers

Bible Focus ▶ Deuteronomy 7:9

Energy Level ▶

iN ◀ Location

Materials

Bibles, blindfold.

Lead the Game

1. Students play a game similar to Marco Polo. Choose and blindfold a volunteer to be "It." At your signal, students begin walking around the room. "It" calls out "God is faithful to. . ." and other students respond by saying their names or the name of someone they know. "It" follows the voices to try to tag a student.

2. When "It" tags another student, student who was tagged answers one of the discussion questions below, says or reads aloud Deuteronomy 7:9 or describes a situation in which we need to trust in God's faithfulness to keep His promises. The student who was tagged then becomes "It" and the game continues for as many rounds as time allows.

Option

If you have a limited space in which to play the game, have students stand still and whisper responses as "It" tries to follow their voices and tag them.

Game Tip

Before the game begins, remind students to walk, not run, as they play the game. If you are concerned that students will become too active, have everyone but student who is "It" tiptoe, crawl or walk in a crouched position.

Discussion Questions

1. **What does Deuteronomy 7:9 tell us about God?** Have a student read the verse aloud.

2. **When might a kid your age need to trust God's faithfulness?** (When he feels afraid. When she does something wrong and asks for God's forgiveness. When family members fight.)

3. **When have you trusted in God's faithfulness? What happened as a result?** Tell your own answer before asking students to respond.

Ship to Shore

Bible Focus ▸ Acts 27

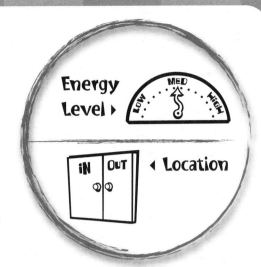

Energy Level ▸

Location ▸

Materials

Bibles; masking tape; five blindfolds; large, open playing area.

Preparation

Use masking tape to make two lines approximately 10 feet (3 m) apart.

Lead the Game

1. **When Paul was traveling to Jerusalem, the ship on which he sailed was destroyed. Paul and his shipmates swam or floated on pieces of the broken ship toward an island. It was a dangerous journey! There were high winds blowing them toward the rocks. They were soaking wet and probably very cold. Let's play a game to see if you can make the dangerous journey from broken ship to sandy shore.**

2. Ask a volunteer to be the Island. Island stands on one side of the playing area. Choose five students to be Shipmates. The remaining players are Rocks. **What sound should our Island make?** Students choose a sound for the Island to make, such as slapping thighs to make the sound of waves lapping against shore, or saying "Welcome!" **What sound should the Rocks make?** Students choose a sound or words to repeat for waves breaking against the rocks ("Crash!" or "Beware of rocks!").

3. Rocks spread out around the playing area and sit on the floor, wrapping their arms around their bent knees. Shipmates put on blindfolds at the opposite side of the playing area from the Island. At your signal, Shipmates attempt to "swim" to the Island without running into any Rocks. The Island makes Island noise to help Shipmates find the shore, and the Rocks make Rock noise to help the Shipmates avoid them. If a Shipmate does run into a Rock, he or she sits down and becomes a rock. When all Shipmates have either become Rocks or arrived at the Island, choose a new volunteer to be the Island. Shipmates and Rocks change roles and play is repeated.

Discussion Questions

1. **When did the people on the ship feel afraid?** (When they were blown off course. When the ship started to break up. When the soldiers wanted to kill them. When they were floating in the water.)

2. **Why wasn't Paul afraid?** (God promised him that they would all live. Paul trusted in God's promise.)

3. **How did Paul help his shipmates to keep on, even when it was hard?** (He kept reminding them of God's promise to keep them all safe.)

Towel Tug-of-War

Bible Focus ▸ Hebrews 10:23

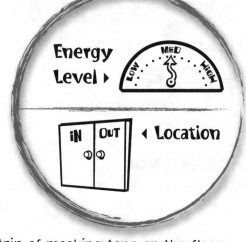

Energy Level ▸ LOW MED HIGH

iN OUT ◂ Location

Materials

Bibles, index cards, marker, small paper bag, masking tape, beach or bath towels.

Preparation

Print each verse reference on an index card: Deuteronomy 31:6; Isaiah 41:10; Lamentations 3:22, 23; Matthew 6:23-31; Romans 8:38-39; 1 Corinthians 10:13; 1 John 1:9. Place cards in a bag. Lay a 1-foot (.3-m) strip of masking tape on the floor for every four students.

Lead the Game

1. Stand on one side of the masking-tape line. Invite a volunteer to stand on the other side of the line. Hold onto one end of a towel while volunteer holds onto opposite end. Have a tug-of-war with volunteer. The first one to pull the other across the tape reads Hebrews 10:23 from his or her Bible.

2. Students form pairs. Each pair moves to one side of the masking-tape line. Give each pair a towel. Pairs play tug-of-war. First pair to win takes a verse card from bag (or call time after 15 seconds and let a volunteer take a verse card from the bag). Pair reads verse from Bible and tells how God keeps that promise in everyday situations. Put cards back in bag. Pairs change partners and continue playing as time permits.

Options

1. For a variation, call out a number and have students form two teams of that number and use a rope to play against each other.

2. To play outside, use rope for the masking-tape line as described.

Discussion Questions

1. **What does it mean to "hold unswervingly"?** (To hold something without letting go or moving.)

2. **What does Hebrews 10:23 tell us to hold onto without giving up?** (Our hope and trust in God and His promises.)

3. **Why can we do this?** (Because God is faithful to His promises and always keeps them.)

Life Application Games

Forgiving Others

Forgiveness Balloons

Bible Focus ▸ Genesis 37; 39; 41:41—45

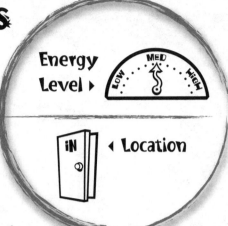

Energy Level ▸

IN ◂ Location

Materials

Bibles, large balloons (at least two for each student).

Preparation

None. (Optional: Inflate balloons before game.)

Lead the Game

1. **We can celebrate the fact that God will always forgive us when we ask Him. His forgiveness helps us want to forgive others. Joseph forgave his brothers, even when they had treated him very badly. In Bible times God asked His people to think about their wrong actions during the 10 days now called the Days of Awe. We'll play a game by trying to tap a balloon 10 times in a row.**

2. Give each student a balloon to partially inflate and tie. Students sit close to each other to form circles of no more than six students. Students sit on the inflated balloons. Give each group an additional inflated and tied balloon.

3. Students in each circle try to tap the balloon 10 times, tapping it to each other in random order without popping the balloons on which they are sitting. Lead students in counting aloud the number of times the balloon is tapped. If balloon touches the floor or if a balloon pops, distribute new balloons as needed and students begin again.

4. After several rounds of play, circles compete to see which circle can keep the balloon in the air the longest. Winning circle earns a letter in the word "forgive." Continue until one circle has earned all the letters or time is up.

Discussion Questions

1. **When has someone forgiven you for doing wrong?** Tell your answer before asking students to answer.

2. **Why does God's forgiveness help us forgive others, even if they don't deserve it?** (God forgives us, even when we don't deserve it. To show our thankfulness to God, we show His love to others by forgiving them.)

3. **When might you need to forgive a friend or family member?** Volunteers tell ideas.

Forgiveness Find

Bible Focus ▸ Philemon

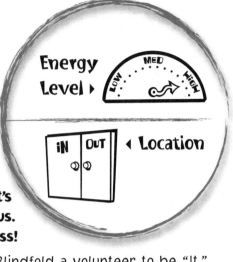

Energy Level ▸ LOW MED HIGH

iN OUT ◂ Location

Materials

Bibles, blindfold.

Lead the Game

1. Because God has forgiven us, we can encourage people to forgive each other and make peace. That's why Paul encouraged Philemon to forgive Onesimus. Let's play a game with messages about forgiveness!

2. Lead students in playing a game like Marco Polo. Blindfold a volunteer to be "It."

3. "It" begins moving around the playing area calling out "God forgives us." Students respond by saying "We forgive others" as they walk around the playing area. "It" moves toward the students by listening to their voices, continuing to say "God forgives us" to hear students respond.

4. When "It" tags another student, that student becomes "It" and game begins again.

Options

1. Play the game outdoors, using traffic cones or masking tape to mark the boundaries of the playing area.

2. Instead of a blindfold, place a large paper grocery bag over the head of "It."

3. After several rounds, ask students to think of a new phrase and response about forgiveness (for example, "Forgiveness from God" and "helps us forgive others"; or "We are forgiven" and "so make peace with others").

4. Students stand still while "It" walks around trying to tag them.

Discussion Questions

1. **How do we know that God forgives us?** (The Bible tells us that God forgives us when we ask for forgiveness and believe Jesus died on the cross to pay for our sins. God always keeps His promises.)

2. **Because God forgives us, we should forgive others and encourage people to forgive each other. What are some ways to encourage people to forgive each other?** (Be an example of forgiving others. Remind them of God's forgiveness.)

3. **How does forgiveness help us make peace?** (When we forgive, we can stop being angry. We can start doing the right things.) **What might your family be like if no one forgave each other? What might your school be like if everyone worked at making peace?**

Sliding Relay

Bible Focus ▸ Genesis 26:1-31; Colossians 3:13

Materials

Bibles, masking tape, large paper plates.

Preparation

Use masking tape to make two lines approximately 10 feet (3 m) apart.

Energy Level ▸

LOW MED HIGH

iN ◂ Location

Lead the Game

1. **Esau's forgiveness of Jacob ended years of angry separation between the two brothers. Let's play a game where we get to think of ways to forgive others.**

2. Divide class into two equal teams: "Jacob" and "Esau." Each team lines up behind one of the lines. Give each team two paper plates. At your signal, first player on each team stands on the paper plates and moves toward the other group's line by sliding feet on the paper plates (see sketch). After reaching the line, the player picks up the paper plates, runs back to the team and hands the paper plates to the next player in line.

3. When both teams have completed the relay, a volunteer from each team stands together between the two lines. Volunteer from the first team to finish the relay tells a situation in which forgiveness needs to be shown ("someone lied," "broke someone's tape player," "lost a friend's soccer ball"). Volunteer from other team tells a way to ask for and give forgiveness in the situation ("offer to pay for something which was broken," "smile and talk to someone to show kindness," "say 'I'm sorry,'" "promise to tell the truth"). Discuss situations and responses. Refer to Colossians 3:13 in your discussion, asking, **What advice does this verse give us about forgiving others? How do forgiving actions help us make and keep friends?**

4. Continue the relay activity as time permits. Vary the relay by challenging students to move sideways or backwards.

Discussion Questions

1. **Why do you think Esau forgave Jacob?**

2. **What might have happened if Esau had not forgiven Jacob?**

3. **What makes it hard to forgive someone?**

Towel Toss

Bible Focus ▸ The Gospels

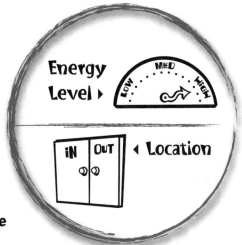
Energy Level ▸ LOW MED HIGH

iN OUT ◂ Location

Materials

Bibles, large towels, balls.

Lead the Game

1. **God's great love in sending Jesus to die for our sins is shown to others when we forgive them. Let's play a game to remind us of the importance of forgiveness.**

2. Group students into teams of five. Give each team a towel and a ball.

3. Four students on each team hold the towel between them at waist height. The other team member stands across the playing area and throws the ball so that the towel holders can catch it with the towel. If the ball is caught, the thrower runs to the towel and switches places with one of the towel holders. The new thrower takes the ball back across the playing area and throws it for the towel holders to catch.

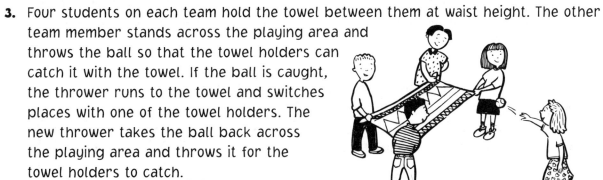

4. Team members continue rotating between throwing and holding, keeping track of the number of times the team catches the ball on the towel. Teams score one letter of the word "forgiveness" each time the ball is caught. The first team to catch the ball 11 times (completely spelling "forgiveness") calls "Stop." Students from that team answer one of the Discussion Questions below.

Options

1. Play game outdoors if possible.

2. Adjust according to students' ages and abilities the distance from which students toss ball.

3. For teams with more than five players, students form a line behind the thrower and rotate in.

Discussion Questions

1. **When has someone forgiven you?** Volunteers respond. **How did it make you feel?**

2. **Why is it important to forgive other people?** (God sent Jesus to Earth to die for us so that our sins could be forgiven. God commands us to forgive people.)

3. **What might happen when you forgive someone?** (You can be friends again. You can show them God's love.)

Who's Forgiven?

Bible Focus ▸ Matthew 18:21-35

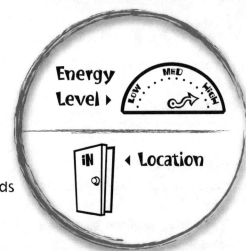

Energy Level ▸ LOW MED HIGH

iN ◂ Location

Materials

Bibles, an index card for each student, marker.

Preparation

On one card print the word "forgiven." Hide all cards around classroom.

Lead the Game

1. **When God forgives the wrong things we've done, it makes us want to forgive others, too. A long time ago, Jesus told a story about a king, and a servant who owed the king lots of money. We're going to play a game that reminds us of what the king did.**

2. At your signal, each student finds one of the hidden cards. Students with blank cards are debtors (people who owe money) and must do 10 jumping jacks to pay their debts. Student with the word "forgiven" on his or her card does not have to do jumping jacks.

3. Repeat game as time permits, each time choosing a different way in which debts are to be paid (do 10 sit-ups, hop across the room, touch toes, pat head and rub tummy for 10 seconds, etc.).

Option

If you are unable to hide cards in your room, give each student a card. At your signal, students begin trading their cards facedown with each other. When time is up, students determine who is forgiven and who are debtors by looking at their cards.

Discussion Questions

1. **How do you feel when someone tells you that you have done something wrong?**

2. **How do you feel when someone says you are forgiven for what you did?**

3. **Why does God's forgiveness of our sins make us want to forgive others?** (God has been kind to us, so we want to be kind to others.)

4. **When might it be hard for a kid your age to forgive someone? Who helps us forgive?**

Life Application Games

Friendship

Balloon Carry

Bible Focus ▸ Ruth

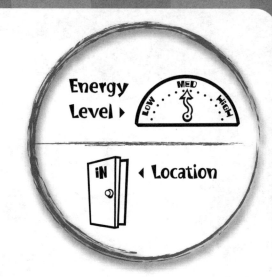

Energy Level ▸ LOW MED HIGH

iN ◂ Location

Materials

Bibles, balloon for each pair of students, large plastic bag.

Preparation

Inflate and tie the balloons. Place them in large plastic bag.

Lead the Game

1. When we make good choices in the things we do and say, we show our faithfulness to God. Sometimes our friends can help us make good choices, just like Ruth did to help Naomi. Today you and your partner can choose the best way to carry a balloon.

2. Students form pairs. Pairs stand at one side of playing area. Give each pair a balloon.

3. Pairs experiment with a variety of ways in which to carry the balloon to the other side of playing area without using their hands to hold the balloon. For example, students may hold balloon between shoulders, heads or hips (see sketch).

4. After students have had time to try several methods of carrying the balloon, ask all pairs to line up at one side of playing area. Each pair chooses the method of carrying the balloon they think will be the fastest. At your signal, pairs carry balloons to the other side of the playing area and back, trying to see who can complete the task first.

Option

For a greater challenge, students increase the number of balloons to carry.

Discussion Questions

1. Ruth helped her mother-in-law, even when it was hard work. How has someone helped you when you had hard work to do?

2. Who is someone you can help when they have hard work to do? How?

3. What is one way God helps you when you have hard work to do? (Gives me courage. Listens to and answers my prayers.)

Bounce It!

Bible Focus ▸ 1 Timothy 6:18

Energy Level ▸ LOW · MED · HIGH

◂ Location iN

Materials

Bibles, large rubber ball or tennis ball, children's music CD and player.

Lead the Game

1. **Remembering to be kind and generous helps us make and keep friends. Let's play a game to help us think of some generous and kind attitudes.**

2. Students stand in a circle and practice bouncing the ball to each other.

3. Ask a volunteer to read 1 Timothy 6:18 aloud. **What does this verse command us to do?** (Do good deeds. Be generous. Be willing to share.) **What are some ways to follow these commands?** Volunteers tell ideas.

4. When you start the music, students begin bouncing the ball to each other. When you stop the music, the student with the ball tells a way to obey 1 Timothy 6:18 or says the verse aloud. Continue play as time allows.

Options

1. Use two balls. Write "2" on one ball and "3" on the other (numbers may be formed with masking tape if needed). When you stop the music, students holding balls name that many ways to obey 1 Timothy 6:18.

2. Play a few rounds in which student holding the ball names a Bible character, a fruit of the Spirit or a book of the Bible.

3. As students bounce ball, they say the words of 1 Timothy 6:18, continuing until the entire verse has been quoted.

Discussion Questions

1. **What are some ways to be generous at school? With friends? With people you don't know?** (Buy lunch for a friend. Talk to a new kid at school. Give offering.)

2. **Why are kind attitudes the best ones for building friendships?**

3. **What actions does the Bible tells us to do?** (Love others. Honor your parents. Tell others about God's love.)

Bucket Brigade

Bible Focus ▸ Matthew 5:9; Romans 14:19

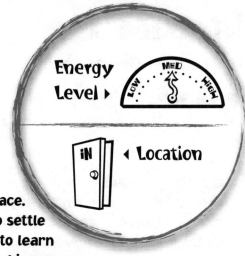

Energy Level ▸ LOW MED HIGH

iN ◂ Location

Materials

Bibles, large disposable cups, two tennis or Ping-Pong balls.

Lead the Game

1. **Jesus taught we are blessed when we make peace. Our friendships are better when we know how to settle arguments and live in peace. Let's play a game to learn one important instruction God gives us about making peace.**

2. Divide class into two equal teams. Each team forms two parallel lines facing each other.

3. Give each student a cup. Give a tennis or Ping-Pong ball to the student at the end of one line of each team. Students put balls in cups.

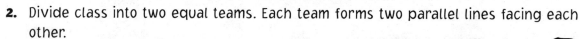

4. At your signal, the students roll (for mostly younger students) or toss (for mostly older students) the balls to the students across from them in line. Those students catch balls in cups and roll or toss balls to the next students opposite them. Students continue tossing or rolling the balls in zigzag fashion down the lines (see sketch) and back to the students who began the brigade.

5. Student from the first team to finish answers one of the questions below or repeats Romans 14:19. Students repeat game as time allows.

Discussion Questions

1. Ask a volunteer to read Romans 14:19 aloud. **What is God's instruction to us in this verse?** ("Make every effort to do what leads to peace.") **What does it mean to "make every effort"?** (To try as hard as you can. To do something to the best of your ability.)

2. **What did we make every effort to do in our game?** (Catch the ball in our cups. Pass it to the other players.)

3. **How can you make every effort to do what leads to peace at home? At school?** (Let your brother or sister be first or borrow something when he or she asks. Ask God for wisdom about how to treat the person who is bothering you at school. Be kind to a person who treats you badly again and again. Don't argue. Don't tease.)

Friend Fun

Bible Focus ▸ 1 Samuel 20; Proverbs 17:17

Materials

Bibles, paper, pencils, kitchen timer or stopwatch.

Energy Level ▸ LOW MED HIGH

iN ◂ Location

Lead the Game

1. **David and Jonathan had a special friendship. Let's play a fun game with our friends to find out what kinds of things we like to do with our friends.**

2. Each student traces one of his or her hands on a sheet of paper.

3. Assign students an action such as "high five," "shake hands" or "pat on the back." Set the timer or stopwatch for 30 seconds. (If you have a larger group, you may want to set the timer for a longer amount of time.)

4. Students move around the room and do the action with as many other students as they can before time is up. When two students have done the action together, they initial the hands on each other's paper. The goal is to collect as many initials as possible.

5. When time is up, students count the number of initials on his or her "hand." Student with most initials tells something he or she likes to do with friends and suggests an action for the next round. Students use reverse side of paper (or new sheet if playing more than two rounds) to trace hand and collect initials for the next round.

Option

Rather than using papers and pencils, students use washable markers to write initials on each other's hands.

Discussion Questions

1. **How do you make friends?** (Be friendly to others. Listen to people. Do things to help others.)

2. Read Proverbs 17:17 aloud. **How has a friend shown love for you?**

3. **What are some ways you show love to your friends?**

Fruit of the Spirit Toss

Bible Focus ▸ Galatians 5:22-23

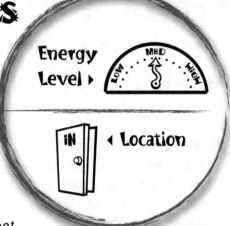

Energy Level ▸ LOW MED HIGH

iN ◂ Location

Materials

Bibles, balloons in a variety of shapes, sizes and colors, permanent markers, masking tape, two bedsheets.

Preparation

Inflate balloons. Print one fruit of the Spirit on each balloon. Tape each set of balloons to a wall, several feet apart. Spread bedsheets on the floor across the room, one opposite each group of balloons. Inflate a few extra balloons to give to students if balloons pop.

Lead the Game

1. **Learning the qualities of the fruit of the Spirit will help you to be a better friend to others.**

2. Divide class into teams of up to 10 players each. Teams stand in lines, with the first players next to the balloons and last players near the sheets.

3. At your signal, the first player on each team takes a balloon off the wall, removes tape and bats it to the next player in line. Players bat the balloon down the line, with the last player batting it onto the sheet. Meanwhile, the first player picks another balloon and passes it down the line. If a balloon pops, give the student last holding it another balloon and quickly write the popped balloon's word on it. The first team to have all its balloons on their sheet wins.

Option

After all the balloons are on their team's sheet, students pick up the balloons and arrange themselves in the Galatians 5:22-23 verse order.

Discussion Questions

1. **The Bible calls these the fruit of the Spirit because they are qualities that God grows in us as we become more like Jesus. How can these qualities help you be a better friend?**

2. **What are some ways to show these qualities to kids older than you? Younger than you?**

3. **What fruit quality do you need most?** Tell an example before asking for students' responses.

Partner Relay

Bible Focus ▸ Judges 4:1-16; 5:1-23

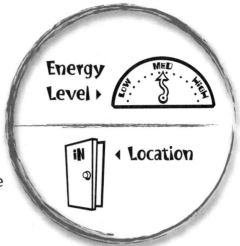

Energy Level ▸ LOW MED HIGH

iN ◂ Location

Materials

Bibles, masking tape, sheets of newspaper.

Preparation

Use masking tape to make a starting line on one side of the playing area.

Lead the Game

1. Sometimes others need our help to trust God and obey Him. In the Bible we read a story about how Deborah helped Barak obey God. It's good to work with others to do good things. Let's play a game to practice helping each other.

2. Divide class into teams of six to eight. Teams line up behind masking-tape line. Students on each team form pairs. Give each pair two sheets of newspaper. (Partner with a student if needed.)

3. To move, student's partner places newspaper sheets on floor for student to walk on. First student in each line moves across the room and back, stepping only on sheets of newspaper. Each pair completes the relay twice with a different student moving the newspaper sheets the second time.

4. Repeat relay as time permits, forming new teams and new pairs.

Options

1. Rectangles made from large paper grocery bags may be used instead of newspapers.

2. If playing this game outdoors, use yarn or string to mark the starting line.

Discussion Questions

1. What are some other games you like to play with friends?

2. How can you help or encourage someone who has something hard to do? (Pray for him or her. Offer to help or go with the person.)

3. When has someone helped or encouraged you to obey God? How?

Peace Path

Bible Focus ▸ Genesis 26:1-31; Romans 12:18

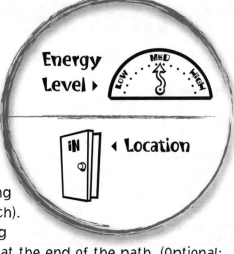

Energy Level ▸

iN ◂ Location

Materials

Bibles, masking tape, construction paper, markers, index cards, number cube; optional—paper bag.

Preparation

Tape sheets of construction paper to the floor, forming a game path with approximately 20 spaces (see sketch). Print the word "START" on the paper at the beginning of the path and print the word "FINISH" on the paper at the end of the path. (Optional: If you do not have a number cube, print the numbers 1,2,3,4 on separate index cards. Place number cards in paper bag.)

Lead the Game

1. **Isaac chose to make peace with his family neighbors. He decided not to let an argument get out of control.**

2. Invite volunteers to complete the question, "What should you do when . . .?" by describing situations in which kids their age need to keep friends by avoiding or ending arguments ("What should you do when you and your friend want to play different video games?" "What should you do when your friend makes fun of you?"). As each question is completed, print it on a separate index card. Continue until at least 8-10 game cards have been made. Ask, **What causes arguments between friends? How can you respond in a way that would stop an argument?** Draw a star on several blank index cards and shuffle them together with the game cards. Place game cards facedown near game path.

3. First player chooses a game card from the stack, stands on square labeled "START" and reads question aloud. Player answers the question (or calls on a volunteer to answer the question), rolls the number cube and advances that number of squares. If the card shows a star, player finds and reads aloud Romans 12:18 from Bible before rolling number cube and moving on the game path. Return game card to bottom of stack after each player's turn. Continue with additional players playing the game until a student reaches "FINISH" square.

Discussion Questions

1. **What does it mean to live at peace with others?**

2. **When are some times people might get into an argument with you?**

3. **What can we do to keep from arguing with others?** (Be careful about what we say. Answer angry words with kind words.)

Peace Practice

Bible Focus ▸ Colossians 3:15

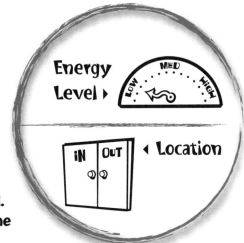

Energy Level ▸ LOW MED HIGH

iN OUT ◂ **Location**

Materials

Bibles.

Lead the Game

1. **Being able to make peace with your friends is something that will help you be a better friend. Let's play a game to work together and spell the word "peace."**

2. Students form teams of up to 10 students each. Students on each team form pairs.

3. Assign each pair a letter of the word "PEACE," giving more than one letter to a pair if necessary. Students figure out how to form their letter(s) using their bodies.

4. Pairs on each team line up in correct order to spell "PEACE." At your signal, the first pair of students on each team links arms, moves quickly to the opposite side of the playing area and forms letter. Pair links arms and returns to team.

5. Next pair on team begins as soon as teammates have returned to team. Pairs continue taking turns until each team has spelled the word "PEACE." Ask one of the Discussion Questions below to volunteers from the first team to finish. Continue discussion with other questions. Play game again as time allows, assigning pairs different letters.

Options

1. Instead of linking arms, pairs move to the opposite side of the playing area while keeping a balloon between their hips or shoulders. Students set down balloon in order to form letter and then put balloon back in place to return to team.

2. Call out a different way for pairs to move on each turn (back-to-back, hopping on one foot with arms linked, skipping with arms linked, etc.).

Discussion Questions

1. **Why does this verse say we should live peacefully with others?** (As followers of Christ we will want to show love for others.)

2. **When are some times kids your age have to work to make peace at school? At home?** (When friends are arguing. When brothers or sisters are angry.)

3. **Why might friendships happen when you work to make peace?** (People like to be around those who are friendly and easy to get along with.)

Quick-Slow Switch

Bible Focus ▸ James 1:19; 3:3-12

Energy Level ▸ LOW MED HIGH

IN ◂ Location

Materials

Bibles, masking tape.

Preparation

On the floor, use masking tape to form three large squares.

Lead the Game

1. **Being careful about what we say shows self-control and helps us be better friends to others. James 1:19 tells us to be "quick to listen, slow to speak and slow to become angry." Let's practice being quick and slow in our game today.**

2. Ask a volunteer to be "It." Form three groups from remaining students. Each group stands in a separate square.

3. Call out either "Quick" or "Slow" and a description such as "kids wearing green" or "kids with brown hair." Students who fit that description move at the called speed to a new square, while "It" moves at same speed to tag students before they reach a new square. Any student who is tagged outside a square becomes "It" also.

4. Continue play, periodically calling out "Quick switch" or "Slow switch," at which time all students must move to a new square at the designated speed. When only a few students have not been tagged, begin a new round of the game with a new "It."

Options

1. Play fast or slow music to indicate the speed at which students should move each time you call out a new description.

2. To challenge older students, review James 1:19 and then say "Listen" to indicate quick movement and "Speak" to indicate slow-motion during the game.

Discussion Questions

1. **When might it be hard to show self-control when you talk to others?** (When you're angry. When you feel like saying something unkind. When you don't like what someone is saying.)

2. **What can you do when you need help showing self-control in your speech?** (Follow James 1:19 and be quick to listen and slow to speak. Pray and ask God for His help. Count to 10 before you speak when you feel upset. Walk away before you say something you shouldn't say.)

3. **How would your (school) be a better place if kids were careful about what they say?**

Stick Together Relay

Bible Focus ▶ Colossians 3:15

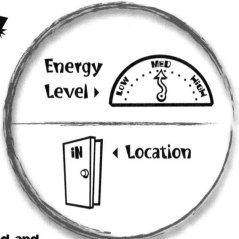

Energy Level ▶

Location ▶

Materials

Bibles, balloons.

Preparation

Inflate one balloon for each team of five students.

Lead the Game

1. Faithfulness to others means being a friend in good and bad times. Let's practice faithfulness by sticking with each other in our game today.

2. Divide students into teams of five. Teams line up on one side of the classroom. Give the first student in each line an inflated balloon.

3. At your signal, the first student in each line taps the balloon up into the air as he or she moves to the other side of the playing area and back. The second student in line then taps the balloon across the playing area and back while holding the wrist of the first student. Game continues until the whole team is holding wrists and moving across the playing area and back as the last student taps the balloon.

4. As teams complete the relay, they sit down. A volunteer from the last team to finish answers one of the Discussion Questions below (or chooses a student from one of the other teams to answer a question). Continue the discussion, asking the remaining questions.

Options

1. Bounce a basketball, kick a tennis ball or carry a Ping-Pong ball on a spoon instead of tapping a balloon across the room.

2. Younger students complete relay in pairs, instead of whole team holding hands.

Discussion Questions

1. **How does this game show us what faithfulness is?** (Faithfulness is sticking with someone or something, no matter what.)

2. Read Proverbs 17:17 aloud. **According to Proverbs 17:17, what does a faithful friend do? Would that be hard or easy? Why?**

3. **Why might a kid your age have a hard time continuing to be a faithful friend to someone?** (When that person moves away. When he or she stops being nice. When we find new friends.) **What can we do to remember to be faithful friends, even when it's hard?** (Ask God's help. Remember the words of Proverbs 17:17.)

Teamwork

Bible Focus ▸ Nehemiah 1-4; 8; 9

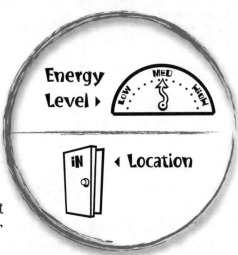

Energy Level ▸ LOW MED HIGH

iN ◂ Location

Materials

Bibles; chair for each student, plus one; sealed bag filled with individually wrapped candies for each team.

Preparation

Arrange chairs so that teams face each other with at least 12 feet (3.6 m) between teams. Place extra chair in the middle (see sketch).

Lead the Game

1. **Working together to complete a job usually makes the job easier, and it's more fun. Let's play a fun game in which we need to work together so that we can each have a piece of candy.**

2. Group students into two equal teams. Students sit in chairs. Give the sealed bag of candy to the first student at the left end of each team. At your signal,

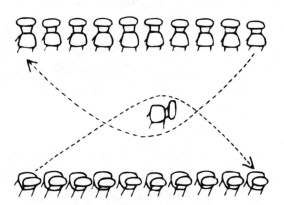

the first student from each team runs around the center chair to the end of his or her team's chairs. While the student is running, the other students move up one seat to fill the runner's chair, leaving the chair at the right end empty for the runner. Runner sits in empty chair and passes the bag of candy up the line toward the first chair. When student sitting in the first chair receives the candy bag, he or she gets up, runs around the center chair and goes back to the end of the line where the chair is again vacant because the students have moved up one chair. Runner passes the bag of candy up the line again. The team whose players are sitting in original chairs first is the winner. Students eat candy.

Discussion Questions

1. **In the Bible, we read about a time when Nehemiah helped God's people rebuild the walls around Jerusalem. Was it hard or easy to help each other in this game? Why?** Could you have played this game by yourself?

2. **What are some other times you work with people?** (On a project at school. On a soccer team. To clean up our classroom or homes.)

3. **How can you show love for God when you work with other people?** (By treating each other patiently and kindly.)

Life Application Games

God's Forgiveness

Believe It or Not

Bible Focus ▸ John 3:16

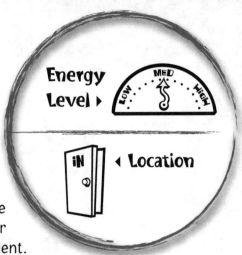

Energy Level ▸ LOW MED HIGH

iN ◂ Location

Materials
Bibles, marker, index cards, children's music CD and player.

Preparation
Print each letter of the word "believe" on a separate index card and mix them together with enough other blank index cards to provide one card for each student.

Lead the Game

1. **Jesus wants us to believe that He is alive and accept His love for us! Let's play a game to remind us of how important it is to believe in Jesus.**

2. Students sit or stand in a circle. Give each student an index card facedown.

3. As you play music, students pass cards facedown around the circle. Stop the music after a short while. When music stops, students look at their cards. Students with blank cards do five jumping jacks. Students with letters on their cards move quickly to stand in correct order to spell "believe." Student holding the letter B answers one of the Discussion Questions below. Collect index cards, mix cards together and redistribute to play again. Continue game as time allows, varying which students are to answer questions and changing the actions of students holding blank cards (high-five a friend, turn around twice, etc.).

Discussion Questions

1. **What does John 3:16 say about believing in Jesus?** Have a student say or read the verse aloud and then invite volunteers to answer the question.

2. **How did Jesus show He loves us?** (Died for our sins. Came to Earth as a baby.)

3. **What can you do to show you believe that Jesus rose from the dead and to show that you want to accept His love?** (Thank Him for His love. Ask Him to forgive my sins and believe that He will. Learn more about Jesus' love for me and how He wants me to live by reading the Bible.)

Favorite Things

Bible Focus ▸ Luke 15:1-2,11-32

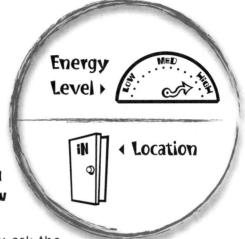

Energy Level ▸ LOW MED HIGH

iN ◀ Location

Materials

Bibles.

Lead the Game

1. The Bible teaches us that God is eager and glad to love and forgive us. Let's play a game to show some things that we are eager about.

2. Students stand in the middle of the room. As you ask the questions below, point to opposite walls of the room as you say each answer. Each student runs and touches the wall that indicates his or her answer.

Ask questions such as "What's your favorite thing to eat—ice cream or cookies?" "What's your favorite game to play—baseball or soccer?" "What's your favorite thing to do—watch TV or play with a friend?" "What's your favorite thing to ride—a skateboard or a bike?" "What's your favorite thing to do with your family—go to a park or go out to eat?" "What's your favorite pet—a cat or a dog?"

Ask additional questions as needed, playing as many rounds as time allows. (Note: Students with answers other than the two given with the question sit down in the middle of the room. Invite these students to say their answers aloud.)

Options

1. Ask an older student to ask the questions or suggest additional questions.

2. Alternate the way in which students move during this game. Instead of running to the wall, students may hop, skip, walk backwards, tiptoe, etc.

Discussion Questions

1. **What does it mean to be eager?** (To be so excited about something you want to do it right away. To look forward to something so much you can hardly stand waiting for it to happen.)

2. **Jesus told a story in the Bible about a father who was eager to forgive his son.** (Optional: Read Luke 15:11-24.) **What is God eager to do for us?** (Love and forgive us.)

3. **How does it make you feel to know God is eager to love and forgive you? Since God forgives us, how should we treat others?**

Forgiveness Frenzy

Bible Focus ▸ Luke 19:1-10

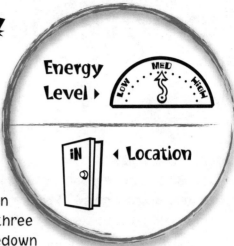

Energy Level ▸ LOW MED HIGH

iN ◂ Location

Materials

Bibles, markers, index cards, children's music CD and player, stopwatch or watch with second hand.

Preparation

Print the word "forgive" on index cards, one letter on each card. Make at least one set of cards for every three to six students. Mix up all cards and place them facedown in a large circle on the floor.

Lead the Game

1. **Let's play a game to celebrate the fact that God's forgiveness is for everyone!**

2. Students form teams of three to six students. Assign a name or number to each team. Members from all teams stand in mixed-up order around the circle of cards.

3. As you play music, students walk around the circle. Stop the music after 15 or 20 seconds. When the music stops, each student picks up the card closest to him or her and finds other team members. Team members compare cards collected, keeping cards with letters needed to spell "forgive" and placing duplicate cards facedown back in the circle. Add blank cards to the circle as needed so that there is always a card for each student.

4. When one or more teams have collected a complete set of cards to spell "forgive," ask one or more of the Discussion Questions below. Repeat game as time allows.

Options

1. Students prepare cards in class.

2. If you have fewer than six students in your class, students form pairs or play individually.

3. For older students, add a few cards with letters not used in "forgive" (s, m, b, etc.).

Discussion Questions

1. **What are some things people might think they have to do to be forgiven?** (Go to church. Read their Bibles.) **Those are all good things to do, but who does Acts 10:43 say can have their sins forgiven?** (Anyone who asks God for forgiveness of sin and who believes in Jesus.)

2. **What does it mean to believe in Jesus?** (To believe that Jesus is God's Son and that He died to take the punishment for our sins.)

3. **How can we be sure our sins are forgiven?** (God always keeps His promises.)

Fresh-Start Tag

Bible Focus ▶ 1 John 1:9

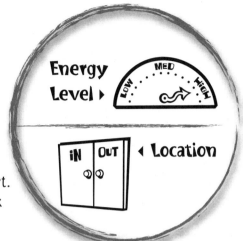

Materials

Bibles, masking tape or chalk, party horn.

Preparation

Make two masking-tape lines about 30 feet (9 m) apart. Make each line at least 10 feet (3 m) long. (Use chalk if you are playing on asphalt.)

Lead the Game

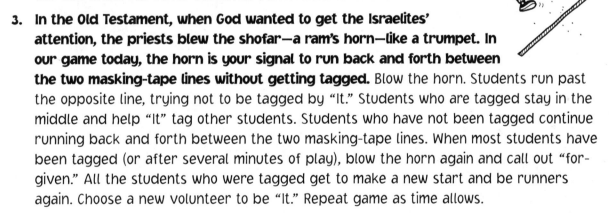

1. **When God forgives the wrong things we have done, we can make a new start. We're going to play a game in which we can practice making new starts, too!**

2. Choose one volunteer to be "It." "It" stands between the two lines. All other students stand behind one line.

3. **In the Old Testament, when God wanted to get the Israelites' attention, the priests blew the shofar—a ram's horn—like a trumpet. In our game today, the horn is your signal to run back and forth between the two masking-tape lines without getting tagged.** Blow the horn. Students run past the opposite line, trying not to be tagged by "It." Students who are tagged stay in the middle and help "It" tag other students. Students who have not been tagged continue running back and forth between the two masking-tape lines. When most students have been tagged (or after several minutes of play), blow the horn again and call out "forgiven." All the students who were tagged get to make a new start and be runners again. Choose a new volunteer to be "It." Repeat game as time allows.

Options

1. If space is limited, students jump or hop between the two lines.

2. Play game outdoors if possible.

Discussion Questions

1. **What happened when I called "forgiven"?** (The game started over. Everyone got a new chance to be a runner.) **How is that like what happens when God forgives us?**

2. **When are some other times we get to make a new start?** (Beginning of a school year. Begin reading a new book. Begin playing a higher level on a video game.)

3. Read 1 John 1:9. **How can we make a new start when God forgives us for the wrong things we have done?** (We can know that our sins are forgiven. We can ask God to help us love and obey Him.)

God's Amazing Plan

Bible Focus ▸ 1 Corinthians 2:9

Materials
Bibles, masking tape, blindfold.

Preparation
Use masking tape to divide playing area into four sections (see sketch).

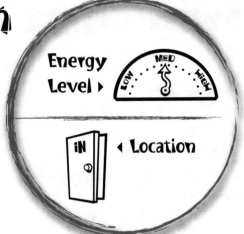

Energy Level ▸ LOW MED HIGH

iN ◂ Location

Lead the Game
1. **The Bible tells us in 1 Corinthians 2:9 that no eye has seen or ear has heard the great things God has prepared for those who love Him. We're going to play a game and talk about the good things God wants to give us!**

2. Choose one volunteer to be blindfolded and one to be "It." Blindfolded volunteer stands in the middle of the playing area.

3. At your signal, "It" and remaining students move randomly (but quietly) around the playing area. Blindfolded volunteer counts to 20 and then says "Stop." All students freeze where they are, and volunteer points toward one of the playing-area sections. If "It" is in that section, "It" reads 1 Corinthians 2:9 aloud or answers one of the Discussion Questions below. If "It" is not in that section, all students in that section move to the side of the playing area. Repeat play until blindfolded volunteer finally points to the section where "It" is standing. Play again with new volunteers as time allows.

Option
If you have a large number of students, choose more than one "It" for each round of the game.

Discussion Questions
1. **What are some good things God gives His followers?** (Forgiveness for sins. Courage to do right. People to care for us.)

2. **What are some good things God promises to help you do?** (Treat others fairly. Be patient with brothers and sisters. Love others.)

3. **When are times that it is hard to live as God wants us to? What can you do then?** (Pray and ask for His help. Read the Bible to learn more of how He wants us to live.)

Jonah's Journey

Bible Focus ▸ Jonah; 1 Timothy 2:3-4

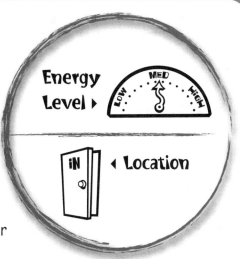

Energy Level ▸ LOW MED HIGH

iN ◂ Location

Materials

Bibles, markers, length of butcher paper, masking tape, small index cards cut in half, blindfold.

Preparation

Draw outlines of a whale (or big fish) and Nineveh on butcher paper (see sketch). Then tape butcher paper on classroom wall.

Lead the Game

1. **In the Old Testament, Jonah went on an unusual journey and as a result people learned about God's forgiveness.** Invite volunteer(s) to tell the story of Jonah's journey to Nineveh.

2. **Let's play a game to remind us of Jonah's journey.** On half an index card, each student draws a stick figure to represent Jonah and attaches a masking-tape loop to the back of the card.

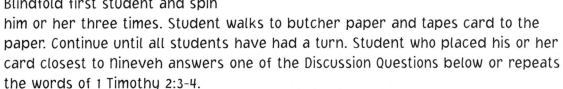

3. Students line up approximately 5 feet (1.5 m) from butcher paper. Blindfold first student and spin him or her three times. Student walks to butcher paper and tapes card to the paper. Continue until all students have had a turn. Student who placed his or her card closest to Nineveh answers one of the Discussion Questions below or repeats the words of 1 Timothy 2:3-4.

Option

If you have more than six to eight students, make additional papers. Students play game in small groups.

Discussion Questions

1. **How can we stop doing wrong things?** (Ask God to forgive our sin and to help us do what's right.)

2. **How do we know that our sin is forgiven?** (The Bible tells us that if we ask God for forgiveness for the wrong things we have done, we will be forgiven.)

3. **What are some ways we can learn the right things God wants us to do?** (Read God's Word. Follow the instructions of people who love God. Pray.)

Reformation Relay

Bible Focus ▸ Ephesians 2:8-9

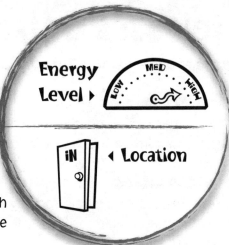

Energy Level ▸ LOW MED HIGH

iN ◂ Location

Materials

Bibles, index cards, marker, cardboard box, pushpins.

Preparation

Print Ephesians 2:8-9 on index cards, one word or short phrase on each card. Prepare at least one card for each student. Place box, pushpins and a set of ordered verse cards on one side of the playing area.

Lead the Game

1. **A long time ago in Germany, a man named Martin Luther wrote some ideas about God's gift of salvation and how no one can earn it. He nailed the paper on a church door for all the people to read. Let's play a game that will help us learn a great verse about God's gift of salvation.**

2. Students line up on one side of the playing area, opposite from box.

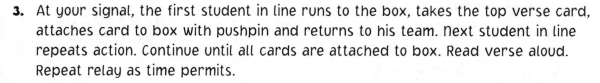

3. At your signal, the first student in line runs to the box, takes the top verse card, attaches card to box with pushpin and returns to his team. Next student in line repeats action. Continue until all cards are attached to box. Read verse aloud. Repeat relay as time permits.

Options

1. For older students or for more challenge, mix up the verse cards so that students must place them in order as they attach cards to box. Review Ephesians 2:8-9 before the game and/or put a Bible opened to verse next to cards.

2. If you have adequate adult supervision, provide a long block of wood, hammer and nails. Students hammer cards to wood to complete the relay.

Discussion Questions

1. **Why can't we boast or brag about being saved?** (We are only saved when we believe in Jesus' death for our sins, not because of any good actions we have done.)

2. **Grace is love and kindness shown to someone who doesn't deserve it. What does Ephesians 2:8-9 say about grace?** (We are saved because of God's grace.)

3. **Why is salvation described as a gift from God?** (It is free. There is nothing we can do to earn it. He gives it to us because He loves us.)

Shoe Search

Bible Focus ▸ Luke 15:1-10

Materials
Bibles.

Energy Level ▸ LOW MED HIGH

iN ◂ Location

Lead the Game

1. **When we find something we've been looking for, it makes us happy. In Luke 15, Jesus told two stories about people who searched for missing items.** (Optional: Read Like 15:1-10 aloud.) **When the people found the missing items, they were joyful! Let's search for something in our game today.**

2. Students form two teams. Students on each team take off shoes and place them in a team pile on one side of the playing area. Students line up in single-file lines on other side of playing area, across from their team's shoe pile. Mix up shoes within each pile.

3. At your signal, the first student on each team skips to shoe pile, finds one of his or her shoes, puts it on and skips back to his or her team. The next student in line repeats the action. Students continue, taking turns until everyone on team has collected and put on both shoes.

Option
Play this game to review Habakkuk 3:18 with students. Stand by one pile of shoes and have a helper do the same by the other pile. When a student comes to shoe pile, begin reading the verse. Stop at any point. Student finishes saying the verse, takes a shoe from the pile and returns to team.

Discussion Questions

1. **What are some of the ways people hear about God's gift of salvation and the joy it brings?** (Friends tell them. They go to church. They read the Bible.)

2. **When we hear about God and accept God's gift of salvation by becoming members of God's family, we experience joy. Why?** (Our sins are forgiven by God. We can have eternal life. We know God loves us.) Talk with interested students about becoming members of God's family (refer to "Leading a Child to Christ" article on p. 11).

3. **The Bible tells us that God is joyful when we become a part of His family. Why?** (He loves us and wants us to be part of His family.)

Son Search

Bible Focus ▸ Luke 15:11-24

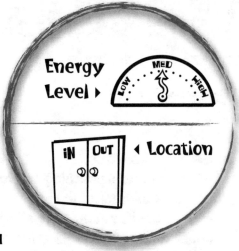

Energy Level ▸

iN | OuT ◂ Location

Materials

Bibles, blindfold.

Lead the Game

1. **When we're sorry for the wrong things we have done, God is always ready to forgive us. To help us learn about God's love and forgiveness, Jesus told a story in Luke 15:11-24 about a forgiving and loving father. Let's play a game to remember that story and God's great love and forgiveness!**

2. **In the story that Jesus told, a son left home and spent all of his money on parties. He was so poor he had to take care of pigs. Finally, he decided to go back home and ask his father to forgive him for his wrong actions. His father was glad to welcome him home.** (Optional: Invite volunteers to tell what they remember about the story.)

3. Students play a game like Marco Polo. Blindfold a volunteer to be the father. Choose another volunteer to be the son. Remaining students are the pigs.

4. Father begins calling out "Welcome home, son." Son responds by saying "I'm sorry, father" while walking slowly around the playing area. The rest of the students oink and snort like pigs while moving around the playing area. Father moves toward son by listening for his response, continuing to say "Welcome home, son" as needed. When the father tags the son or after several minutes, choose two new volunteers to be the father and son and repeat game as time allows.

Options

1. Be sure to clear playing area of tables and chairs, or play game outdoors and use yarn to indicate boundaries.

2. If playing game with younger students, students representing the son and pigs stand still while the father tries to find the son.

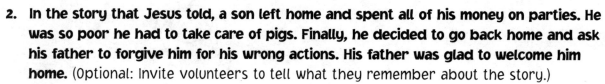

Discussion Questions

1. **When does God forgive us?** (When we are sorry for our sins and ask Him to forgive us. When we believe Jesus took the punishment for our sins through His death on the cross.)

2. **When is a good time to ask God to forgive us?** (Whenever we realize we have sinned, are sorry for the wrong things we have done and want to start doing right things.)

3. **What are some ways to celebrate God's forgiveness of our sins?** (Sing songs to thank Him. Thank Him in our prayers. Forgive others. Tell others about God's forgiveness.)

Life Application Games

God's Help

Alphabetical Help

Bible Focus ▸ Philippians 4:19

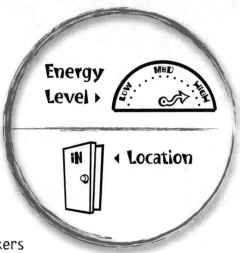

Energy Level ▸ LOW MED HIGH

iN ◂ Location

Materials
Bibles, masking tape, large sheets of paper, markers.

Preparation
Use masking tape to make a starting line on one side of the room. Print alphabet down one side of large sheet of paper, making one paper for each group of up to eight students. Place alphabet papers and markers on the other side of the room.

Lead the Game
1. Divide class into teams of up to eight students each. Teams line up behind starting line. Each team sends one person at a time to its large sheet of paper to write a name of something God made next to the letter of the alphabet with which the word begins. Teams attempt to name something that begins with each letter of the alphabet. Call time after several minutes.

2. Team with the most words on its alphabet paper chooses one item on the paper. Ask the Discussion Questions below. Repeat with additional words and questions. Students find Philippians 4:19 in their Bibles. **How does this verse say that God takes care of us?** (He meets all our needs.)

Option
Students play relay game again with several different categories of items God uses to meet our needs (things in the room, animals, plants, foods, things you can buy, etc.), using a different color marker on the same alphabet paper, or new paper, as time permits.

Game Tip
When putting students in groups, make sure to include at least one good reader and/or writer in each group. And don't worry about words getting spelled correctly. The most important part of this game is seeing how God helps us.

Discussion Questions
1. **Why do you think God made this item?**

2. **How does this item help us?**

3. **What are other ways God helps us?** (Helps us when we face bullies. Helps me forgive a friend who has hurt me.)

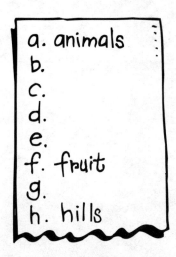

a. animals
b.
c.
d.
e.
f. fruit
g.
h. hills

Balance Relay

Bible Focus ▸ Psalm 55:16-17

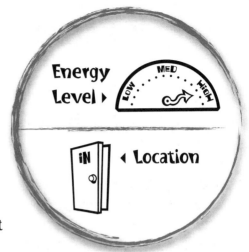

Energy Level ▸ LOW MED HIGH

iN ◂ Location

Materials

Bibles, paper cups and plates, marker.

Preparation

Divide Psalm 55:16-17 into six sections. Print each section and the reference on a cup or plate, alternating cups and plates (see sketch a). Make one set for each group of no more than six students.

Lead the Game

1. Divide class into teams of no more than six students. Each team lines up, half on one side of the room and half on the other side of the room (see sketch b). Set out plates and cups as shown.

2. At your signal, first player of each team finds the plate with the first phrase in Psalm 55:16-17. Player carries plate to other side of the room and gives plate to first player in that line. This player finds the cup with the second phrase from the verse, places it on the plate and carries cup and plate across the room, giving them to the next player in line. Continue until all the cups and plates are stacked together in the proper order. If plates and cups fall, student restacks them and continues carrying them to the other side of the room.

3. First team to finish reads Psalms 55:16-17 aloud together and answers one or two Discussion Questions below.

a. Psalm 55: 16,17 — he hears my voice — I cry out in distress — Evening, morning and noon — and the Lord saves me. — I call to God

b. cups — plates

Options

1. Teams sit together at tables and compete to see which team is the first to stack cups and plates in verse order. Discuss as above.

2. If the game seems too easy, add the rule that only one hand can be used to carry the cups and the plates.

Discussion Questions

1. **When does Psalm 55:16-17 say that God will hear us?** Students read verses in their Bibles.

2. **When are some times kids your age might ask God for help?** (Arguments. Homework too difficult. Driving with parent in a storm.)

3. **How could talking to God about the problem help?** (Reminds us that God knows what is best for us.)

Ball Bounce

Bible Focus ▸ Ruth

Energy Level ▸ LOW MED HIGH

Location ▸ iN

Materials

Bibles, container (wastebasket, large bowl, cardboard box), ball.

Lead the Game

1. **In the Bible we read the story of Ruth. Ruth helped and cared for someone in her family. God gives us people to guide us and care for us, too. Let's play a game to think of some of those people He gives us!**

2. Students line up approximately 3 feet (.9 m) from container.

3. Students take turns bouncing a ball at least once while attempting to get ball into container. If the ball goes into the container, student tells the name of someone who guides and cares for him or her. If ball does not go into the container after three tries, next student takes a turn. Continue play as time allows.

Options

1. Instead of naming people who care for them, older students give clues ("This person taught me to ride a bike." "This person helps me do math problems.") about the people for others to guess.

2. Consider the age and ability of your students and adjust distance students stand from container accordingly.

3. If you have more than six students in your group, provide additional balls and containers in order to limit the time students spend waiting in line.

Discussion Questions

1. **How does (your mother) guide and care for you?** Volunteers respond. Repeat with other people named by students.

2. **What are some ways we need to be cared for? What are some good reasons to have people to guide us?** (To help us know what to do in our lives. To teach us good ways to live.)

3. **Who are some people who teach you about God? What can you do to thank God for giving you people to guide you in knowing Him?**

Balloon Bat

Bible Focus ▸ Mark 4:35-41

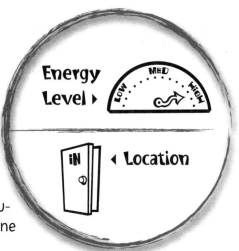

Energy Level ▸

◂ Location

Materials

Bibles, masking tape, ruler, inflated and tied balloon, chair or cone.

Preparation

Tear off 3-inch (7.5-cm) strips of tape, two for each student. Place a chair or cone representing the goal at one end of the playing area.

Lead the Game

1. **In Mark 4, we read about a time Jesus' disciples were in a difficult situation. They were in danger of drowning in a storm. What did the disciples discover?** (They could count on Jesus to help them.) **No matter how bad things look or how stuck we feel in a certain situation, we can depend on God because He is in control and promises to help us. We're going to play a game in which we're stuck in one place, but we can still help each other.**

2. Students stand evenly scattered around the playing area. Each student tapes a masking-tape X where he or she is standing.

3. Bat the balloon into the playing area at the opposite end from the goal. Students begin batting the balloon toward the goal, keeping one foot on their Xs at all times. Each student must touch the balloon at least once, and if the balloon touches the floor, it must be restarted. After the balloon goes past the goal, begin a new round by batting the balloon into the playing area again.

Options

1. Adjust size of playing area according to number of students, making sure that students stand at least an arm's distance away from each other. If playing in a small area, students must keep both feet on their Xs at all times.

2. Play this game outside on a paved area. Students use chalk to draw Xs.

Discussion Questions

1. **Even if in our lives we feel stuck in certain situations that make us feel worried, we can be sure God is able to help us in that situation. What can you do to depend on God's help during hard times?** (Pray and ask for His help. Believe God will help. Ask other people who love God for their help.)

2. **What are some reasons to depend on God for help? What is He like?**

3. **How has God helped you or your family in the past? How do you need God's help today?**

Balloon Fears

Bible Focus ▸ Exodus 13:17—15:21

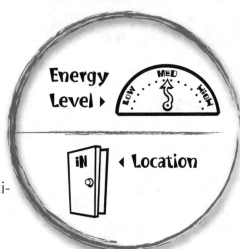

Energy Level ▸ (LOW · MED · HIGH)

Location ▸ IN

Materials
Bibles, masking tape, balloons, two pushpins.

Preparation
Mark two masking-tape squares on the floor approximately 8 to 10 feet (2.4 to 3 m) apart. Each square should be large enough for a student to stand in.

Lead the Game

1. **God freed the Israelites from Egyptian slavery. But as the Israelites came to the Red Sea, the Egyptian army raced toward them. The people were afraid until God parted the sea and all the Israelites crossed over. Let's play a game in which we talk about fears.**

2. Divide the class into two teams. Each team chooses a captain who stands in one of the squares. Give each captain a pushpin. Team members kneel on floor in the playing area between the two captains, positioning themselves evenly throughout the playing area and facing toward the middle of the playing area. No one other than the captain may enter a captain's square.

3. Blow up and tie a balloon. Tap the balloon above heads of teams. Team members, while remaining on their knees, try to tap the balloon toward their own captain so that he or she may catch and pop the balloon. (If you need students to calm down while playing this game, add the rule that each one must not only stay on his or her knees but also must keep one hand on the floor at all times.) When the balloon is popped, a volunteer from the team who popped the balloon answers one of the Discussion Questions below.

4. Continue activity as time permits with new balloons and different captains for each round of play. When time is up, lead students in a brief time of prayer, inviting volunteers to thank God for His love and help.

Discussion Questions

1. **How might the words of Exodus 15:11 help someone who is in a fearful situation?**

2. **When might the kids you know feel worried or afraid?**

3. **How can God help you with your fears?** (He gives help to do right when friends want us to cheat at school, reminds us of His power and love when we're feeling afraid.)

Basket-Wall

Bible Focus ▸ Acts 9:20-30; 11:19-26; 13:1-3

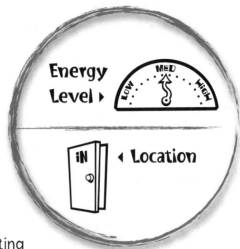

Energy Level ▸ LOW MED HIGH

iN ◂ Location

Materials

Bibles, markers, butcher paper, masking tape, small rubber kickball; optional—toy basketball hoop (over-the-door or suction-cup mounted, or child's-size hoop with stand).

Preparation

On butcher-paper sheet draw a large oval with netting hanging down to suggest a basketball hoop (one hoop for each team), and tape paper to the wall about 4- to 5-feet (1.2- to 1.5-m) high. (Optional: Use toy basketball hoop instead of drawing hoop on paper.) Place a masking-tape line on the floor 4 feet (1.2 m) away from the wall.

Lead the Game

1. Divide class into two or more teams. Choose one volunteer on each team to be the Slam Dunker. Volunteer stands behind masking-tape line and faces basketball hoop. All other team members line up behind the player. Give the ball to the last person in line. Demonstrate the different methods of passing the ball that you will call out during the game (see below).

Basket-Wall Passing

- **Down the Line:** Hand ball to the next player.

- **Behind the Back:** Pass ball behind the back.

- **Under/Over:** Alternately pass ball between the legs and over the head.

2. At your signal, players pass the ball up the line to the Slam Dunker who takes the ball to the hoop on the wall, reaches up to touch the ball on the hoop, and runs with the ball to the end of the line. Then the ball is passed up the line again, with the player at the head of the line becoming the next Slam Dunker. Periodically, call a time-out and have students answer a Discussion Question about Paul's story in Acts. After an answer, call out a new method of ball passing.

Discussion Questions

1. **How did God's people help Paul?** (They helped him escape in a basket through the city wall.)

2. **Why did Paul need encouragement?** (He was a new follower of Jesus. People were afraid of him and didn't believe him.)

3. **What was Paul able to do because his friends helped and encouraged him?** (He traveled to many countries, telling the good news about Jesus.)

Battle of Jericho

Bible Focus ▸ Joshua 1; 3; 6

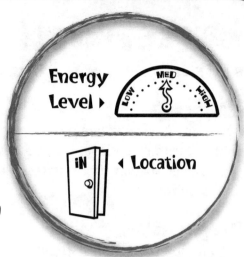

Energy Level ▸ LOW MED HIGH

iN ◂ Location

Materials

Bibles, children's music CD and player, a chair for each student less one, wooden or cardboard blocks.

Preparation

Place chairs in a circle, facing out. Several feet away from the chairs, stack blocks to make a wall.

Lead the Game

1. **No matter how hard things look, God is always available to help us. When the Israelites faced Jericho, they needed God's help. We're going to play a game to act out what happened in this story.**

2. Students walk around the chairs as you play music on CD.

3. When you stop the music, each student tries to sit in a chair. The student without a chair removes one of the blocks from the wall. Continue playing until wall has been dismantled. Play additional rounds of the game as time permits.

Options

1. If wooden or cardboard blocks are not available from preschool classes, draw a block wall on chalkboard or whiteboard. Students erase blocks as game is played.

2. If possible in your location, student without a chair knocks down the entire wall instead of removing a block. Student and another volunteer quickly rebuild the wall before the next round of the game.

Discussion Questions

1. **When are some times kids your age need encouragement?**

2. **Why might someone forget to depend on God and His encouragement?**

3. **God provides people to encourage us. If you needed courage, what could someone do or say to help you?**

Boat Tag

Bible Focus ▸ Matthew 8:23-27;
Mark 4:35-41; Luke 8:22-25; John 14:27

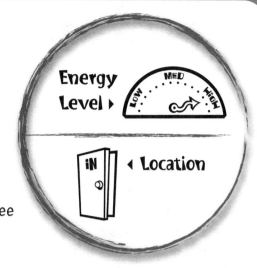

Energy Level ▸

iN ◂ Location

Materials

Bibles, masking tape.

Preparation

On the floor, use masking tape to form at least three shapes representing boats large enough to fit the number of students in your class. (For example, if you have 20 students, make four boats large enough for five students to stand in each shape.) Make shapes 4 to 5 feet (1.2 to 1.5 m) apart.

Lead the Game

1. **Because God's power is greater than anything, He can help us when we're afraid. Jesus' disciples learned about His power when they were in boats during a big storm. Jesus made the storm stop. Let's play a game that reminds us of Jesus' power.**

2. Ask a volunteer to be "It." Form three groups from remaining students. Each group stands in a separate boat marked on the floor.

3. One at a time call out such descriptions as "kids wearing red" or "kids in second grade." Students who fit each description run to new boats while "It" tries to tag them before they are inside their new boats. Any student who is tagged becomes "It" also. Continue play, periodically calling out "Boats are sinking," at which all students must run to new boats. When only a few students have not been tagged, begin a new round of the game with a new "It."

Options

1. If you have a large group, choose more than one student to be "It."

2. If space is limited, play this game outside on a paved area. Draw the boats with chalk.

Discussion Questions

1. **What are some powerful things that kids your age might be afraid of?** (Storms. Earthquakes. Tornadoes.)

2. **Why can God help us when we are afraid of these things?** (Because He is the one true God. God created everything. He is more powerful than anything He created. He loves us and wants to help us.)

3. **How does God help us when we are afraid?** (Answers our prayers. Gives us adults to help us feel safe. Helps us remember His power. Gives us courage and peace.)

Care-Full Question

Bible Focus ▸ Mark 5:21-43; Luke 8:40-56

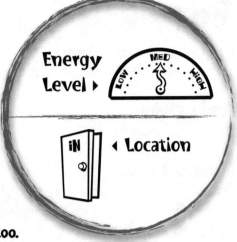

Energy Level ▸ LOW MED HIGH

iN ◂ Location

Materials

Bibles, large sheet of paper, marker, masking tape, blindfold.

Lead the Game

1. In the Bible we read a story about a time Jesus cared for a sick woman and a young girl who had died. God knows us and helps us with our needs, too. One way God helps us is to provide caring people who help us. Let's play a game to name some of the people who care for us.

2. Students name specific people who care for them. List students' responses on a large sheet of paper. Display paper for students to refer to during the game.

3. Students stand in a circle. Volunteer stands in the middle of the circle, and puts on a blindfold or closes his or her eyes. Students standing in the circle begin walking clockwise. When volunteer stamps his or her feet twice, students stop moving. Volunteer points in any direction and says, "Good morning, Mr. Brown. Who cares for you?" (Note: Volunteer may substitute any last name for "Brown.")

4. Student to whom volunteer pointed responds by saying "(My parents) care for me," referring to list made earlier if needed. If volunteer can identify the speaker, they change places. If not, play another round of the game. If volunteer does not identify speaker after two rounds, allow another student to have a turn.

Option

Before the game, review students' names by grouping students in pairs and asking each student to introduce his or her partner to the whole group. Or play game in groups of no more than eight so that students will easily be able to remember each others' names.

Discussion Questions

1. How have some of the people we talked about in this game cared for you?

2. As you grow older, how do you think parents and teachers will continue to care for you? (Help me learn to do new things like driving a car. Help me choose which college to attend.)

3. What can you do this week to thank someone who cares for you?

Cereal Spell-Off

Bible Focus ▸ Matthew 6:25-34; John 14:27

Energy Level ▸ LOW MED HIGH

Location ▸ iN

Materials

Bibles, bowls, alphabet-shaped cereal.

Preparation

Pour a large amount of cereal into two bowls. Place bowls on the far side of the playing area.

Lead the Game

1. **Jesus' words in the Bible help us know that we can have peace because God knows what we need and promises to help us. Let's find a reminder of that during our game today.**

2. Divide group into two teams. Students line up in the playing area, across from the bowls of cereal letters.

3. At your signal, the first student on each team moves quickly to his or her team's bowl of cereal letters and digs through it to find a P. Student returns to team with letter. The next student moves to the bowl and searches for an E. Relay continues in this manner with each student finding the next letter of the word "PEACE." Continue playing until all students have had a turn and each team has formed the word "PEACE" as many times as possible.

4. Students from the team that formed "PEACE" the most times answer one of the Discussion Questions below. Continue discussion with other questions.

Discussion Questions

1. **God knows what we need and promises to care for us. Why can we depend on God's help?** (God always keeps His promises. God promises to answer our prayers. God's love for us never changes or fails.)

2. **What does John 14:27 tell us about peace from God?** (He gives us peace so that we do not need to be worried or afraid.)

3. **How can we get the peace that Jesus said He left with us?** (Ask Jesus to forgive our sins and tell Him that we want to be members of God's family. Keep trusting God, even when we're worried.) Talk to interested students about salvation (see "Leading a Child to Christ" article on p. 11).

Choose Your Way

Bible Focus ▸ Psalm 46:1

Energy Level ▸ LOW MED HIGH

Location ▸ iN

Materials
Bibles, scrap paper, marker, masking tape.

Lead the Game
1. Volunteers suggest two categories of people (baby, mom, teacher, etc.), four places (home, soccer field, school hallway, store, park, etc.), and six objects (soccer ball, necklace, sock, milkshake, CD, etc.). Write named people, places and items on separate sheets of scrap paper. Place papers on floor as shown in sketch.

2. Volunteer walks across papers, stepping on one paper from each category. Using words volunteer chose, students suggest situations in which a kid might need God's love and protection. (A boy at the park kicks a soccer ball and it hits an old man.) Ask the discussion questions below after each situation.

3. Repeat with other students and new situations as time permits.

Option
1. Students add words that describe feelings (happy, angry, fearful, etc.). Students then use person, place, object and feeling words to suggest situations.

2. Instead of the group working together to suggest situations, volunteer makes up the situation as he or she steps on the words.

Game Tip
Use large index cards if no scrap paper is available.

Discussion Questions
1. **What are some words in Psalm 46:1 that would help someone in this situation? Why?**

2. **What can we say to God when we feel like we need His help? What would you say to God if you were in this situation?**

3. **How would you want God to help you if you were in this situation?**

Colorful Costumes

Bible Focus ▸ Genesis 37; 39—45

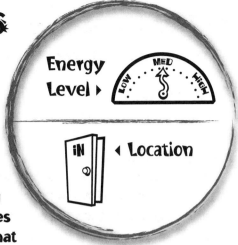

Energy Level ▸

LOW   MED   HIGH

iN   ◂ Location

Materials

Bibles, rolls of tape, colored newspaper comics, colored construction paper, colored tissue paper.

Lead the Game

1. Getting a coat of many colors was the beginning of a long adventure for Joseph. There were times when Joseph had to go through hard times in that adventure, but God was still with him. We're going to have an adventure making our own colorful costumes that look like coats.

2. Divide class into groups of no more than four. Give each group a roll of tape and some comics, construction paper and tissue paper.

3. Each group chooses one student to dress in a costume that will look like a "coat" of paper. Students make coats by taping paper together. Each coat must have a front, a back and two sleeves. Groups dress volunteers.

Options

1. If you have older students, students compete to see which group can make the best coat costume in five minutes.

2. Take instant-photo of each student wearing a coat.

3. Invite students wearing coats to participate in a "fashion show" of coats; describe the coats as students walk in front of group, commenting on the ways coats have been constructed.

Discussion Questions

1. No matter what happened to him, Joseph remembered that God was with him. When are some times kids your age need to remember that God is with them?

2. When has God helped you or your family in the past?

3. When do you need to remember God's love and help?

Family Ball

Bible Focus ▸ Matthew 28:16-20; Acts 1:1-11

Materials

Bibles, volleyball or tennis ball.

Energy Level ▸ LOW MED HIGH

iN ◂ Location

Lead the Game

1. Shortly before Jesus returned to heaven, He promised to be with the members of His family both now and in the future. Because of this promise, we know Jesus will always care for us. Let's play a game where we call out each other's names to remember that we can all be members of God's family.

2. Students stand in a circle. Choose one volunteer to stand in the center of the circle and be the Ball Tosser. Ball Tosser throws the ball straight up into the air and calls the name of one of the students. Student whose name was called moves to get the ball, becoming the Ball Catcher. All other students move around the playing area, attempting to move away from the Ball Catcher. When the Ball Catcher gets the ball, he or she calls out "Freeze" and all the other students must freeze.

3. Ball Catcher rolls the ball at any of the other students who must stay standing on one foot but can lean out of the way of the ball. The student who is first touched by the ball answers one of the Discussion Questions below and becomes the Ball Tosser for the next round. If the ball does not touch any student, the Ball Catcher becomes the new Ball Tosser. Students return to circle position and the new Ball Tosser throws the ball again, calling out the name of a different student. Repeat play as time allows.

Options

1. Students wear name tags or review names of classmates before playing this game.

2. For older students, challenge the Ball Catcher to catch the ball before it hits the floor or after just one bounce. If the Ball Catcher does not catch the ball, he or she becomes the new Ball Tosser and throws the ball for another student, forfeiting the opportunity to roll the ball at anyone.

Discussion Questions

1. **How does Jesus show that He cares for the members of His family?** (Loves us. Is with us. Helps us make wise choices. Prepares a place for us in heaven.)

2. **How can we become members of God's family?** (Believe in Jesus' death and resurrection and ask Jesus to forgive our sins.)

3. **Why is it so important to know that Jesus is always ready to care for us?**

Frisbee Bowling

Bible Focus ▶ Exodus 16—17:7

Energy Level ▶ LOW · MED · HIGH

◀ Location iN

Materials

Bibles, paper cups, markers, Frisbee.

Lead the Game

1. As God's people moved through the desert, He provided a bread-like food called manna to fall from the sky. The people always had enough to eat. And God also gives us everything we need. Let's play a game to remember the good things He provides for us.

2. **What are some of the needs people have?** (Family. Friends. Clothes. Help. Shelter. Food. Transportation.) Print each category on a separate paper cup. On one side of the classroom, set cups up like bowling pins (see sketch).

3. Students stand in a line at least 6 feet (1.8 m) from cups. Students take turns rolling the Frisbee on its edge toward cups. When a student knocks over a cup, student names one specific thing God has given him or her from category on that cup (Family: mom, grandpa, sister), and then places cup back in correct position. Repeat play as time allows.

Options

1. Instead of paper cups, collect empty soda cans or plastic liter bottles. Print categories on separate index cards and tape cards to cans or bottles. Set up cans or bottles as above.

2. Make one set of cups for every six to eight students. Set up bowling areas for each group of students.

3. Adjust distance from which students roll Frisbee according to age of students. Older students may stand further back than younger students.

4. If students continually knock down all the cups, spread cups further apart or let students choose one of the cups which have been knocked down.

Discussion Questions

1. **What are some times in the Bible when God gave people what they needed?** (Manna and water to the Israelites in the desert. A dry sea for the Israelites to get away from Pharaoh. Instructions for Noah to build an ark, so he could be safe during the flood.)

2. **With the things God has given us, how can He use us to help provide for other people's needs?** (Share what you have with people who need it. Help serve food to people at a homeless shelter. Give offering at church, so the church can use the money to help people with their needs.)

Numbered Needs

Bible Focus ▸ Mark 2:1-12; Luke 5:17-26; Philippians 4:19

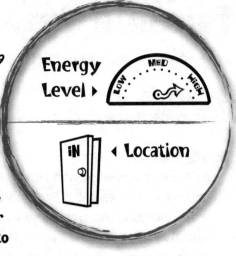

Materials

Bibles, sock (or eraser), chalkboard, chalk.

Lead the Game

1. **Jesus healed a paralyzed man when the man's friends brought him to Jesus. No matter what we need, we can depend on God to help and care for us. We're going to play a game in which we race to get something we need.**

2. Play a game like Steal the Bacon. Divide class into two equal teams. Each team stands in a straight line facing the other team, leaving about 10 feet (3 m) between the teams. One team numbers off from one end of the line, while the other team numbers off from the opposite end (see sketch).

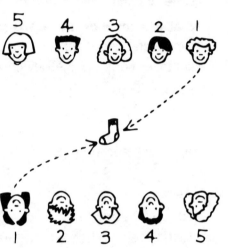

3. Hold up sock (or eraser). **We're going to pretend this is something we need. What is something we need that this (sock) could represent?** (Water, food, air, warm clothes, shelter, etc.) Place the sock in the center of the playing area, reminding students of what it represents.

4. Call a number. Students on both teams with that number run to grab the item in the center. Student who gets the item first runs back to his or her team. Student who does not get the item tells a new need that the item could represent for the next round. Print each suggested need on the chalkboard. Call a new number each round.

Options

1. If you have a wide variety of ages in the group, assign numbers so that students compete against students of similar ages.

2. Play this game using objects which more closely represent needs students may have: water bottle, jacket, apple, book, photo of family or friends, etc.

Discussion Questions

1. **How is something you need different from something you want?**

2. Read Philippians 4:19 aloud. **How does God help and care for our needs? In what way might God use you to meet another's need?**

3. **How does God care for some of our wants?**

Partner Play

Bible Focus ▸ Matthew 28:16-20; Acts 1:1-11

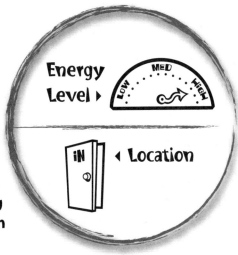

Energy Level ▸ LOW MED HIGH

iN ◂ Location

Materials

Bibles, several tennis balls.

Lead the Game

1. **Because Jesus is alive, we know He will keep His promise to always be with us, helping us to obey His commands. Let's play a game we can only win if we have a partner helping us.**

2. Divide group into equal teams of at least six students each. (Join a team yourself if needed.) Teams line up in single-file lines on one side of the playing area with plenty of space between teams. Students become partners with team member behind or in front of them in line.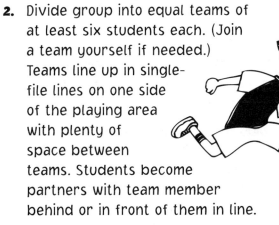

3. Give the first partners in each line a tennis ball. At your signal, first partners on each team roll ball back and forth to each other while moving to the opposite side of the playing area and then back to line. Next partners in team repeat action. Continue until all partners on each team have had a turn. Switch partners and repeat play.

Options

1. If you have fewer than 12 students, time partners with a stopwatch. Partners race against their own or other partners' times.

2. For a variation during repeat play, have partners bounce or gently kick ball back and forth.

Discussion Questions

1. **What would happen if you had no partner for this game?** (You wouldn't be able to get the ball back quickly or follow the rules of the game.)

2. **What are some of the ways Jesus helps us?** (Helps us remember His Word. Helps us know what to do to obey Him. Forgives us.)

3. **How does it make you feel to know that Jesus promises to always be with you?**

Peace Hop

Bible Focus ▸ Psalm 29:11

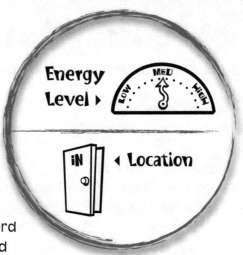

Energy Level ▸ LOW MED HIGH

iN ◂ Location

Materials

Bibles, butcher paper, measuring stick, markers, masking tape.

Preparation

Draw a large grid on butcher paper, forming at least 20 10-inch (25-cm) squares. Print one letter of the word "PEACE" in each square, as shown in sketch. Tape grid to floor in center of playing area.

Lead the Game

1. **Psalm 29:11 tells us that God gives His peace to people. God's peace helps us to trust in God's care instead of worrying. Let's play a game about peace and talk about some times when we need to ask God for peace.**

2. To play game, students stand around edges of the grid. Starting at any P square on the grid, first student hops on squares to spell "PEACE," and then he or she thinks of a time when kids his or her age might worry or not have peace. Student writes that situation in any square with a P in it. To finish this round of the game, repeat activity with four other students, instructing them to write situations in squares with E, A, C and E.

3. Play several rounds of the game, until all squares have situations written in them or until time is up. As students suggest situations, ask the Discussion Questions below.

Options

1. Prepare a grid for each group of six to eight students.

2. To make the game more challenging, students may not hop in any square that has a situation written in it.

3. Instead of writing situations, students say Psalm 29:11 aloud (or find and read it in a Bible) and then write their names in squares.

P	E	A	C	A
E	C	E	E	C
P	A	P lost my homework	P	E
E	C	E	E	A

Discussion Questions

1. **What does it mean to say that we have God's peace?** (We can depend on God's love and care for us. We know He will help us in any situation.)

2. **When have you seen someone have God's peace because he or she remembered God's promise of care?** Share your own example before students answer.

3. **What might a kid do instead of worrying if he prayed and trusted God about (lost homework)?** (Do his homework again. Have courage to talk to teacher.) Repeat question with other situations students wrote in grid.

Picture Hunt

Bible Focus ▸ Acts 2

Materials
Bibles, old birthday cards, scissors, markers.

Preparation
Cut the back off of each card, leaving only the front design.

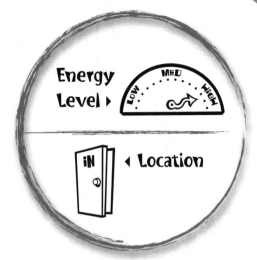

Energy Level ▸ LOW MED HIGH

iN ◂ Location

Lead the Game
1. **God gives us the Holy Spirit to guide us and to help us tell others about Jesus. When God first gave the Holy Spirit to Jesus' followers, the Church began as a place where people could learn about Jesus! Let's play a game to celebrate the birthday of the Church.**

2. Ask volunteers to suggest sentences or phrases which describe the Holy Spirit ("Helps us," "Teaches us," "Guides us," "Sent from God," "Promised by Jesus"). As sentences or phrases are suggested, print them on separate birthday cards. Make enough cards so that there is a card for every two students. Repeat sentences or phrases as needed.

3. Students cut cards into two puzzle pieces.

4. Collect all puzzle pieces and mix them up. Then distribute puzzle pieces to students. At your signal, students race to match up their puzzle pieces. When students match pieces, they call out "Happy Birthday" and sit down. When all pieces have been matched, pair of students who first sat down read the message on their puzzle pieces aloud. Collect puzzle pieces and play again. Continue game as time permits.

Options
1. Instead of using birthday cards, cut squares of a variety of styles of birthday wrapping paper.

2. After cards have been cut into puzzle pieces, keep one puzzle piece of each card and hide the other puzzle piece in your room. Give each student one puzzle piece. At your signal, each student hunts around the room to find the puzzle piece that fits his or her piece. After finding the piece, student calls out "Happy Birthday" and sits down.

Discussion Questions
1. **Why did God send the Holy Spirit?** (To help members of His family love and obey Him.)

2. **What are some ways the Holy Spirit can help us?** (Guides us in knowing the right things to do. Reminds us of and helps us follow God's commands in the Bible. Helps us know the words to say when we tell others about Jesus.)

Take the Challenge!

Bible Focus ▸ 1 Kings 17—19; Nahum 1:7

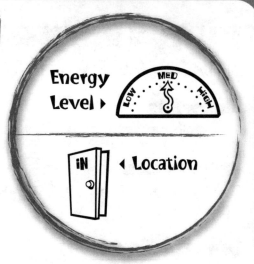

Energy Level ▸

iN ◂ Location

Materials

Bibles, materials for one or more of the challenges suggested below.

Lead the Games

Lead students to participate in one or more of the following challenges:

Ping-Pong Challenge

Students form teams of four and hold a towel stretched out between them. Students work as a team to bounce a Ping-Pong ball up into the air without the ball falling onto the floor. Teams challenge each other to see who can keep the ball off the ground the longest.

Balloon Challenge

Give each student a balloon. Student writes initials on balloon. Student blows up balloon and pinches end to make sure no air escapes. All students stand shoulder-to-shoulder on one side of the playing area. At your signal, students let go of balloons and watch to see where balloons land. Student whose balloon lands farthest from the group gets to give the signal for the next round. (Variation: Blow up and tie balloons ahead of time. Students write their initials on balloons. Students hit the balloons as far as possible with one hit.)

Feather-Blowing Challenge

Students kneel around a table. Students on each side of the table form a team. Set a craft feather (or cotton ball) in the middle of the table. Students blow the feather toward the other side of the table while trying to keep the feather from falling off their own side of the table. (Variation: If you have small tables, students form pairs or trios. Teams rotate as in a tournament so that winners are challenging winners and vice versa.)

Discussion Questions

1. **What made the challenge(s) hard? How did you feel if your team won?**

2. **How do you think Elijah felt when God showed His power and answered Elijah's prayer in the challenge with the Baal worshipers?** (Thankful to God. Glad that God proved He is the one true God.)

3. **What kinds of challenges might a kid your age need God's help to overcome?** (Telling the truth. Being patient with a brother or sister.)

Life Application Games
God's Love

Action Relay

Bible Focus ▸ Psalm 105:2

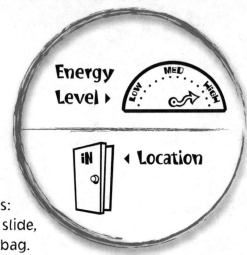

Energy Level ▸ LOW MED HIGH

Location ▸ iN

Materials
Bibles, index cards, marker, paper bag; optional—paper.

Preparation
Print each of these motions on separate index cards: skip, jump, tiptoe, walk backward, hop on one foot, slide, walk heel-to-toe, crawl. Put index cards in a paper bag.

Lead the Game

1. **God's actions show His love for us. To celebrate His love for us, we're going to play a game in which we tell about God's great actions.**

2. Group students into two equal teams. Teams line up on one side of an open area in your classroom. Place bag of prepared index cards on other side of open area.

3. **What has God done that you have read about in the Bible?** (Sent Jesus to die for our sins. Healed people. Provided food and water for the Israelites in the desert. Provided bread and fish for the people in Galilee.) (Optional: If children in group are unfamiliar with Bible information, list responses on paper for use in the relay.) **To take a turn in our game today, tell one of God's great actions!**

4. At your signal, the first student on each team runs to the other side of the room and announces to the group one of God's great actions. Then student moves to bag of index cards, picks one card from the bag, reads card, returns it to the bag and then returns to his or her team in the manner written on the card. Continue until all students have had a turn. Teams sit down when all members have completed turns. Ask the Discussion Questions below.

Discussion Questions

1. **When is a time a kid your age might experience God's loving care?** (When He answers prayer. When He provides food.)

2. **What are some good ways to learn more about God's loving acts?** (Read the Bible. Ask older people who love God about His great acts.)

3. **What can you do to tell others about God's loving acts?** Read Psalm 105:2 aloud.

Beat the Ball

Bible Focus ▸ 1 John 3:16

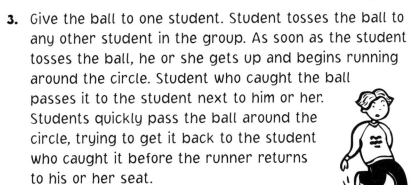

Energy Level ▸ LOW MED HIGH

iN ◂ Location

Materials

Bibles, foam ball or tennis ball.

Lead the Game

1. Read 1 John 3:16 aloud. **We learn what love is like by looking at Jesus' life. Let's play a game to think about some of the different ways Jesus showed love.**

2. Students sit in a circle in the middle of the playing area.

3. Give the ball to one student. Student tosses the ball to any other student in the group. As soon as the student tosses the ball, he or she gets up and begins running around the circle. Student who caught the ball passes it to the student next to him or her. Students quickly pass the ball around the circle, trying to get it back to the student who caught it before the runner returns to his or her seat.

4. Student who gets beaten (either the student who first tossed the ball or the student who first caught the ball) names one thing Jesus did to show love while He was here on Earth. Repeat game as time allows, giving ball to a different student to start each round. Between each round, ask one of the Discussion Questions below.

Options

1. If you have more than 15 students, form two groups to play the game.

2. As a challenge, have older students toss the ball to one another instead of passing it. Each student in the circle must still handle the ball as the runner returns to his or her seat.

Discussion Questions

1. **What are some ways Jesus showed love to people?** (Cared for people's needs. Helped them get well. Gave them food. Was kind to them. Taught them.)

2. **What is one way to show love like Jesus did when you are at school? In your neighborhood?** (Forgive someone when he or she says something rude or mean to you. Invite kids whom other people usually ignore to play with you.)

3. **What might happen if we show love in some of the ways Jesus showed love?**

Footloose Relay

Bible Focus ▸ Genesis 2:4—3

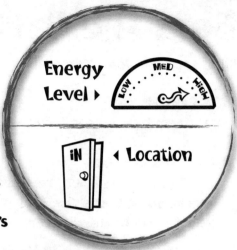

Energy Level ▸ LOW MED HIGH

iN ◂ Location

Materials

Bibles, large sheet of butcher paper, pencils.

Lead the Game

1. When God made us and the world, He showed His love for us. One of the ways He showed His love is that He created us each a little differently. Let's find out one way we are each special.

2. Each student traces one of his or her feet (with shoe on) on the butcher paper.

3. Students line up across the room from the paper. (If you have more than 10 students, students form two or more teams and race against each other.)

4. At your signal, the first student(s) in line runs to the paper, finds his or her shoe outline, removes his or her shoe and leaves it in the outline. Student returns to line, hopping on the foot that still has a shoe on it. Students in line repeat the process until everyone has had a turn.

5. If you have time, play another round, with each student tracing his or her hand this time. Student runs to paper, finds his or her handprint and writes his or her initials in it with a pencil. Student then skips back to line. Students in line repeat the process until everyone has had a turn.

Option

If you have older students, play another round with students hopping back to paper to retrieve a teammate's shoe.

Discussion Questions

1. How did God make you the same as others? Different than others?

2. If everyone in our class was created exactly alike, how might your parents find you after church?

3. How did God show His love for us when He created the earth, the animals and you? (He made the sun, so that we have heat and light. He gave animals ways to protect themselves. He made our bodies in amazing ways.)

Full of God's Love

Bible Focus ▸ Acts 2; Romans 5:5

Energy Level ▸ LOW MED HIGH

◂ Location iN OuT

Materials

Bibles; for each team of six students: two containers (buckets, bowls or plastic tubs), a small plastic cup and water, uncooked rice or uncooked beans.

Preparation

Fill half of the containers with an equal amount of water, rice or beans. For each team, set an empty container and a full container next to each other on one side of the playing area.

Lead the Game

1. **Let's play a pouring relay to remind us of the Bible verse that tells us that God poured out His love by sending the Holy Spirit.**

2. Group students into teams of no more than six. Teams line up in single-file lines across the room from containers. Give a cup to the first student in each line.

3. At your signal, the first student in each line runs to the filled container opposite from his or her team, takes one full scoop with cup and pours contents of cup into empty container. Student returns to line and gives cup to next student who repeats process. Several times during the game, call out "Full Cups." Each student with a cup in his or her hand when "Full Cups" is called must go to another team's container and transfer a scoop for that team instead. The first team to transfer all its contents wins.

Option

Play game outdoors and fill containers with 1/2 cup water. Give the first student in each team a straw. Student runs to team's containers, puts straw into water and then places finger over one end of the straw. Student then withdraws straw, positions it over the empty container and takes finger off the top of the straw to release water. Student runs back to line and gives straw to next student in line.

Discussion Questions

1. **God has given us the Holy Spirit because He loves us. What are some other ways God has shown love to us?** (Sent Jesus to take the punishment for our sins. Created a beautiful world for us to enjoy. Answers our prayers.)

2. **The Holy Spirit helps us show God's love and care to others. What are some things we can do for others with the help of the Holy Spirit?**

Human Bowling

Bible Focus ▸ Matthew 19:13-15; Mark 10:13-16;
Luke 18:15-17; 1 John 3:1

Energy Level ▸ LOW MED HIGH

iN ◂ Location

Materials
Bibles, masking tape, playground ball or basketball.

Preparation
Use masking tape to mark a starting line.

Lead the Game

1. **You and every other child are important to God! Jesus showed His love for children when He told them to come to Him. Jesus' disciples tried to stop the children from seeing Jesus by sending them away. Let's play a game to remind us how much Jesus loves children and to remember that each of us is important to God!**

2. Select a volunteer to be the bowler. The remaining students—the human bowling pins—stand approximately 10 feet (3 m) away from the starting line in bowling-pin formation (see sketch). Students stand one arm's length apart (when arm is extended, student's fingertips touch a nearby student's shoulders).

3. Bowler names a way God shows love (answers prayer, forgives sins, gives courage, helps us do right) and rolls ball, trying to hit the feet of one of the human bowling pins. The "pins" must keep their left feet on the floor, but they may move their right feet to avoid being hit by the ball. First student hit with the ball becomes the bowler for the next round. Continue game as time permits.

Options

1. For groups larger than eight or nine students, form more than one game.

2. For each new round, "pins" reform with students who were in the back moving to the front.

Discussion Questions

1. **How are important people usually treated?** (Given a red carpet. Given a special seat. Get driven around in a special car. Have people to help them do everything.)

2. **How do we know that we are important to God?** (The Bible tells us. We are called His children.) Have an older student read 1 John 3:1 aloud.

3. **What things does God do to show you that you are important to Him?** (Listens to and answers my prayers. Sent Jesus to take the punishment for my sins so that I can live forever with God. Gives me people who love and care for me.)

Ladder Leap

Bible Focus ▸ Genesis 25:19-34; 27—33; Psalm 136:1

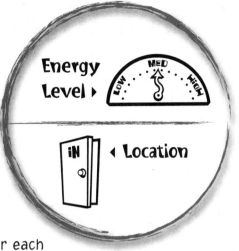

Energy Level ▸ LOW MED HIGH

iN ◂ Location

Materials

Bibles, masking tape, sheets of paper, marker.

Preparation

1. Make a masking-tape ladder on the floor, with at least 10 rungs or spaces (make one ladder for every 10 students).

2. Print actions on separate sheets of paper—one for each ladder space: "touch your toes," "turn around three times," "do five jumping jacks," "shake hands with everyone in line," etc. Place papers outside ladder outline next to each space.

Lead the Game

1. **Jacob and Esau were two brothers who didn't get along and spent many years apart. The two brothers caused problems because of the many things they did wrong to each other. But God allowed the brothers to forgive each other and make peace. God loves us even when we do wrong. Let's play a game to remind us that God doesn't give up on us!**

2. Students form a single line. First student hops on one foot through ladder spaces, while saying the sentence "My name is (P-E-T-E-R) and God does not give up on me!" and hopping one space for each word and for each letter of his or her name. Student hops up and down the ladder as many times as needed to complete sentence.

3. On the word "me," student stops and reads what the paper says in that space. Student leads all students in doing whatever action the paper says to do.

4. Repeat game with each student in line.

12"(30 cm)

Discussion Questions

1. **When might a kid your age feel like God doesn't love him or her?**

2. **What should we do when we've disobeyed God?** (Ask God for forgiveness and ask His help in doing right.)

3. **Read Psalm 136:1 aloud. How do we know that God will never give up loving us?** (He loves all people. He is more powerful than anyone. He is the only true God.)

String Hunt

Bible Focus ▸ Psalm 130:7

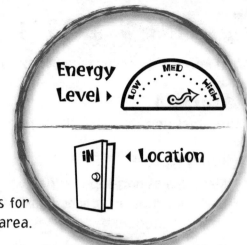

Energy Level ▸ LOW MED HIGH

iN ◂ Location

Materials

Bibles, string (or yarn), scissors, stopwatch or watch with second hand.

Preparation

Cut string into varying lengths (at least two lengths for each student). Hide string in classroom or outdoor area.

Lead the Game

1. Read Psalm 130:7 aloud. **Let's play a game to remind us of God's great love for us. In our game, the string we collect will get bigger and bigger to remind us that God's love is bigger than all the wrong things we have done.**

2. Group students in two or more teams of four or five students each.

3. At your signal, students look for and collect string, trying to find as many pieces as they can in 30 seconds.

4. After time is called, team members lay out end-to-end the pieces of string they have collected. Team who collected the longest length wins. Play additional rounds of this game as time permits. (Volunteers take turns collecting and hiding string.)

5. At the end of the game time, teams use string to spell out the words "God's Love."

Options

1. If space is limited, students roll string into balls to see who collected the most string.

GOD'S LOVE

2. Depending on the number of students in your class, vary the amount of time students have in which to collect string.

3. To help students become better acquainted, form new teams for each round of the game.

Discussion Questions

1. **What are some big things that might remind you of how big God's love is?** (The ocean. A tall redwood tree. A huge waterfall. The sky.)

2. **How does God's love get rid of our sin?** (Because God loves us, God forgives us. Jesus loves us so much He took the punishment we deserve.)

3. **What are some ways Jesus showed God's love in the Bible?** (He made sick people well. He taught others about God. He died on the cross.)

Towel Travel

Bible Focus ▶ Mark 2:1-12; Psalm 106:3

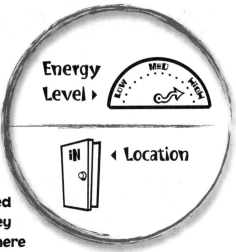

Energy Level ▶ LOW MED HIGH

IN ◀ Location

Materials

Bibles, two of each of the following: towels, stuffed animals, balloons.

Lead the Game

1. **A paralyzed man's four friends were so convinced that Jesus could help their friend get better, they carried him on a mat all the way to the house where Jesus was.**

2. Students form two teams. Teams line up in single-file lines on one side of the playing area. Give a towel and a stuffed animal to each team.

3. At your signal, the first four students on each team grasp the corners of the towel and place the stuffed animal in the center. Students walk together, carrying the animal across the playing area and back. If the stuffed animal falls off, students return to the starting point and try again.

4. When first group of students is finished, the next foursome carries the stuffed animal on the towel across the room and back. Relay continues until all students have had a turn. (Note: Some students may need to take more than one turn to provide a foursome for each turn.) Ask one of the Discussion Questions below to a volunteer from the first team to finish.

5. **Now let's try to carry something a little bit tougher.** Give each team a balloon. One student on each team inflates balloon. Students repeat relay, carrying a balloon instead of a stuffed animal on the towel.

Options

1. Invite students to tell other Bible story details if they have already heard the story.

2. If you have fewer than 20 students, students may work in pairs instead of foursomes to carry the towel.

Discussion Questions

1. **Jesus showed God's love as He healed the paralyzed man. In what ways can God's love help kids your age?** (Help them feel better about how they look. Help us love both parents going through a divorce.)

2. **What are some of the ways sharing God's love can help people in your family? People at school? People in your neighborhood?** Read Psalm 106:3 aloud.

Who Does God Love?

Bible Focus ▸ Acts 9:1-31; Romans 6:23

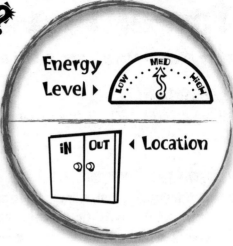
Energy Level ▸ LOW MED HIGH

iN OUT ◂ Location

Materials
Bibles, blindfold.

Lead the Game

1. **To become a Christian, we must make a choice to accept Jesus' love and be a part of God's family. The game we're going to play will remind us of God's love for us.**

2. Play a game like Marco Polo. Ask a volunteer to stand on one side of the playing area. Blindfold the volunteer. Students quietly position themselves at random around the playing area. Volunteer begins calling "God loves . . ." Rest of students answer "me."

God loves...

3. Blindfolded volunteer moves toward students by listening to their voices. As he or she continues calling "God loves . . ." students around the room must respond each time. Depending on the size of your playing area, the students who respond to the blindfolded volunteer may stay frozen in one spot or may move around as they respond. (If you have a large playing area or a large number of students, students should stay frozen.)

4. When the volunteer finds and tags a student, that student (or a student who hasn't had a turn yet) is blindfolded for the next round. Continue game as time permits.

Options

1. Instead of responding "me," students may respond with names of friends or family members.

2. A paper bag may be used instead of a blindfold.

Discussion Questions

1. **What are some choices kids your age make every day? What are some hard choices? Some easy ones?**

2. **What might be one of the most important choices anyone can ever make?** (Whether or not to become a Christian and be a part of God's family.)

3. **How can we choose to become part of God's family?** (By asking Jesus to forgive our sins and to be with us forever.)

Life Application Games

God's Power

ע = gimel (take all)

ה = hei (take half)

ש = shin (add one)

נ = nun (do nothing)

Dreidel Power

Bible Focus ▸ 1 Kings 5—8

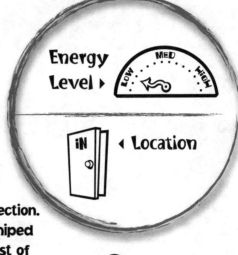

Energy Level ▸ [LOW MED HIGH]

iN ◀ Location

Materials

Bibles, a dreidel for every four to six students, game pieces (small candies, nuts, paper squares or pennies); optional—large sheet of paper, marker.

Lead the Game

1. **We can worship God for His great power and protection. In New Testament times, the Hebrew people worshiped God at the Temple during a holiday called the Feast of Dedication, now called Hanukkah. This holiday reminded God's people of God's power. Let's play a game that is played by people today to celebrate Hanukkah.**

2. Students form groups of four to six. Give each group a dreidel and give each student at least six game pieces.

3. Groups sit in circles. Each student puts one game piece into the center of the circle. Students take turns spinning the dreidel and following the directions for the letter the dreidel lands on: gimel (GIH-mel)—take all pieces from the center; hei (HEH)—take half of the pieces; shin (SHIHN)—add one; nun (NOON)—do nothing. (Optional: Print game instructions on paper for students to refer to.) **The letters on the dreidel are the first letters from the Hebrew words for "a great miracle happened there." God's people believed God had done a miracle when during the Temple's rededication a one-day supply of oil for the menorah lights lasted for eight days.** If all game pieces are taken, each student puts in one game piece. The game ends when one player has all the game pieces or when time is called.

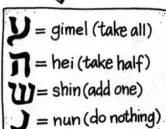

= gimel (take all)
= hei (take half)
= shin (add one)
= nun (do nothing)

Option

Play dreidel as part of a Hanukkah party. Decorate room with blue and white streamers, play Hebrew songs, serve a holiday snack such as latkes (potato pancakes) or powdered donuts and use chocolate foil-wrapped coins as game pieces for the dreidel game.

Discussion Questions

1. **What stories about God's power have you read in the Bible?** (The parting of the Red Sea. Elijah being fed by ravens. Jesus healing the blind man.)

2. **When have you been helped by God's power? How has God cared for you?**

3. **How do you need God's help and care today?**

Exodus Relay

Bible Focus ▸ Exodus 12

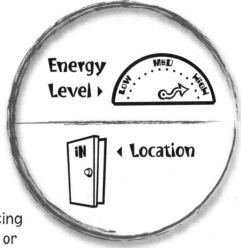

Energy Level ▸

iN ◂ Location

Materials

Bibles, two bathrobes with ties, two pairs of adult-size sandals, two walking sticks or canes, two paper plates, crackers (matzos or saltines).

Preparation

On one side of the playing area make two piles, placing one bathrobe, a pair of sandals and a walking stick or cane in each pile. On the other side of the playing area, put a paper plate across from each pile and place half the crackers on each paper plate.

Lead the Game

1. **Whenever we need help, we can depend on God's power! That's what the Israelites did when they got ready to leave Egypt where they had been slaves for many years. Let's play a relay game to remember what the Israelites did!**

2. **Guess where we're going to find the directions for today's game—in the Bible! Let's listen to the command God gave the Israelites when they were getting ready to leave Egypt.** Read, or have a volunteer read, Exodus 12:11. **For our relay, we're going to put on this cloak (bathrobe), put on the sandals and carry the staff across the room to get a cracker from the plate. Then we eat the cracker and return to our team for the next player to have a turn.** (Optional: volunteer demonstrates how to wear the clothing as you explain.)

3. Have students form two teams. Each team lines up by one pile of clothing. At your signal, students begin relay. Continue until all students have had a turn.

Option

If you have more than 16 students, form additional teams and bring additional game supplies.

Discussion Questions

1. **When are some times kids your age need to trust God's power?**

2. **When are some times God's power has helped you?** Tell your own answer before volunteers respond.

3. **What can we do to receive God's help?** (Pray to God and ask for His help. Read what God tells us to do in the Bible.)

Slow-Motion Relay

Bible Focus ▶ Psalm 29:11

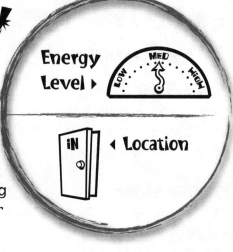

Energy Level ▶ LOW MED HIGH

iN ◀ Location

Materials

Bibles, masking tape, two chairs, children's music CD and player.

Preparation

Set up a relay course: Make a starting line with masking tape on one side of the room and place two chairs (or other objects) on the other side of the room for students to move around during race.

Lead the Game

1. Divide class into two equal groups. Each group lines up behind masking-tape line for a relay race. At your signal, first person in each line walks quickly to the other side of the room, around a chair and back to tag the next person in line. Periodically, play a song from the CD. While music is playing, students must turn around and walk backwards in slow motion.

2. First team to finish relay chooses one person to answer the following question: **When is a time kids your age need to trust in God's power?** (When we need God's help to study for a test. When a family member is sick. When we need courage to tell the truth.) Repeat game as time permits.

3. After several rounds, ask the Discussion Questions below. Repeat relay as time permits.

Option

For variety, change ways students move across the room while the music is playing (walk, hop, crawl, tiptoe, etc.).

Discussion Questions

1. **What does Psalm 29:11 say that God does for His people?** Students read verse in their Bibles and tell answers in their own words.

2. **How can knowing about God's power give you peace or help you?**

3. **How does someone who trusts in God's power act when he or she is in a difficult situation?** (Talks to God about the situation. Remembers God's promise of help.)

Target Practice

Bible Focus ▸ John 9

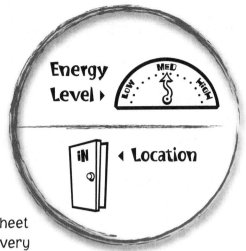

Energy Level ▸

iN ◂ Location

Materials

Bibles, large sheets of paper, markers, masking tape, index cards, scissors; one blindfold for every eight students.

Preparation

Draw several circles inside of each other on a large sheet of paper (see sketch), making one paper target for every eight students. Tape target(s) onto wall at eye level of students. Cut index cards in half.

Lead the Game

1. **We want to worship God when we see His great power. The Bible tells about a blind man who saw Jesus' power and realized He is God. Let's play a game to find out what it might be like to be blind.**

2. Give each student half of an index card. Student draws a large X on the card and writes initials in one corner. Students make masking-tape loops to put on the backs of their cards.

3. Play a game similar to Pin the Tail on the Donkey. Students stand in single-file lines of no more than eight students each, approximately 5 feet (1.5 m) away from a target. Blindfold the first student in each line. Each blindfolded student walks to the target and tries to stick his or her X onto the center of the target. Then student takes off blindfold and returns to the end of the line. Next student in line is blindfolded and takes a turn. Repeat activity until all students have had a turn.

Options

1. If you are unable to use blindfolds, put a large paper bag over students' heads or simply ask students to close their eyes while playing the game.

2. Assign points to each section of the target. Students take several turns each to see who can accumulate the most points.

Discussion Questions

1. **What are some ways we see God's power?** (A thunderstorm. A beautiful sunset. Jesus' miracles.)

2. **What has God made that shows His power?**

3. **In what ways can we worship Jesus for His power?** (Sing songs about how great He is. Tell Him what we love about Him when we pray to Him. Thank Him for being our God.)

Throwing Power

Bible Focus ▸ 1 Kings 17:7-16

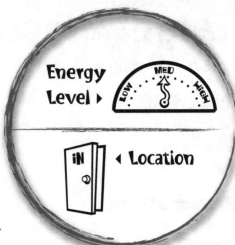

Energy Level ▸ LOW · MED · HIGH

iN ◂ Location

Materials

Bibles, masking tape, cardboard box, watch with second hand, two colors of scrap paper.

Preparation

Make two masking-tape lines 15 feet (4.5 m) apart. Place cardboard box in the center area (see sketch).

Lead the Game

1. **God's power was displayed when Elijah helped a poor widow have food to eat. Let's play a game about God's power.**

2. Divide class into two equal teams. Teams sit behind opposite masking-tape lines.

3. Give each team one color of paper (at least 10 sheets for each student on the team). At your signal, students begin making paper balls and throwing them into the box. Call time after 30 seconds.

15 feet (4.5 m)

4. One volunteer from each team collects team's paper balls from the box and counts them. Another volunteer from each team collects the paper balls landed outside the box and returns them to his or her team. Student from team with the most paper balls in the box tells one way in which God shows His power by helping us in everyday situations. If team members need help in thinking of answers, ask the Discussion Questions below.

Options

1. Use newspapers and magazines instead of colored paper. Or if you only have white scrap paper, mark each team's paper with a different-colored marker.

2. Laundry basket or other container may be used in place of cardboard box.

Discussion Questions

1. **How do you see God's power in the things He made?**

2. **What are some stories you have heard about God showing His power to people today?**

3. **What kinds of problems might kids your age have? How might God show His power by helping with those problems?** (Helping a kid overcoming temptation to drink or take drugs. Help to stop fighting with family members.)

Life Application Games

God's Word

Drop and Freeze

Bible Focus ▶ Psalm 32:8; Acts 8:26-40

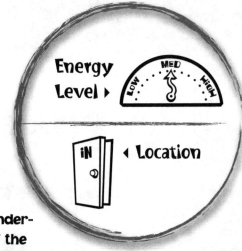

Energy Level ▶

◀ Location

Materials

Bibles, children's music CD and player, identical small object for each student (stackable block, plastic spoon, beanbag, eraser, etc.).

Lead the Game

1. **A disciple of Jesus named Philip helped a man understand the good news of Jesus from the words of the prophet Isaiah that he was reading. Let's play a game to remember the good things we learn from the Bible.**

2. Group students in two teams. Identify each team as team one or team two. Give each student a small object. Students practice balancing object on head while walking around the room.

3. Tell students a way in which to move (heel-to-toe, tiptoe, baby steps, hop etc.). Play a song from the CD as students (hop) around the playing area, balancing object on head. If a student's object falls off his or her head, student immediately freezes and does not move until music stops.

4. Stop music after 8 to 10 seconds. Students with objects remaining on heads when music stops raise one or both hands (one hand if on team one or both hands if on team two). Count the number of students with hands raised on each team. A volunteer from the team with most people with hands raised tells some good news he or she has learned from God's Word. Repeat play as time allows, sometimes asking a volunteer from the team with the fewest people with hands raised to tell good news from the Bible or answer a Discussion Question below.

Discussion Questions

1. **What good news do you learn about Jesus from reading the Bible?** (He died on the cross to pay for our sins. He rose from the dead. He healed and cared for many people.)

2. **How does the Bible help us grow in God's family?** (The Bible tells us how to become a part of God's family: believe that Jesus died for our sins and ask for forgiveness. When we read the Bible, we can learn the good things God wants His family members to do.)

3. **What are some of the ways the Bible tells us to live?** (Love God. Love our neighbors. Be kind and help others. Tell the truth. Obey our parents. Tell about God.)

Duck, Duck, Verse

Bible Focus ▸ John 3:36

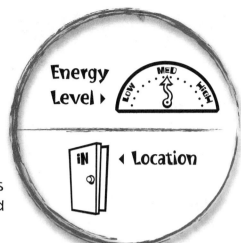

Energy Level ▸

iN ◂ Location

Materials
Bibles, index cards, marker.

Preparation
Print the first phrase of John 3:36 ("Whoever believes in the Son has eternal life".) on index cards, one word on each card.

Lead the Game
1. Show cards you prepared. **How would you put these words together to make a sentence?** Students work together to make a sentence with the words. **Let's find out how these words are used in the Bible.** Students read John 3:36 in their Bibles.

2. Play a game similar to Duck, Duck, Goose. Students sit in a circle with one volunteer standing outside of the circle. Distribute verse cards randomly to students sitting in the circle. Students place cards faceup on the floor in front of them. Volunteer walks around outside of circle, tapping each student lightly on the head and saying the words of the first phrase of John 3:36 (one word each time he or she taps a person on the head).

3. When volunteer comes to a student with the word he or she is saying, student with the card tells a situation in which a kid his or her age would need God's forgiveness. (After three rounds, volunteer chooses any student in circle to tell a situation.) Repeat activity with different volunteers as time permits.

Discussion Questions
1. **How do people feel when they need forgiveness? Why is God's forgiveness important?** (Because only God can forgive sins.)

2. **What did God do to give us forgiveness?** (The Bible tells us Jesus died on the cross to pay for our sins. God rose Jesus from the dead.)

3. **What do we need to do in order to be forgiven?** (Believe in Jesus.)

On Your Guard

Bible Focus ▸ Psalm 119:11; Matthew 4:1-11; Luke 4:1-13

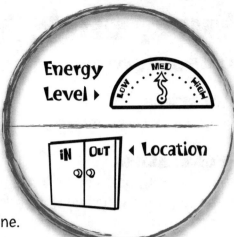

Energy Level ▸

iN | OuT ◂ Location

Materials

Bibles, masking tape, one paper cup for each student, at least two soccer balls, volleyballs or tennis balls.

Preparation

Divide the playing area in half with a masking-tape line.

Lead the Game

1. **Knowing God's Word can protect and help us when we are tempted to do something wrong. In the game we're going to play, we're going to protect something, too.**

2. Group students into two equal teams, one group on each side of the dividing line. Give each student a paper cup. Each student places the cup somewhere in his or her team's playing area, no more than 20 feet (6 m) from the dividing line. Student then stands about halfway between his or her cup and the dividing line.

3. Give a ball to one of the teams. A volunteer from that team rolls the ball across the dividing line, trying to knock down the other team's cups. Students standing in front of the cups attempt to protect cups, blocking balls with their hands or feet. Student who catches ball rolls it back across the center line toward the opposite team's cups. (Note: If no cups are knocked down after several minutes of play, add another ball or two so that more than one ball is in play at the same time.) Call time after three or four minutes. Ask one or more of the Discussion Questions. Set up cups again and begin a new round of play.

Discussion Questions

1. **What did you do to protect your cup?** Read Psalm 119:11 aloud. **What does the Bible tell us we can do to protect ourselves from doing wrong, or sinning?** (Read and learn God's Word.)

2. **What wrong things are kids your age tempted to do? How can God's Word help and protect you when you are tempted?** (Help me know what is right.)

3. **In His Word, God promises to never leave His children. How can knowing this promise help you when you are tempted to do something wrong?**

Picture Puzzle Relay

Bible Focus ▸ Psalm 119:130; John 20:31

Energy Level ▸ LOW MED HIGH

iN ◂ Location

Materials

Bibles, puzzles with about a dozen pieces each (one puzzle for every six to eight students).

Lead the Game

1. **We put together the pieces of a puzzle to see the picture that it makes. Reading the Bible is like putting together a puzzle. All the stories we read in the Bible help us see a true picture of what God is like, so we can know and love Him.**

2. Divide group into teams of six to eight students.

3. Teams form lines. Mix up puzzle pieces and place them about 20 feet (6 m) from the teams, keeping each team's puzzle pieces separate.

4. At your signal, the first student from each team runs to his or her team's puzzle pieces, gets a piece, returns to his or her line and tags the next student to run to the puzzle and get a piece. Students continue until all puzzle pieces have been collected. Then students on each team work together to assemble their puzzle. Play additional rounds as time allows, trading puzzles each round.

Option

Borrow puzzles from students or preschool classes. If puzzles are not available, print Psalm 119:30 or John 20:31 on index cards, one word on each card. Play relay as instructed above, substituting index cards for puzzle pieces and having teams put cards in correct verse order.

Discussion Questions

1. **What was the hardest puzzle you ever put together?**

2. **What was the longest story or part of the Bible you ever read?**

3. **What have you learned about God from the Bible?** (He loves all people. He is more powerful than anyone. He is the only true God.)

Rhythm Relay

Bible Focus ▶ 2 Timothy 3:16-17

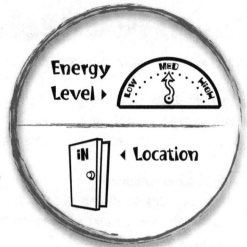

Energy Level ▶ LOW MED HIGH

Location ▶ iN

Materials

Bibles, children's music CD and player.

Lead the Game

1. **When we know God's Word, it shows in our lives! Let's celebrate that now!**

2. Group students into at least two even-numbered teams. Students form pairs within teams.

3. Demonstrate a grapevine step, moving sideways by bringing left foot behind right foot (see sketch below). Students practice the step in pairs, holding their arm over their partners' shoulders as they try the step. After practice, students form teams again on one side of an open playing area.

4. Play music from CD. At your signal, the first pair on each team takes grapevine steps to the opposite side of the playing area and back, tagging the next pair in line to repeat the action. When all students on a team have had a turn, volunteers from winning team answer one of the Discussion Questions below. Repeat relay as time permits.

Options

1. If you have space or can play this relay game outdoors, students form pairs and all pairs race each other at once.

2. Students may do steps as individuals rather than in pairs.

3. Play a CD of upbeat Hebrew music during the relay.

Discussion Questions

1. **When might kids your age read and think about God's Word?** (When hearing a Bible story at church. When reading a Bible story with parents.)

2. **Who has helped you learn from God's Word?** (Parents. Grandparents. Teachers.)

3. Read 2 Timothy 3:16-17 aloud. **What do we learn from reading God's Word?** (How to love and obey God. How to show His love to others. How to become members of God's family.)

Sheep's Tail

Bible Focus ▸ Joshua 23:14

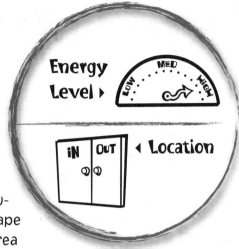

Energy Level ▸

Location ▸

Materials

Bibles, fabric strips, ruler, scissors, masking tape; optional—rope.

Preparation

Cut one 2×10-inch (5×25-cm) fabric strip for each student. Mark off a large area of the classroom with tape (Optional: Mark boundaries of an outdoor playing area with rope.) Mark some of the following verses in Bibles, so students can find them quickly: Deuteronomy 31:8; Psalm 34:17; Psalm 100:5; Isaiah 41:10; Jeremiah 29:12; Jeremiah 31:3; Jeremiah 32:27; John 1:12; John 14:23; Hebrews 13:8; 1 John 1:9; 1 John 5:14.

Lead the Game

1. Lead students to play a game called "Sheep's Tail." Attach tails to the back of clothing with masking tape. At your signal, students try to capture each other's tails (see sketch) while moving only within the boundaries ("sheep pen"). When a student's tail gets taken, he or she cheers for others from outside the sheep pen until the next game begins.

2. The last student with his or her tail in place reads aloud a verse from one of the Bibles you have marked, telling one of God's promises to His children. **What promise does this verse tell about?** Extend your discussion about God's promises by asking the Discussion Questions below. Students play as many rounds of the game as time allows.

Option

Play a slow-motion version by having the players blindfolded.

Game Tip

Explain rules clearly and simply step by step. You might want to offer a "practice round." When playing a game for the first time with your class, play it a few times "just for practice."

Discussion Questions

1. Read Joshua 23:14. **What do you learn about God and His promises from His Word?**

2. **What does God promise when we ask for forgiveness?** (In 1 John 1:9. He promises to forgive us when we admit that we have done wrong things.)

3. **How do God's promises in His Word encourage you?**

Treasure Hunt

Bible Focus ▸ Psalm 119:127; Jeremiah 1:4-10; 36—40

Materials

Bibles, coins, small plastic bags.

Preparation

Around the playing area, hide at least two coins for each student.

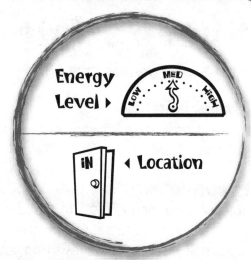

Energy Level ▸

iN ◂ Location

Lead the Game

1. **God's words are valuable because they tell us the best way to live. Let's go on a treasure hunt to remind us that God's Word is like a treasure.**

2. Students pair off. Each pair determines a signal they will use to call each other (three claps, calling out a certain word, a whistle, a howl, etc.). Within each pair, one student becomes the "scout," who looks for the treasure, and one becomes the "collector." Give each collector a small plastic bag.

3. At your signal, the scouts move around the playing area to begin searching for the "treasure" (coins). When a scout finds a coin, he or she cannot touch it but instead must use the pair's pre-determined signal to call the collector. When the collector hears the signal, he or she must go and pick up the treasure and put it in his or her plastic bag. Continue game until each pair has located a coin.

4. Begin a new round of the game with students trading roles. Hide additional coins if needed.

Options

1. Have students count their "treasure" to determine the winning pair; then invite the winning pair to read Psalm 119:127 aloud.

2. Substitute gold-wrapped chocolate coins for coins.

Discussion Questions

1. **How do God's words help us more than money or gold?** (They show us the best way to live. They tell us about God's love.)

2. **How can we show our love for God's Word?** (Pay attention to what it says. Try to obey it.)

3. **Who helps you learn about God's Word?**

Life Application Games
Holidays and Special Days

Candy Heart Relay

Bible Focus ▸ 1 Corinthians 13:4

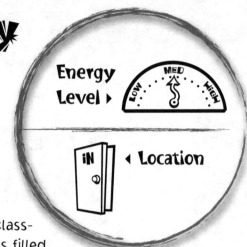

Energy Level ▸ LOW MED HIGH

iN ◂ Location

Materials

Bibles, disposable bowls, small Valentine's Day conversation hearts, plastic spoons, sandwich-sized plastic bags.

Preparation

Place two empty bowls on one side of open area in classroom. On the other side of the room, place two bowls filled with equal amounts of candy.

Lead the Game

1. **God's love for us is the greatest love of all. On Valentine's Day, people talk a lot about love, send cards and eat candy; but often they forget God's love! Let's play a game with candy to celebrate God's love!**

2. Group students into two teams. Teams line up by empty bowls. Give the first student on each team a spoon.

3. At your signal, the first student on each team walks quickly to his or her team's bowl of candy, fills spoon with candy and returns with the candy, dumping candy into team's empty bowl. If student drops any candy, student picks it up and returns to the candy bowl to begin again with new candy. (Students throw away dropped candy.) Next student in line repeats the action. Play continues until both teams have transferred all candies from one bowl to the other. Volunteer from the first team to complete the relay answers one of the Discussion Questions below. Repeat relay as time permits.

4. Students take home candy in plastic bags.

Option

Limit number of students on each team to six. If you have more than 12 students, form additional teams and provide additional materials.

Discussion Questions

1. **What are some ways God's love is different than the love people have for one another?** (God always loves us no matter what. We don't have to do anything to earn God's love for us. God's love is shown by His forgiveness of our sins.)

2. Have an older student read 1 Corinthians 13:4-7 aloud. **How do these verses describe love? Volunteers name characteristics. These are the ways God loves us!**

3. **What are some ways we can show God's love to others?**

Christmas Go-Fish

Bible Focus ▸ Psalm 130:7; Luke 2:1-20

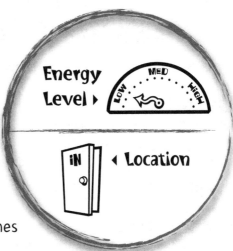

Energy Level ▸ LOW MED HIGH

iN ◂ Location

Materials

Bibles, large sheet of paper, marker, index cards (six for each student), pencils; optional—Christmas stickers.

Preparation

Print Psalm 130:7 on large sheet of paper, drawing lines to divide the verse into six sections.

Lead the Game

1. Give each student six index cards. Students copy verse onto cards, dividing verse as shown on large sheet of paper (see sketch). (Optional: Students decorate cards with Christmas stickers.) Collect all cards and shuffle them together.

2. Lead students in playing a game similar to Go Fish. Place all cards facedown in a pile. Each student takes a turn to choose four cards. Students look at their cards to see what they need in order to complete the verse. First player asks any student for a card he or she needs. If student has the card, he or she must give the card to the player, ending the first player's turn. If student does not have the card, the first player chooses a card from the pile. Play continues until one student has collected all the words of Psalm 130:7 and places the cards in order faceup on table or floor.

3. Player who won finds Psalm 130:7 in his or her Bible, reads the verse aloud and tells why Jesus' birth fulfilled Israel's hope for love and redemption. Ask the Discussion Questions below. Repeat game as time permits.

Psalm 130:7	"Oh Israel, put your hope	in the Lord,	for with the Lord	is unfailing love and with	him is full redemption."

Option

Gather old Christmas cards. Cut pictures on cards to the same size. Students write verse on back of picture and use as game cards in the game above.

Discussion Questions

1. **When might someone your age need to know about God's love? Need God's forgiveness?**

2. **When might we need help in knowing what to do?**

3. **How does the meaning of Christmas give you hope?** Give an answer before asking students to respond.

Christmas Hunt

Bible Focus ▸ Psalm 9:1; Luke 2:22-38

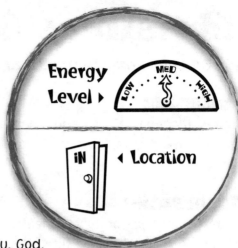

Energy Level ▸

iN ◂ Location

Materials

Bibles, large sheet of paper, marker, small Christmas object (Christmas sticker on a small piece of paper, small pinecone or unbreakable ornament or nativity figure).

Preparation

Print several prayer starters (for example, "Thank You, God, for . . ." and "Jesus, You are . . .") on the large sheet of paper. Leave space for students to complete the prayer starters and write other sentences. Hide the Christmas object somewhere in your classroom.

Lead the Game

1. **There is a (Christmas sticker) hidden somewhere in the classroom. When you see it, quickly sit down in the center of the room without telling where the object is.** When two or three students have located the object and are seated, call the remaining students back to the center of the room. Ask the student who was the first one seated to bring the object to the center of the room. Review the story of Simeon and Anna by asking the Discussion Questions below.

2. **One way we can show God we are thankful that He sent Jesus to be our Savior is by telling Him in prayer.** Read Psalm 9:1 aloud as a prayer. Show students prayer starters you prepared. Ask the student who brought the object back to complete one of the prayer starters, praising Jesus for who He is or thanking God for sending Jesus. Student writes prayer on paper.

3. Students close their eyes while student who wrote prayer hides the object again. Repeat activity as above. First student seated retrieves the object and writes another sentence of prayer before hiding the object again. Repeat hiding and adding sentences to prayer as time allows.

4. Lead students in reading the completed prayer aloud together.

Discussion Questions

1. **Who did Simeon and Anna find at the Temple?** (Baby Jesus, the Savior for all people.)

2. **What does it mean to say that Jesus is the Savior for all people?** (He saves us from the punishment we deserve for the wrong things we do.)

3. **What did Simeon and Anna do when they saw Jesus?** (They thanked and praised God. Told others who Jesus is.)

Christmas Scrolls

Bible Focus ▸ Luke 2:1-20

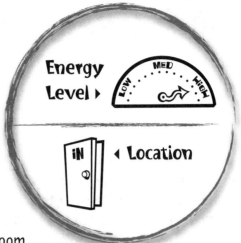

Energy Level ▸ LOW MED HIGH

iN ◂ Location

Materials

Bibles, masking tape, three large sheets of butcher paper, two lengths of yarn, 3x5-inch (7.5x12.5-cm) pieces of red and green construction paper, markers, two rolls of transparent tape.

Preparation

Make a masking-tape line on one side of your classroom. Roll up two of the sheets of butcher paper to make two scrolls and tie with yarn.

Lead the Game

1. Invite students to list as many ways to celebrate Jesus' birth as they can (singing Christmas carols, decorating, making cookies, sending Christmas cards). List ideas on remaining sheet of butcher paper. Each student writes one idea from the list on a piece of red or green paper.

2. Divide class into two teams. (Students keep their own pieces of paper.) Teams line up behind masking-tape line. Place one scroll and roll of tape opposite each team on the other side of the room. At your signal, first player on each team runs with his or her piece of paper to a scroll, unties and unrolls it, then tapes the paper onto the scroll before rolling it back up and tying it again. Continue until all players have completed the relay.

3. Two volunteers from the winning team unroll the team's scroll and hold scroll open for others to read. One at a time, read aloud the ways of celebrating Jesus' birth attached to the scroll. Discuss the ways by asking the Discussion Questions below. Two volunteers from the other team unroll the scroll and hold it open to see if there are any additional ways of celebrating Christmas mentioned. Encourage students to write additional items on the scroll.

4. Invite each student to write his or her initials on at least one way he or she plans to help others celebrate God's gift of Jesus at Christmas.

Discussion Questions

1. **How does (singing Christmas carols) remind you of God's gift of Jesus at Christmas?**

2. **How can this way or celebrating help you share the good news of Jesus' birth?**

3. **What are some other ways we can help others celebrate God's gift of Jesus at Christmas?** (Send a Christmas card about Jesus to someone who doesn't know about Him. Invite a friend to come to a special Christmas event at church.)

Christmas-Tree Relay

Bible Focus ▸ Luke 2:1-20

Energy Level ▸ LOW MED HIGH

iN ◂ Location

Materials
Bibles, colored paper cups.

Lead the Game

1. At Christmastime, we worship God because He loves us and promised to send Jesus, our Savior. Some people celebrate Christmas by decorating Christmas trees, singing special songs and giving gifts to one another. Let's play a game to build our own Christmas trees!

2. Group students into teams of no more than six students each. Teams line up in single-file lines on one side of the playing area. Give each team six cups.

3. Demonstrate to students how to stack cups to build a Christmas tree (see sketch). At your signal, the first student on each team runs to the opposite side of the playing area, sets down his or her cup, returns to his or her team and tags the next student in line. Team members repeat actions. Volunteer from the first team that finishes building Christmas tree answers one of the Discussion Questions below.

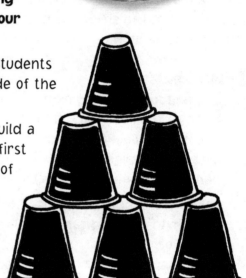

Options

1. Use Christmas cups for the relay.

2. For older students, provide 10 cups for each team. Print the letters of the sentence "Worship God" on paper cups, one letter on each cup. Team members complete relay in the correct order to build a tree that spells "Worship God" from the top down.

Discussion Questions

1. **What fun things do you and your family do to celebrate Christmas?**

2. **What can we thank God for at Christmastime?** (His love. Sending Jesus, the Savior.)

3. **How does giving and receiving gifts help us celebrate Jesus' birth?** (Jesus is God's gift to us.)

Coin Toss

Bible Focus ▸ Matthew 2:1-12

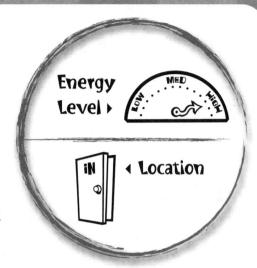

Energy Level ▸ LOW MED HIGH

iN ◂ Location

Materials
Bibles, large sheet of paper, marker, coins, paper, pencils.

Preparation
Draw, divide and number a large star on the sheet of paper (see sketch). Place paper on the floor in the middle of the playing area.

Lead the Game

1. **God showed His faithfulness in keeping His promise to send the Savior. When the wise men saw a bright star, they traveled to worship Jesus, the great King God had promised. Let's play a game to remember God's faithfulness.**

2. Group students into teams of three to four. Teams gather around the paper, standing at least 4 feet (1.2 m) from the paper. Give each group a coin, a paper and a pencil.

3. Silently choose a number over 30. Teams take turns tossing coins onto the paper, one student at a time. One student on each team keeps track of team's points, adding them up and announcing the point total after each toss.

4. Call stop when a team gets close to or scores the exact number you chose. Announce what your number was. Volunteer from the team who got closest or scored the exact number you chose tells a way God shows His faithfulness. Continue discussion by asking questions below. Repeat game as time allows, choosing a new number for each round.

Discussion Questions

1. **What have you heard or read about in the Bible that shows God's faithfulness?** (God kept His promise to send Jesus, the Savior. God kept His promise to Noah that a flood wouldn't destroy the earth. God rescued the Israelites from slavery in Egypt.)

2. **How does God show His faithfulness to people today?** (Answers prayers. Forgives us.)

3. **Why is it important to know God kept His promise to send us a Savior?** Talk with interested students about becoming a member of God's family. Refer to guidelines in "Leading a Child to Christ" on page 11.

Full of Life

Bible Focus ▸ Mark 16:1-7

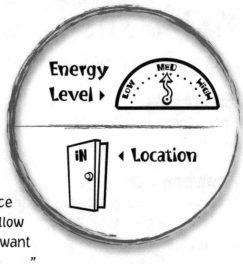

Energy Level ▸ LOW MED HIGH

iN ◀ Location

Materials

Bibles, five large sheets of paper, markers, masking tape, small slips of paper, paper bag, pencils.

Preparation

On large sheets of paper, print the following sentence starters, one sentence starter on each paper: "I can follow Jesus by . . . ," "I'm glad Jesus is alive because . . . ," I want to praise God by . . . ," "I thank God for His Son because . . . ," "I will celebrate Jesus' resurrection by . . . " Attach large sheets of paper to a wall. Place markers near papers. On small slips of paper print different ways to move ("crabwalk," "skip," "hop on one foot," "walk backwards," "crawl," etc.). Place slips of paper in a bag.

Lead the Game

1. Distribute blank slips of paper and pencils to students. Students choose one of the sentence starters and write or draw sentence completion on their papers.

2. Students line up across from large sheets of paper. First student picks a slip of paper from the bag you prepared, reads it, places it back in the bag and moves in that manner to the paper with the sentence starter matching the one he or she completed. Student writes or draws his or her sentence completion on the large piece of paper and then continues movement back to the line. Next student repeats the process.

3. When all students have completed the activity, ask the Discussion Questions.

Discussion Questions

1. **Why was Jesus the only One who could take the punishment for our sins?** (Jesus is the only person who never sinned. He is the One God promised to send.)

2. **When we choose to become members of God's family, what does He give us?** (Forgiveness for our sins. Eternal life.)

3. **What are some ways we remember Jesus' death and celebrate His resurrection?** (Thank Jesus for His love. Sing special songs. Celebrate Easter with our church families at special worship services.)

4. **How does your family celebrate Jesus' resurrection at Eastertime?**

Journey to Bethlehem

Bible Focus ▸ Matthew 2:1-16; John 8:12

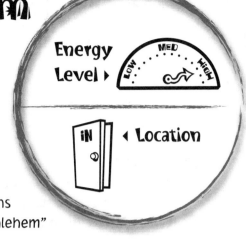

Energy Level ▸

iN ◂ Location

Materials

Bibles, butcher paper, markers, measuring stick, colored construction paper, beanbags.

Preparation

Draw a 4-foot (1.2-m) star on a section of butcher paper. Draw lines to divide the star into five sections and then label star as shown in sketch a. Print "Bethlehem" on a sheet of construction paper.

Lead the Game

1. **We can worship Jesus as the Savior whom God sent for the whole world! Some of the first people who worshiped Jesus—the wise men—went on a long journey to find Jesus in Bethlehem. Let's play a game to take a journey to Bethlehem, too.**

2. Give each student three or four sheets of construction paper. Students draw stars on each sheet of paper.

3. Students place their star papers on the floor to form a game path. Place star you prepared near the path and place the Bethlehem paper at the end of the game path. Choose one student to be the gofer.

4. Students line up at the beginning of the game path. Students take turns tossing beanbag onto the star you prepared and moving the number of star papers written in the section that the beanbag landed in (see sketch b). The gofer retrieves the beanbag and moves the star around for students as needed. (If a star paper is already occupied, student moves to the next unoccupied star paper.) The first student to reach the Bethlehem paper answers one of the Discussion Questions below. Repeat game with a new gofer.

Discussion Questions

1. **How do we know that God sent Jesus as the Savior for the whole world?** (Jesus said He came to offer salvation to all people.) Have an older student read John 8:12 aloud.

2. **What are some reasons to worship Jesus?** (He died on the cross to forgive our sins. He is God. He loves and cares for all people.)

3. **What gifts can we give Jesus?** (Sing songs to praise Him. Tell Jesus the things we are thankful He did. Do the things Jesus told people to do in the Bible.)

Joyful Relay

Bible Focus ▸ Psalm 95:1; John 20

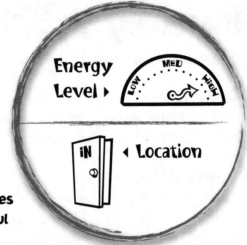

Energy Level ▸ LOW MED HIGH

iN ◂ Location

Materials

Bibles, index cards, marker, two paper bags, children's music CD and player.

Lead the Game

1. Read Psalm 95:1. **Knowing that Jesus is alive gives us great joy! Let's play a game using some joyful actions to remind us to celebrate.**

2. **What are some actions people do to show that they are full of joy?** (Smile. Sing. Jump. Clap. Cheer. High-five. Skip.) List each student's idea on two separate index cards to create two identical sets of cards. Put one set in each bag.

3. Group students into two equal teams. Teams line up single file on one side of the playing area. Place a bag of cards across playing area from each team.

4. Play an upbeat song from a CD. When the music begins, the first student on each team runs to the paper bag, takes out an index card, reads action, returns card to bag and performs that action during the entire time it takes to return to his or her team. Student then tags the next student in line. Game continues until each student has had a turn.

Option

If you have fewer than eight students, make one set of action cards and one set of directional cards (forward, backward, in a circle, sideways, by the table, etc.). Place each set of cards in a separate bag. Students spread out around the playing area. While you play music each student takes a turn picking a card from each bag. The student holds up both cards, so all students can see and perform actions as a group (for example, smile while moving in a circle). Continue until all students have had a turn picking cards.

Discussion Questions

1. **What can we do to celebrate the fact that Jesus died for our sins and rose again?** (Sing songs about it. Thank Jesus in our prayers. Accept Jesus' forgiveness and become a member of His family.) Talk with interested students about salvation (see "Leading a Child to Christ" article on p. 11 of this book).

2. **What can we do to share with others the joy that comes from knowing that Jesus is alive?** (Tell them Jesus loves us and rose again because He wants to give us eternal life. Invite them to church on Easter. Ask God to help us show joy to others and explain why we have that joy.)

Palm-Branch Pass

Bible Focus ▸ Matthew 21:1-17; Mark 11:1-11;
Luke 19:28-40; John 12:12-19

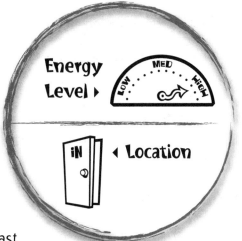

Energy Level ▸

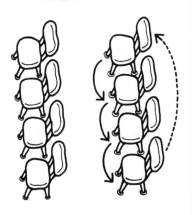

iN ◀ Location

Materials

Bibles, a chair for each student, small branch from a tree or bush for every six to eight students, garden clippers.

Preparation

Set the chairs in lines of four to eight, creating at least two lines of chairs as shown in the sketch. Trim off any sharp twigs from branches.

Lead the Game

1. **We can't help but praise Jesus because of whom He is and what He came to do! When Jesus entered Jerusalem the week before He died, people praised Him by waving palm branches in the air. Let's play a game with branches to remember a way Jesus was praised!**

2. Group students into teams of four to eight. Assign each team a line of chairs. Students sit on chairs.

3. Give a branch to the student sitting in the first chair on each team. At your signal, the student passes the branch down the row. When the branch reaches the last student in the row, he or she carries the branch and runs to the first chair in the row. While student is running, all the other team members move down one chair, leaving the first chair empty for the running student to sit on. After he or she is seated, student passes branch to the next student and branch is passed down the row again. Process is continued until all students have returned to their original chairs.

4. A volunteer from the first team to finish the relay answers one of the questions below. Mix up teams and play game again if time allows.

Discussion Questions

1. **What are some of the reasons we want to praise Jesus?** (He is God's Son. He was willing to die on the cross to pay the punishment for all people's sins. He rose from the dead. He loves us all. He taught us the best way to live.)

2. **What are some ways we can praise Jesus?** (Sing songs to Him. When we pray, tell Him why we love Him or what we are thankful for. Tell others how wonderful He is.)

3. **What is your favorite way to praise Jesus?** Volunteers respond.

Palm-Branch Pickup

Bible Focus ▸ Matthew 21:1-17; Mark 11:1-11;
Luke 19:28-40; John 12:12-19

Energy Level ▸

iN ◂ Location

Materials

Bibles, green construction paper, scissors or paper cutter, markers.

Preparation

Cut construction paper into small squares, making at least 10 squares for each student.

Lead the Game

1. **When Jesus was entering Jerusalem, people gave Him praise by covering the ground with branches from palm trees. We're going to play a game and give praise to Jesus, too.**

2. Give each student 10 squares of paper and a marker. Students number squares 1 to 10 and then randomly place squares, numbered side down, in center of playing area.

3. Divide students into two teams. Teams line up shoulder-to-shoulder on opposite sides of the playing area. Assign numbers to students as in the game Steal the Bacon (see sketch).

4. Call two numbers. Students with those numbers from each team have five seconds to collect as many green squares as possible. Call "stop" when time is up; students return to teams with the squares they collected. Volunteer(s) from team who collected the square with the highest number tells a reason to praise Jesus.

5. To play another round, volunteers return squares to playing area, numbered side down. Play as many rounds as time allows.

Discussion Questions

1. **Instead of laying palm branches on the ground, how might we show praise to an important person today?** (Putting down a red carpet where that person is going to walk. Clapping for a person.)

2. **What are some ways we can give praise to Jesus today?** (Sing songs to Him. Pray to Him and tell Him what we praise Him for. Tell other people how great He is.)

3. **What are some reasons Jesus is so great?**

Pumpkin Praise

Bible Focus ▸ Matthew 21:1-17; Mark 11:1-11;
Luke 19:28-40; John 12:12-19

Energy Level ▸ LOW MED HIGH

iN ◂ **Location**

Materials

Bibles, four to eight pumpkins of any size for every 10 students, black permanent markers.

Preparation

Arrange pumpkins to create an obstacle course in your playing area (see sketch). Create one obstacle course for every 10 students. Place a marker next to the last pumpkin in each course.

Lead the Game

1. **Thanksgiving time reminds us to give thanks to God for His care for us. Let's play a game to thank God for the great things He has given us.**

2. Students line up in a single-file line at the beginning of the obstacle course. Demonstrate how to complete the obstacle course (which order and direction to run around each pumpkin, whether to circle around each pumpkin or just pass by it, etc.). **When you reach the last pumpkin in your course, use the marker to write or draw on the pumpkin something for which you are thankful. What is something that you are thankful for?** Print volunteer's response on the pumpkin as an example.

3. At your signal, first student in line begins obstacle course. When student has finished course and written on pumpkin, he or she tags the next student in line who begins obstacle course. Continue until each student has had a turn. Then ask volunteers to tell their responses from the pumpkins.

Discussion Questions

1. **What are some ways God cares for your family?**

2. **How can you show God that you are thankful for His love and care?** (Name the things you are thankful for when you pray. Write God a thank-you prayer. Sing praise songs to Him.)

3. **What is your favorite way to tell God thank you?**

Purim Gamefest

Bible Focus ▶ Psalm 33:11; Esther

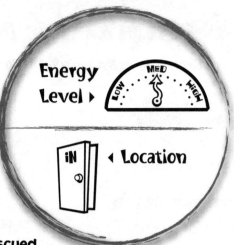

Energy Level ▶ LOW MED HIGH

iN ◀ Location

Materials

Bibles, materials needed for one or both of the games.

Preparation

Prepare games as directed below.

Lead the Game

1. **Long ago in Old Testament times, Queen Esther rescued her people to keep them safe, as God had planned. God's power and Esther's brave actions are celebrated with a holiday called Purim (POO-rihm). Children today often celebrate this holiday by playing games. Let's play some games to remind us of this holiday.**

2. Lead students in one or both of the games.

Beanbag Toss

Before class, draw a large face on a 4-foot (1.2-m) or larger cardboard square. Cut out a mouth and two eye shapes large enough for a beanbag to fit through. Add a triangle-shaped hat to represent Haman (see sketch). Place target on one side of the playing area, propped up against a table or chairs. During class, students line up about 5 feet (1.5 m) from the target and take turns tossing beanbags through the target. Have a volunteer collect the beanbags for the students.

Ring Toss

Set up six to eight water bottles, filled and capped, in any type of geometric shape (circle, square, triangle, etc.). Students stand about 3 feet (.9 m) from the bottles and take turns tossing rings made from paper plates onto the bottles.

Discussion Questions

1. **What did Esther and her people celebrate on Purim?** (Esther's brave actions. The defeat of Haman. God's power and care for them.)

2. **What are some of the good things God has helped you do?** (Be kind to a brother or sister. Tell others about Him. Help someone who was in danger.)

3. **What are some ways to learn more of the good things God has planned for you to do?** (Read God's commands in the Bible. Ask teachers or older Christians. Pray to God.)

Resurrection Toss

Bible Focus ▸ Matthew 28; Mark 16; Luke 24; John 20

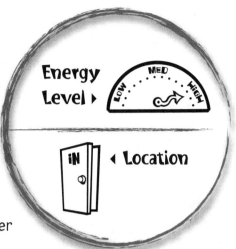

Energy Level ▸ LOW MED HIGH

iN ◂ Location

Materials
Bibles, paper plates, markers.

Preparation
Print the letters from the sentence "Jesus is alive," printing one letter on each paper plate. Make one set for every 12 students. Use a different-color marker each time you print the sentence.

Lead the Game
1. **God's promise of salvation came true in Jesus' death and resurrection. Let's play a game where we are reminded of Jesus' resurrection.**

2. Divide class into teams of no more than 12. Each team lines up single file at one side of the playing area. Give each student a paper plate written in his or her team's color. (If teams are small some students may have more than one paper plate.)

3. Students take turns throwing the paper plates like Frisbees. Then, at your signal, first student in each line runs to collect one of his or her team's paper plates. Next students in line repeat process.

4. When all of the paper plates have been collected, teams put them in order to read "Jesus is alive."

Options
1. If you have a small playing area, challenge students to skip or hop (or another way of movement) to collect the plates and return to line.

2. Students retrieve the plates in order. The first team to complete the sentence gives an example of how we know Jesus is alive.

Discussion Questions
1. **What are some other ways to complete the sentence "Jesus is . . . "?**

2. **What are some ways we can show Jesus we are thankful for the wonderful news that He died to take the punishment for our sins and that He is alive today?** (Sing praise songs to Him. Invite a friend to an Easter service or event at church.)

3. **How does your family celebrate Jesus' resurrection at Eastertime?**

Ring Toss

Bible Focus ▸ Isaiah 9:1-7; Micah 5:2-4

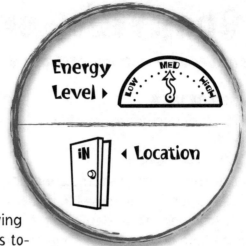

Energy Level ▸ LOW MED HIGH

iN ◂ Location

Materials

Bibles; paper plates; scissors; measuring stick; stapler; butcher paper; marker; filled, small plastic water bottle; scratch paper; pencils.

Preparation

Cut the center section out of two paper plates, leaving at least a ring 1-inch (2.5-cm) wide. Staple the plates together, one on top of the other, to create a sturdy ring (see sketch a). On a 3x3-foot (.9x.9-m) square of butcher paper, draw and number sections and place water bottle as shown in sketch b.

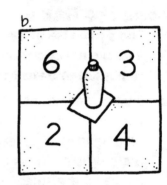

Lead the Game

1. **The prophets Isaiah and Micah told people about God's promise to send a Savior. The season when people get ready to celebrate the birth of Jesus, the promised Savior, is called Advent. Let's play a game with things that will remind us of Advent and help us think about getting ready to celebrate Jesus' birthday.**

2. Students line up approximately 4 feet (1.2 m) from prepared paper. Give the paper-plate ring to the first student in line.

3. At your signal, the first student tosses the ring at the bottle. Student determines points based on where ring lands, retrieves ring and gives it to next student in line. (Note: A ring that circles the bottle scores 10 points.) Next student repeats action. Students keep track of points on scratch paper. Student with the highest score when you call stop answers one of the Discussion Questions below. Repeat play as time allows.

Discussion Questions

1. **What do you do to get ready for school? To go on a trip? To celebrate Christmas?**

2. **What do you and your family do to get ready to celebrate Christmas? Which of those celebrations especially remind you of Jesus' birth?**

3. **How can you get ready to celebrate Jesus' birth?** (Thank God that He sent Jesus. Sing songs to worship God. Prepare gifts for others to celebrate Jesus' birth.)

Shepherd Relay

Bible Focus ▶ Luke 2:1-20; 1 John 4:9

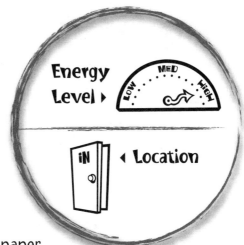

Energy Level ▶ LOW MED HIGH

Location ▶ iN

Materials

Bibles, one shepherd costume (towels, bathrobes, fabric lengths, sandals, walking sticks, etc.) for each group of six to eight students, large paper bags.

Preparation

Place the materials for each costume in a separate paper bag at one end of an open playing area.

Lead the Game

1. **The birth of God's Son, Jesus, the Savior, is reason for the whole world to celebrate! Let's play a game to dress up as some of the people who were among the first to celebrate Jesus' birth—the shepherds!**

2. Using the materials from one paper bag, demonstrate how to dress as a shepherd. When you are completely dressed up, hold the walking stick and call out, "Jesus the Savior is born today!" Return materials to bag.

3. Students form teams of no more than six to eight. Teams stand in single-file lines across the playing area from paper bags. At your signal, the first student on each team runs to his or her team's bag, dresses up in shepherd clothes, holds up the walking stick and calls out, "Jesus the Savior is born today!" Student puts clothes back in bag and returns to his or her team. The next student in line repeats the action. Students continue taking turns until all students have had a turn. A volunteer from the first team to finish answers one of the Discussion Questions below. Play again as time allows.

Discussion Questions

1. **Why should the whole world celebrate Jesus' birth?** (He came as the Savior for all people. God showed His love for the whole world when He sent Jesus.)

2. **What are some ways you've seen or heard the Christmas story?**

3. **What are some ways you, your family or your church tell other people that Jesus has been born?**

Surpriseball

Bible Focus ▸ Matthew 1:18—2:23; Luke 1:26-56; 2

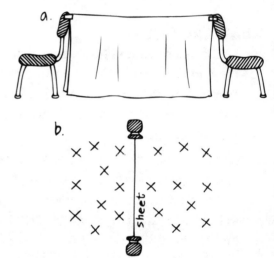

Energy Level ▸ LOW MED HIGH

iN ◂ Location

Materials

Bibles, flat bed sheet, two chairs, masking tape, inflated and tied balloon.

Preparation

In the middle of the playing area, spread a bed sheet between two chairs, taping it so that it is hanging vertically (see sketch a). Prepare one playing area for each group of up to 20 students.

a.

b. sheet

Lead the Game

1. **God's people were expecting God to keep His promise to send the Savior. They were probably surprised by the humble way the Messiah was born. We're going to play a game where we get surprised!**

2. Divide group into two teams of no more than 10 students each, sending teams to opposite sides of the sheet. Students sit on the floor, spacing themselves evenly around the playing area and sitting so that they cannot see over the sheet (see sketch b).

3. Students play a game like volleyball, but they remain seated during the game and do not rotate positions. Give one team a balloon. With no advance warning, student from the team with the balloon hits the balloon over the sheet from anywhere in the playing area. Students on the receiving team, who are waiting for the balloon to come over at any time, catch the balloon and tap it twice to teammates before hitting it back over the sheet to the other team. Teams see how many times they can hit the balloon over the sheet without the balloon hitting the ground.

Discussion Questions

1. **What did you wait for in this game? What did you expect would happen?** (The balloon would come.)

2. **What other kinds of things do kids your age wait for, expecting that they will happen?** (For things ordered in the mail. For dinner to be ready to eat. For birthdays to come.)

3. **Why is waiting for and expecting the birth of Jesus more important than waiting for all these things?** (He came to save people from their sins. He is God's Son.)

Life Application Games

Leadership

Hands-on Leaders

Bible Focus ▸ Old Testament Leaders

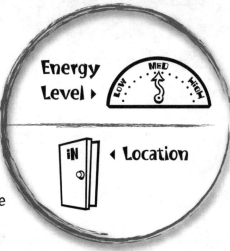

Energy Level ▸ LOW MED HIGH

iN ◂ Location

Materials

Bibles, butcher paper, tape, marker, children's music CD and player.

Preparation

Cover tabletop with butcher paper. Draw lines to divide the paper into sections, one section for each student. Print these Bible references in separate sections: 1 Samuel 10:1; 16:13; 1 Kings 17:2-4; 2 Kings 18:5; 2 Chronicles 5:1; 34:1-2; Nehemiah 8:2-3. Make one table for each group of seven students.

Lead the Game

1. **These are the people God chose to be the leaders of His people. We can read true stories about what these people did in the books of History.**

2. Students walk around table while you play music. When you stop the music, each student puts hand on one section and finds the Bible reference printed in the section. Invite students to read the verses aloud and tell the names of Bible characters they have read about and in which book of the Bible the characters are written about. Ask the Discussion Questions to explore the leaders.

Option

Provide several Bible dictionaries (or encyclopedias). Students find names of leaders in dictionaries and tell information about the leaders.

Discussion Questions

1. **What did this leader do?**

2. **How can the leader's example help you?**

3. **What ways can you be a leader for God?** (Help serve at church. Be a good example for a younger brother or sister. Commit to reading my Bible regularly.)

Leader Hunt

Bible Focus ▸ Old Testament Leaders

Energy Level ▸ LOW MED HIGH

iN ◂ Location

Materials

Bibles, 16 slips of paper, basket or other container, pencils, a 3-foot (.9-m) butcher-paper square for each student.

Preparation

Number slips of paper from 1-16 and place them in the basket.

Lead the Game

1. **The first 17 books of the Bible tell us about the first people God made and the people who became leaders of God's people. Let's find and read about some of the people who were God's leaders.**

2. Each student folds a butcher-paper square in half four times, then unfolds paper to reveal 16 squares. Student numbers the squares randomly from 1-16, writing the numbers small in the corners of squares (see sketch).

3. Play a game similar to Bingo. Choose a number from the basket and read the number aloud, designating this square as the one to be used for the first round. Then say, **Genesis 2:20**. Each student finds and reads the verse in his or her Bible, identifying the name(s) of the Bible character(s) mentioned in the verse. Student writes the name(s) of the Bible character(s) in the designated square. Continue activity, choosing new numbers for the following references: Genesis 3:20; 6:8; 12:1; 21:3; 24:15; 25:25; 25:26; 37:3; Exodus 2:10; Joshua 1:1; Judges 4:4; 6:12; 13:24; Ruth 1:16; 1 Samuel 3:10. After each Bible character is named, invite students to tell information about the leader. Play continues until one student has written names in four squares in a row.

Option

Repeat game as time permits, using reverse sides of butcher-paper squares or folding new papers.

Discussion Questions

1. **How would you describe this leader?**

2. **What things can you learn from this leader?** (How to love God more. How to stand up to negative pressure from friends. Make sure our words and actions match.)

3. **What did this leader do that was not good?**

Lead Me On

Bible Focus ▸ 2 Kings 6:8-23; 1 Timothy 4:12

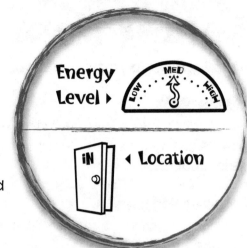

Energy Level ▸

iN ◂ Location

Materials
Bibles, chair, table.

Preparation
In the middle of the playing area, place a chair and table where students can easily walk around them.

Lead the Game
1. **The prophet Elisha guided blinded soldiers to the king of Israel, where the Lord opened their eyes. Elisha told the king to send the soldiers back to their country, and peace was restored between Israel and the surrounding peoples. When we do what's right, we can help others do good, too. In the game we're going to play, your words and actions will help lead others on a safe path.**

2. Have three volunteers line up behind you and place their right hands on the shoulders of the people in front of them (see sketch). Volunteers close their eyes. Give verbal directions for students to follow as you lead students on a walk around room, between the chair and the table and back to your starting position.

3. Repeat activity, with a student acting as the leader and six to eight students lined up behind the leader. Each time the activity is repeated, choose a different leader and rearrange chair and table if possible.

Options
1. Create additional obstacles: step over a book or box of crayons, walk in and out of a doorway or walk a certain number of times around a chair.

2. If you have a large number of students, form several groups. Each group's leader guides his or her group on a different route around the room.

Walk straight and then turn left.

Discussion Questions
1. **How did the right actions of the leaders in this game help others?** (Helped others walk safely around the room.)

2. **Whose good example have you followed? Who might follow your good example? How?** (Younger brother might help someone who is hurt after he sees you help someone who is hurt.)

3. Read 1 Timothy 4:12 aloud. **How does this verse encourage you to be a leader, even though you are young?**

Line Leaders

Bible Focus ▸ Joshua 1

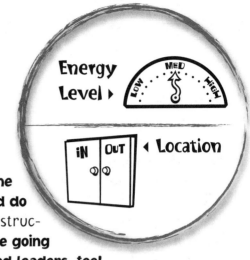

Energy Level ▸

Location ▸

Materials

Bibles.

Lead the Game

1. **God's Word helped Joshua get ready to lead the Israelites into the Promised Land. What did God do to help Joshua be a good leader?** (God gave instructions and promises to help Joshua.) **Today we're going to play a game in which we will need to be good leaders, too!**

2. Students play a game similar to Follow the Leader. Students stand in a single line as shown in sketch. The first student in line is the leader. The leader stays in one place and begins motion (moves legs, moves arms, bends to the side, etc). The second student follows the leader; the third student follows the second; and so on (see sketch). There will be a ripple effect similar to the wave performed at a sporting event.

3. After several motions have been successfully completed, ask a volunteer to name something God's Word teaches us to do. Ask the Discussion Questions to extend your discussion about ways we can depend on God's Word to guide us. Repeat several times with new leaders as time permits.

Options

1. Divide group into two single-file lines with the line leaders facing each other. The leader of one line begins a motion, immediately followed by the leader of the other line.

2. Play this game outside if possible and allow students to walk around as part of motions.

3. If you have a large number of students, form several groups. Each group's leader guides his or her group on a different route around the room.

Discussion Questions

1. Read Joshua 1:6-9 aloud. **What are some of the instructions God gave Joshua? Which of these instructions can we follow today?**

2. **What are some things kids your age depend on for guidance?** (Parents. Maps. Friends. Teachers. Computers.)

3. **When are some times that you might need God's Word to guide you?** (When a friend hurts your feelings. When you feel afraid. When you want to tell a lie. When you feel all alone.)

Loud Leaders

Bible Focus ▸ 2 Chronicles 34

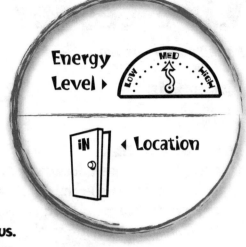

Energy Level ▸

Location ▸ iN

Materials

Bibles, blindfolds.

Lead the Game

1. Even though Josiah was a young boy when he be-came king, he loved God. Good leaders do all they can to obey God and help others do what is right. God gives us people who will be good leaders for us. Let's play a game to practice being good leaders for each other.

2. Designate a playing area. Students form pairs. Three pairs play each round.

3. One student in each of the first three pairs puts on a blindfold. The partner of each blindfolded stu-dent takes off a shoe and places it somewhere in the playing area.

4. Shoeless partner and blindfolded partner stand at the edge of the playing area. At your signal, shoeless partner sends blindfolded partner to find his or her shoe, giving directions such as, "Walk three small steps forward" or "Turn to your right and bend down." Student giving directions remains in place.

5. Once the blindfolded partner finds the correct shoe, the shoeless partner directs him or her back toward his or her partner. (Optional: The blindfolded partner must also put the shoe on the partner's foot.) Repeat play until all students have had a turn to be blindfolded.

Options

Make a separate playing area for each group of three pairs. Mark off playing areas with masking tape, rope or yarn.

Discussion Questions

1. How did your partner act as a good leader? What would happen if you didn't fol-low your partner's directions?

2. Would you rather be a leader and help people know what to do or be a follower and do what a good leader says to do? Why?

3. How can people who love God be both good followers and good leaders? (Follow and obey God. Help others learn to obey Him, too.)

Life Application Games

Obeying God

Balloon Challenge

Bible Focus ▸ Proverbs 3:3; Daniel 6

Energy Level ▸ LOW MED HIGH

iN ◂ **Location**

Materials

Bibles, balloons.

Lead the Game

1. **Daniel had formed a habit of praying three times each day. When we form habits of faithfulness to God, it is easier to do what is right when trouble comes. We form habits when we practice doing something again and again until we can do it without even thinking about it. Let's practice this fun activity and see how good we can get at it!**

2. Students form pairs. Give each pair a balloon. Students inflate and tie balloons and practice hitting them back and forth to each other.

3. **Now that you've practiced hitting the balloon, count how many times you can hit the balloon back and forth before it touches the floor.** Pairs complete task. **Imagine how much easier hitting the balloon would be if you had a habit of doing it every day.** Pairs continue activity, challenging themselves to increase the number each time.

Options

1. Students may vary distance between themselves and their partners and try different hitting techniques to discover what works best for them.

2. Challenge older students to use their heads, knees or elbows instead of their hands to hit balloon back and forth.

Discussion Questions

1. **What are some things kids your age try to get in the habit of doing?** (Doing homework. Riding bike or skateboard. Brushing teeth. Practicing a sport. Playing an instrument.)

2. **What kinds of habits could you form that would show your faithfulness to God?** (Reading the Bible to learn more about God. Praying to God every day. Obeying God's commands in the ways you treat others.)

3. Read Proverbs 3:3 aloud. **How can these words help you when things are hard?** (Knowing God's Word will help you know the right thing to do even in difficult situations. Praying to God will comfort you when you are scared or sad.)

Choice Moves

Bible Focus ▸ John 14:15

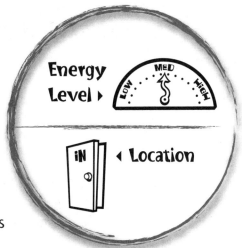

Energy Level ▸ LOW MED HIGH

Location ▸ iN

Materials

Bibles, children's music CD and player, large sheet of paper, construction paper, markers, masking tape.

Preparation

Print the letters *C, H, O, I, C* and *E* on separate sheets of paper. Tape papers to the floor in a large circle.

Lead the Game

1. **Jesus teaches that one way we show our love to God is when we obey Him. Let's play a game in which we tell ways we can obey God.**

2. Each student stands on or near one of the letters. (More than one student may stand on or near any letter.) As you play music students move to new letters, making sure they are not standing next to the same two students. Stop the music. Call out any one of the letters. The students standing on or near that letter tell situations in which kids their age might 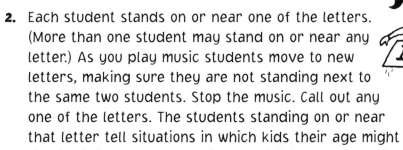 find it difficult to make a right choice ("Parent asks if I've done my homework when I'm watching TV" or "Coach asks if I touched the ball last before it went out of bounds in a soccer game"). Print a brief description of the choice on large sheet of paper. Use the Discussion Questions to enhance the conversation. Repeat the activity until all students have had turns, or all letters have been chosen.

3. Tell students about a time you prayed, asking God's help in making a right choice. Lead students in prayer, mentioning the choices on the list and asking God for help in following Him.

Option

If you have fewer than six students in your class, students walk around the circle as you play the music instead of trading places.

Discussion Questions

1. **What are some ways we can show trust in God when making choices?** (Ask God for courage to do right. Remember His commands.)

2. **Which of these choices might be the hardest for you to make?**

3. **How can God help you when it's hard to obey Him?**

Coin Toss Relay

Bible Focus ▸ 1 Samuel 15:1-26

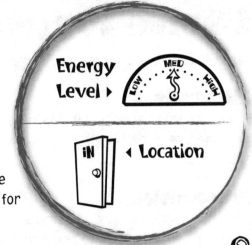

Energy Level ▸

in ◂ Location

Materials
Bibles, masking tape, coins.

Preparation
Using masking tape to make two curvy paths on the ground or floor in your playing area, leaving room for students to line up behind the paths.

Lead the Game

1. **God wants us to obey Him because He knows His commands are the best way to live. King Saul decided to follow his way rather than God's way, which led to God choosing a new king. We are going to do a coin toss relay to remind us of the difference between choosing our own way and obeying God's way.**

2. Group students into two teams. Each team lines up behind one of the masking-tape paths. **In this game, when your coin lands heads up, you'll get to move along the path in an easy way to remind you of how good it is to obey God's wise commands. If your coin lands tails up, you'll have to move along the path in a harder way to remind you that disobeying God causes trouble.**

3. Student at front of each line flips a coin. If the coin lands heads up, tell the student(s) to move along the masking-tape path in an easy manner (skipping or walking). If the coin lands tails up, tell the student(s) to move along the path in a more difficult manner (crab-walking or putting one foot behind the other to move backwards).

4. After first student has completed the path, next student in line flips the coin and moves along the path. Continue play until all students on one team have completed the path. If time allows, begin a new round of the relay with students doing new movements.

Discussion Questions

1. **What are some commands God wants us to obey?** (Forgive others. Help needy people.)

2. **What is one way you can obey one of these commands?**

3. **What excuse might a kid your age give for not obeying God?** (It's too hard. No one else obeys.)

Color Your Actions

Bible Focus ▸ Matthew 5—7; Luke 6:17-49

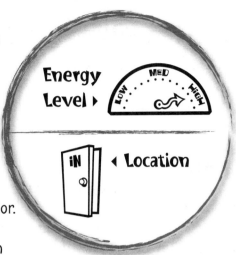

Energy Level ▸ LOW MED HIGH

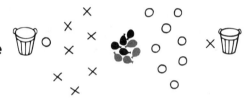

iN ◂ Location

Materials

Bibles, balloons in two colors, plastic garbage bag, two large boxes or garbage cans.

Preparation

Inflate and tie balloons, an equal number of each color. (Prepare one balloon for each student. If you have a small group, prepare more than one balloon for each student.) Place balloons in garbage bag for storage.

Lead the Game

1. **Jesus teaches us to live in ways that show we belong to Him and follow Him. In the game we're going to play your actions will show which team you're on. Let's also see if your attitude when you play can show you belong to Jesus.**

2. Play a game similar to soccer, using multiple balloons. Place balloons on the floor in the middle of a large playing area.

3. Students form two teams. Teams line up shoulder-to-shoulder at opposite ends of the playing area. Assign each team a balloon color and choose a student from each team to be a scorer. Scorer stands behind opposing team, in front of a large box or garbage can (see sketch).

4. At your signal, all team members run to the middle of the playing area and try to kick balloons of their team's color to their scorer. (Optional: Students remove shoes.) Scorer grabs his or her team's balloons and puts them into the box or can. At your signal, scorer counts balloons in box or can. Team with most balloons in the box or can wins. Repeat as time permits, blowing up additional balloons to replace any popped balloons.

Discussion Questions

1. **How did you show which team you belonged to in this game?** (Kicked balloons of only one color.)

2. **What are some actions you can do every day to show that you belong to and follow Jesus?** (Read the Bible. Say kind words. Forgive others. Share with others. Be honest. Pray.)

3. **Why is it important to live in ways that show we belong to Jesus and want to follow Him?** (Because we love God. So that others can learn about God through our actions.)

Connect the Part

Bible Focus ▸ Psalm 119:60

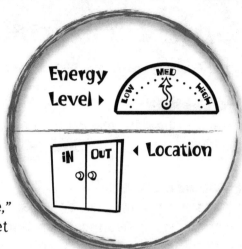

Energy Level ▸

Location

Materials

Bibles, index cards, marker.

Preparation

Print the following words on index cards, one word per card: "elbow," "foot," "hand," "shoulder," "knee," "back," "wrist," "toe," "head," "finger." Make one set of cards for every six students.

Lead the Game

1. The words in Psalm 119:60 tell us it is good to obey God eagerly. Let's play a game in which we eagerly follow some funny commands to connect groups of people together.

2. Group students into teams of six. Distribute a set of cards to each team.

3. One student on each team acts as the cardholder. This student mixes up the cards and then holds cards so that the other students cannot see words. Another student from the team picks a card and reads it aloud. Everyone on the team quickly connects the body part written on the card (for example, group stands in a circle with elbows connected in the middle). Cardholder mixes up cards and allows a different student to pick a card while group stays in position. Group tries to connect new body part as well as keeping command from the first card. When the group falls or can no longer stay connected, begin a new round with a new cardholder.

Option

If you have a small class, make one set of cards. Students form pairs. Choose two cards and read them aloud. Students in each pair connect the named body parts (such as wrist to ear). Mix up the cards and choose two new cards.

Discussion Questions

1. **What made it hard to stay connected? What made it hard to follow the commands?**

2. **In what ways can we learn about God's commands? What are some of God's commands you remember?** (Treat others fairly. Be patient.)

3. **When might a kid your age find it hard to obey one of God's commands?**

Fish and Sharks

Bible Focus ▸ Exodus 23:2

Materials

Bibles, masking tape, large sheet of paper, marker.

Preparation

Make two masking-tape lines approximately 20 feet (6 m) apart.

Energy Level ▸ LOW MED HIGH

Location ▸ iN OUT

Lead the Game

1. **We're going to play a game of tag, but first we need to make a list of situations to use in the game. What are some situations in which kids your age might be tempted to do the wrong thing?** (Taking a test at school. Not having enough money to buy something at a store.) List students' ideas on large sheet of paper.

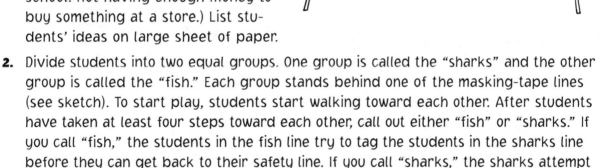

20 feet (6m)

2. Divide students into two equal groups. One group is called the "sharks" and the other group is called the "fish." Each group stands behind one of the masking-tape lines (see sketch). To start play, students start walking toward each other. After students have taken at least four steps toward each other, call out either "fish" or "sharks." If you call "fish," the students in the fish line try to tag the students in the sharks line before they can get back to their safety line. If you call "sharks," the sharks attempt to tag the fish. Anyone who is tagged joins the other team. Play several rounds.

3. Play the game again; but this time at the end of each round, the first student tagged chooses one of the situations listed on the large sheet of paper and tells what he or she thinks would be the right thing to do in God's eyes.

4. After the last round, ask a student to find Exodus 23:2 in his or her Bible and read it aloud. Ask one or more of the Discussion Questions below.

Discussion Questions

1. **How does God want us to act toward others? How is this different from following the crowd?**

2. **When are some times that kids your age don't do what is right in God's eyes? When might a kid your age be tempted to follow the crowd in doing wrong?**

3. **How can you do what is right in God's eyes instead of doing what other kids are doing?** (Pray. Remember what God's Word says. Don't hang around people who usually do wrong things.)

Follow the Guide

Bible Focus ▶ Genesis 12:1-9; Jeremiah 17:7

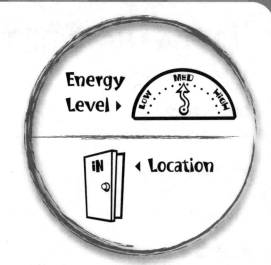

Energy Level ▶ LOW MED HIGH

iN ◀ Location

Materials

Bibles, large sheets of paper in three or four colors, tape.

Preparation

Tape the sheets of paper to the wall at varying locations around an open playing area.

Lead the Game

1. **Abram followed God's guidance as he left his land and went to a new place God showed him. God has promised to guide and protect us, and we can always trust God's promises! Let's play a game in which you need to listen to a guide to succeed.**

2. **Listen carefully to what I say as your guide and follow my instructions.** Students begin walking around the playing area. Call out a number between two and four and instruct students to quickly gather in groups of that number, linking arms. Call out a manner of moving (hopping on one foot, skipping, tiptoeing, giant steps, baby steps, etc.). Groups move in this manner, keeping arms linked. Then call out a color of one of the sheets of paper. Groups quickly move to the closest paper of that color, keeping arms linked and moving in the manner called. As each group gets to the named paper, each member of the group touches the paper and sits down on the floor as a group.

3. A volunteer from the first group to be seated tells a time he or she can trust God's promise to guide and protect us or names one of God's promises or repeats Jeremiah 17:7. Continue playing as time allows, varying the instructions for each round of play.

Discussion Questions

1. **How do your parents or teachers give you guidance or instruction?** (Tell what to do. Write lists. Show how to do things.)

2. **In what ways does God guide us?** (By His instructions in the Bible. By giving us people who tell us the right ways to love God and others. By answering our prayers.)

3. **What are some ways to show we trust God to be our guide?** (Ask His help when making choices. Read God's Word to discover His commands.)

"Here I Am!"

Bible Focus ▸ 1 Samuel 3

Materials

Bibles, blindfold.

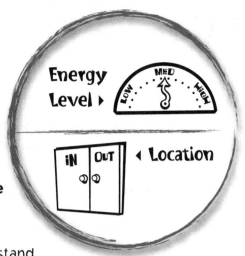

Energy Level ▸ LOW MED HIGH

iN OUT ◂ Location

Lead the Game

1. Samuel was a man who listened to God his whole life. We're going to play a game that shows how important listening is.

2. Play a game like Marco Polo. Ask a volunteer to stand on one side of the playing area. Blindfold the volunteer. Students quietly position themselves at random around the playing area. Volunteer begins calling, "Samuel, Samuel." Rest of students answer with the phrase, "Here I am."

3. Blindfolded volunteer moves toward students by listening to their voices. As he or she continues calling, "Samuel, Samuel," students around the room must respond each time. Depending on the size of your playing area, the students who respond to the blindfolded volunteer may stay frozen in one spot or may move around as they respond. (If you have a large playing area or a large number of students, students should stay frozen.)

4. When the volunteer finds and tags a student, that student (or a student who hasn't had a turn yet) is blindfolded for the next round. Continue game as time permits.

Option

Play the game outdoors if possible. Make the boundaries of game area larger for an additional challenge.

Discussion Questions

1. **What are ways we can listen to God and find out what He wants us to do?** (Read the Bible. Listen to Bible stories. Pray. Talk with adults who know and love God.)

2. **What do you think a person is like who listens to and obeys God?** (Treats others in kind ways. Is honest. Reads God's Word.)

3. **What's one way you have listened to God today?**

On Guard

Bible Focus ▸ Judges 16:4-22

Energy Level ▸ LOW MED HIGH

iN ◂ Location

Materials

Bibles, masking tape, measuring stick, cardboard box, scrap paper in two or three different colors.

Preparation

Use masking tape to make a 5-foot (1.5-m) square in the middle of the playing area. Place the box in the middle of the masking-tape square.

Lead the Game

1. **Samson made some bad choices when he was tempted. God's Word tells us to be on our guard so that we won't make bad choices in tempting situations. We can ask God for self-control to help us always make the best choice. Let's practice being on our guard in this game.**

2. Students form two or three teams. Teams stand on different sides of the playing area. Give each team one color of scrap paper. Students wad paper into balls. Invite one volunteer from each team to be a guard. Guards stand inside the masking-tape square in front of any team except their own.

3. At your signal, students attempt to throw their paper balls past the guard and into the box, making sure to stay behind the masking-tape line at all times. The guards try to block the paper balls.

4. After a short time, signal students to stop throwing the paper balls. Ask another volunteer from each team to collect their paper balls from the box, counting how many balls of their team's color are in the box. A volunteer from the team with the most balls in the box answers one of the Discussion Questions below. Students collect paper balls and play game again, choosing new volunteers as guards for the teams.

Discussion Questions

1. **When might you find it hard to show self-control and need to remember to be on guard? Why?** Volunteers respond.

2. **Not having self-control and not being on our guard against tempting situations often gets us into trouble. What might happen if you don't have self-control when you are tempted to (copy someone's homework)?** Volunteers respond.

3. **What kinds of good choices might you make when you depend on God for self-control?** (You can control your temper. You can obey God's Word by treating others kindly and not lying or stealing.)

Patience Tag

Bible Focus ▸ Jeremiah 36

Materials
Bibles, masking tape or chalk.

Preparation
Make two parallel masking-tape lines at least 15 to 25 feet (4.5 to 7.5 m) apart and at least 10 feet (3 m) long. (Use chalk if you are playing on asphalt.)

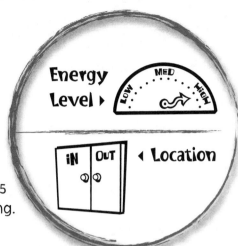

Energy Level ▸ LOW MED HIGH

iN OuT ◂ Location

Lead the Game
1. **Jeremiah patiently had scrolls of God's Word remade after a king destroyed them. Just like Jeremiah, we need to patiently keep doing what God wants us to do. Let's try out our patience during a game of tag.**

2. Choose one volunteer to be "It." "It" stands between the two lines. All other students stand behind one line.

3. At your signal, students run past "It" and across the opposite line, trying not to be tagged by "It." If a student is tagged, that student freezes in place and begins touching his or her head, shoulders, knees and then toes, repeating movements over and over again.

4. At your signal, students who successfully crossed run back to opposite line, tagging any frozen students to unfreeze them. Any new students who are tagged by "It" must freeze in place and repeat the motions until they are freed by another student.

5. Continue giving signal for students to run back and forth between the masking-tape lines. Every few minutes, substitute a new volunteer to be "It." Continue game as time allows.

Discussion Questions
1. **When did you have to be patient while you were playing this game?** (While repeating the motions and waiting for someone to tag and unfreeze you.)

2. **What are some of the things we know God wants us to do?** (Show love to others. Speak kind words to others. Tell the truth. Pray to Him.) **When would kids your age need patience to keep doing those good things?** (When they don't feel like being kind. When people aren't being kind to them. When people make fun of them.)

Pharaoh, Pharaoh

Bible Focus ▸ Exodus 8—11

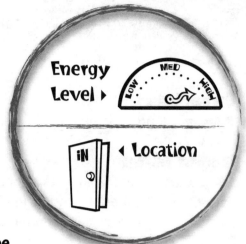

Energy Level ▸ LOW MED HIGH

iN ◂ Location

Materials
Bibles, masking tape or chairs.

Preparation
Use masking tape or chairs to mark a "safe" area.

Lead the Game

1. **Moses kept going to Pharaoh to ask him to let the Israelites leave Egypt. It was hard to keep asking Pharaoh, but God helped Moses. Let's play a game to act out what happened.**

2. Choose a volunteer to be Pharaoh. All the other students act as Moses and the Israelites.

3. Explain to the students where the safe area is. Pharaoh should start walking outside the safe area. Other students follow him and ask in unison, "Pharaoh, Pharaoh, can we go?" If Pharaoh answers "No," students continue following and keep repeating the question. If Pharaoh answers "Yes," Pharaoh turns and chases the students back to the safe area. The first student  Pharaoh tags becomes Pharaoh for the next round of play. If all students reach the safe area before they are tagged by Pharaoh, Pharaoh continues in his position or a new volunteer is chosen.

Discussion Questions

1. **What are some things kids your age do to love and obey God?** (Be patient. Help an older neighbor.)

2. **Why might it be hard for a kid your age to do what's right?** (No one else is doing right. Afraid of what friends might think.)

3. **How might God help someone your age do what's right?** (Give courage. Help the person think of a right action.)

Ready or Not

Bible Focus ▸ Esther

Materials

Bibles, masking tape, rope or yarn.

Preparation

Mark out a playing area with masking tape, rope or yarn (playing area should only allow minimal movement).

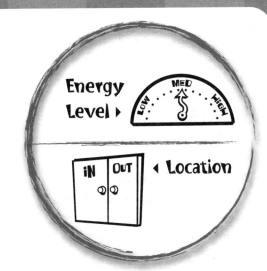

Energy Level ▸ LOW MED HIGH

iN OUT ◂ Location

Lead the Game

1. God helped Esther get ready for an important job. Even though we may not know it, God is helping us get ready to do good things for Him. Let's play a game about getting ready.

2. Students move around the playing area randomly. Call out "Get ready" so that students know to listen; then immediately clap your hands a certain number of times. For example, if you clap your hands three times, students form groups of three and sit down. Repeat play, clapping a different number of times each time. Continue play as time permits.

Option

1. Instead of saying "Get ready," blow a whistle to get students' attention and then bang on a metal pot with a metal spoon to communicate the number of students needed to form a group.

2. An older student may lead this game.

Discussion Questions

1. **What did you have to do to get ready in this game?** (Stop and listen for the claps.)

2. **What kinds of things do you do to get ready for school? For a trip?**

3. **How can we get ready for the good things God wants us to do?** (Pray every day. Read and think about God's Word. Follow the example of people who love God.)

Repetition Relay

Bible Focus ▸ Galatians 6:9

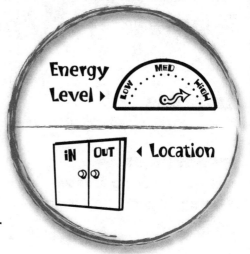

Energy Level ▸ LOW · MED · HIGH

IN | OUT ◂ Location

Materials

Bibles.

Lead the Game

1. **One way to show faithfulness is by continuing to do what God wants us to do without giving up when we're tired or bored. Let's practice continuing to do something during our game today.**

2. Students form two equal teams. Teams line up on one side of the playing area.

3. At your signal, the first student on each team runs to the other side of the playing area, does 10 jumping jacks and runs back to his or her team. The next student in line repeats the action.

4. Students continue until everyone has completed the relay. Have a volunteer from the first team to complete the relay answer one of the Discussion Questions below.

5. Repeat relay with a new action such as clapping 10 times, touching toes or hopping on one foot.

Option

For older students, play this game with two hula hoops: each team stands in a circle and holds hands. One pair of students on each team holds hands through the hula hoop. At your signal, one of the students from each pair begins moving the hula hoop around the circle without unclasping hands—each student slides hula hoop over his or her head, steps through and slides it along arms and over the next person's head. Teams race to move hula hoop around the circle three times.

Discussion Questions

1. Have a student read Galatians 6:9 aloud. **What does Galatians 6:9 say that we should continue doing?** (Good.)

2. **We can do good by obeying what God wants us to do. How do we find out what God wants us to do?** (Read the Bible. Listen to our pastors and teachers. Ask our parents or other people who love God.)

3. **What are some of the things you already know that God wants you to do?** (Show love to God and others. Be kind. Treat others as you want to be treated. Forgive others.) **When can you (be kind) to others at home? At school?**

Scrabble Scramble

Bible Focus ▸ *Psalm 119:11*

Materials

Bibles, index cards, marker, large sheet of paper.

Preparation

Print 8 to 10 key words about ways to remember God's Word on index cards, one letter on each card (memorize, sing, read, think, talk, draw, write, posters, friends, parents). Also list words on large sheet of paper. Make one set of cards for up to 12 students. Mix up cards. Spread cards facedown at one end of the room.

Energy Level ▸

iN ◂ **Location**

Lead the Game

1. Students find and read Psalm 119:11 in their Bibles. **How many different ways can you think of "hiding God's Word in your heart"?** (Memorize Bible verses, sing verses, read the Bible, think and talk about what God says, look at posters that tell things the Bible says, etc.). **Which of these ways will best remind you to do what is right even when you're tempted to disobey?** Divide class into four groups. Distribute three blank cards to each group. At your signal, one student from each group runs to the card pile, takes seven cards and returns to his or her group.

2. Groups play Scrabble game together, taking turns spelling out words on the floor and connecting their words as shown in sketch. (Show words lettered on paper for students to refer to.) Students may use blank cards as "wild cards," substituting them for missing letters. As each word is formed, volunteer uses the word in a sentence describing a way to learn about and remember God's instructions.

3. If a group cannot spell a word, it sends a runner to the card pile to take another card. Continue until a word can be formed. (If all the cards have been taken from the pile, group loses its turn.) The game ends when one group has played all its cards, or when no group is able to form additional words. Words may only be used once.

Discussion Questions

1. Read Psalm 119:11. **What does it mean to hide God's Word in your heart?**

2. **How can learning and memorizing God's Word help you make right choices?** (We can remember what God wants us to do. If we know God's Word, we can make good choices.)

3. **When are some times it would help a kid your age to know a Bible verse to help him or her make right choices?**

Self-Control Toss

Bible Focus ▸ 1 Samuel 24; Proverbs 29:11

Materials

Bibles, large sheet of paper, marker, masking tape, large container, soft ball or beanbag.

Energy Level ▸ LOW MED HIGH

iN ◂ Location

Preparation

Print the word "self-control" across the top of a large sheet of paper. Draw a line down the center of the paper. Print "Team 1" on one side of the line and "Team 2" on the other. Display in classroom. Place container on the floor on one side of the playing area.

Lead the Game

1. **David did not let his feelings get out of control when he was hunted by King Saul. David chose not to kill King Saul. God can help us control our angry feelings so that we can treat others in ways that please Him. Let's play a game to help us remember how we need self-control.**

2. Divide class into two teams. Play a ball-tossing game similar to H-O-R-S-E. Students stand about 5 feet (1.5 m) from the container and take turns attempting to toss the ball or beanbag into it. Each time the ball lands in the container, the tossing team writes one letter of the word "self-control" on its side of the paper. First team to complete the word wins.

3. Ask a volunteer from the winning team to answer one of the Discussion Questions below. Repeat game as time allows.

Discussion Questions

1. **When are some of the times angry feelings are hard to control?** (When someone is continually mean or rude to you. When someone makes you feel bad.)

2. **Read Proverbs 29:11. How can we control our angry feelings?** (Pray and ask God for His help. Walk away. Take a deep breath and wait before speaking.)

3. **When God helps us have self-control, how will we act toward others?** (We won't act angrily. We will treat them in ways that please God, being kind to them instead of treating them in the way they treated us.)

Shuffle Feet

Bible Focus ▸ Daniel 1; Acts 5:29

Energy Level ▸ *LOW MED HIGH*

iN ◂ Location

Materials

Bibles, index cards, marker, two paper bags, four empty shoe boxes or large tissue boxes.

Preparation

Print the following commands on separate index cards: "Do three jumping jacks," "Smile and say hello to your teacher," "Clap seven times," "Wink at your team," "Turn around twice." Make two sets of cards. Place one set in each bag. Remove lids or tops of boxes.

Lead the Game

1. **Daniel chose to obey God by refusing to eat the king's food that was sacrificed to idols. One way we can show our love for God is by choosing to obey Him, even when it is hard. Let's play a game to obey some instructions, even if they are hard to do!**

2. Divide group into two teams. Teams line up on one side of the playing area. Place one bag of index cards on the opposite side of the playing area from each team.

3. Give the first student on each team two boxes. At your signal, the first student on each team steps into his or her boxes and shuffles to his or her team's bag. Student takes out an index card, reads card and returns it to the bag and then performs the action on the card, stepping out of the boxes if necessary. Student steps back into boxes, shuffles back to his or her team and steps out of boxes for the next student to begin the relay. Game continues until all students have had a turn.

Discussion Questions

1. **What was hard about this relay?** (Moving quickly or completing a command with the boxes on our feet.)

2. **What are some of God's commands from the Bible?** (Love others. Don't lie. Care for people who are different from you.) **When are some times it is hard to obey God's commands?** (When everyone else is disobeying God's commands. When we don't feel like being kind or loving.)

3. **Read Acts 5:29 aloud. Why is it most important to obey God?** (His laws are the best, even when they are hard. He loves us. He is God, the maker of everything. His laws tell us how to follow God's plans.)

Standing Firm

Bible Focus ▸ Nehemiah 1—8:12; 1 Corinthians 15:58

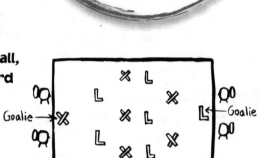

Energy Level ▸ LOW MED HIGH

iN OUT ◂ Location

Materials

Bibles, masking tape, chairs, tennis ball or soft foam ball.

Preparation

Tear off masking-tape strips (two for each student). Position chairs as shown in sketch.

Lead the Game

1. **Nehemiah led the rebuilding of Jerusalem's wall, even when others tried to stop him. God's Word tells us to patiently continue to do what is right in all situations. One way the Bible describes this is by telling us to stand firm. We're going to practice standing firm as we play a game of human Foosball.**

2. Divide group into two teams. Position students as shown in sketch, both teams facing away from their respective goalie. Students should stand at least an arm's length from each other. Give each student two strips of masking tape. Students on one team make masking-tape Xs on floor to mark their positions. Students on other team make masking-tape Ls on floor.

3. Gently roll the ball toward the middle of the playing area. Students try to kick the ball toward their team's goal, each student keeping at least one foot on his or her masking-tape mark at all times and not touching the ball with his or her hands.

4. Students continue kicking ball until a goal is scored. (Note: Goalies only use their feet to defend goal.) After each goal, ask a volunteer from the team that scored the goal to answer a question below. Begin again by giving ball to a player from the team that did not score.

Discussion Questions

1. **During this game, you stood firm by not moving off the tape. Listen to what the Bible says about standing firm.** Ask a volunteer to read 1 Corinthians 15:58 aloud. **What does it mean to "stand firm" and "let nothing move you"?** (Keep on doing what is right, even when other people around you are doing wrong things.)

2. **What is "the work of the Lord"?** (Loving others. Obeying God's commands.)

3. **Name one time (at school) that it is hard to do what is right. How can you patiently keep doing right in that situation?** Repeat question, substituting other places or situations for the words "at school."

Strong Obstacles

Bible Focus ▸ Judges 14—16

Materials
Bibles.

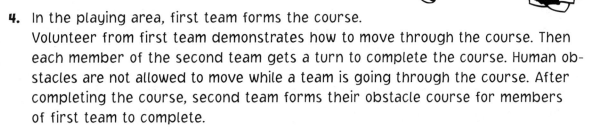

Energy Level ▸ LOW MED HIGH

iN OuT ◂ Location

Lead the Game

1. Samson kept doing things that made it hard for him to follow the instructions God had given him. His wrong actions were obstacles—things that kept him from obeying God. We're going to play a game where we form an obstacle course with our bodies.

2. Divide the group into two teams.

3. Each team plans a human obstacle course for the other team to move through. Obstacles might be a student on hands and knees to hop over, a student standing with legs apart to form a tunnel to crawl through or two students lying next to each other to jump over.

4. In the playing area, first team forms the course. Volunteer from first team demonstrates how to move through the course. Then each member of the second team gets a turn to complete the course. Human obstacles are not allowed to move while a team is going through the course. After completing the course, second team forms their obstacle course for members of first team to complete.

Option
Students use classroom or outdoor objects to create obstacle courses.

Discussion Questions

1. **When do kids your age sometimes find it hard to obey God's instructions?** (When friends make fun of you for obeying God. When I want to do things my way.)

2. **What are some obstacles (problems, people, etc.) that sometimes get in the way of obeying God?**

3. **What can we do when we need help to obey?** (Pray to God. Ask parents for help.) **When we have disobeyed and need to be forgiven?**

Switcheroo

Bible Focus ▸ Matthew 4:18-22; Mark 2:13-14; 3:13-19

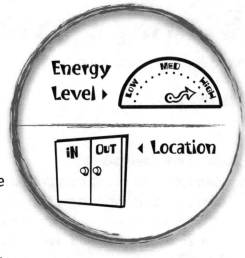

Energy Level ▸

Location

Materials

Bibles, masking tape.

Preparation

On the floor, use masking tape to form at least three shapes large enough to fit the number of students in your class. (For example, if you have 20 students, make four squares or rectangles large enough for five students to stand in each shape.)

Lead the Game

1. **Jesus chose 12 disciples who came from many different backgrounds. It's great that God chooses all kinds of people to learn from Him. Let's play a game where a leader chooses all kinds of people to play.**

2. Ask a volunteer to be "It." Form three groups from remaining students. Each group stands in a separate shape marked on the floor.

3. One at a time call out such descriptions as "kids wearing blue" or "kids wearing tennis shoes." Students who fit each description run to new shapes while "It" tries to tag them before they are inside their new shapes. Any student who is tagged becomes "It" also. Continue play, periodically calling out "Switcheroo" at which all students must run to new shapes. When only a few students have not been tagged, begin a new round of the game. Begin the new round with a new "It."

Options

1. If you have a large group, choose more than one student to be "It."

2. If space is limited, students jump, hop or tiptoe instead of running between shapes.

3. Play this game outside on a paved area. Draw the shapes with chalk.

Discussion Questions

1. **In this game, how did we choose the people who had to switch places?**

2. **What kinds of people did Jesus choose to be His disciples? What did they do to learn about Jesus?** (Traveled with Him. Listened to Him teach.)

3. **What are some ways we can learn what God wants to teach us?** (Read our Bibles. Listen to teachers and parents. Ask God to help us learn about Him.)

Target Relay

Bible Focus ▸ Esther; Galatians 6:10

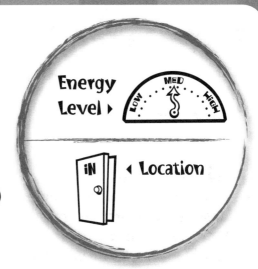

Energy Level ▸

iN ◂ Location

Materials
Bibles, masking tape or yarn, several Frisbees.

Preparation
For every four to six students, make a 2-foot (.6-m) masking-tape or yarn square on one side of the playing area.

Lead the Game
1. **Queen Esther used her opportunity to save God's people from destruction. We can please God by using every opportunity we have to do what is right. Let's practice doing what is right in our game today.**

2. Group students in teams of four to six. Teams line up across the playing area from the targets. Give the first person on each team a Frisbee. **For each round of the game, we'll have a different way to "do what is right," or correctly get the Frisbee onto the target. The first way is to hang the Frisbee by its rim on your fingertip and toss it onto the target.** Demonstrate the motion.

3. At your signal, the first student on each team hangs the Frisbee by its rim on his or her fingertip, runs across the room and tosses the Frisbee onto the team's target. Whether or not the Frisbee lands on the target, student retrieves the Frisbee and runs back to line. The next student in line repeats the action.

4. When all students have completed the relay in this manner, announce a new way to get the Frisbee onto the target and begin game again. Continue as time allows, announcing a new way to "do right" each round (for example, rolling Frisbee onto the target, tossing Frisbee from a standing position, tossing Frisbee back over the shoulder, rolling the Frisbee between the legs, etc.).

Discussion Questions
1. **What are some ways to learn the right things to do?** (Read the Bible. Listen to parents or teachers. Watch older people who love Jesus.)

2. **What are some ways to show goodness by doing what is right at home? At school?** Volunteers tell ideas.

3. **What are some ways you can remember to do what is right when you have the opportunity?** (Pray and ask God to help you remember. Think of a slogan or a question to ask yourself when you have to make a choice.)

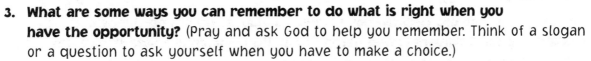

Turn and Run

Bible Focus ▸ 2 Chronicles 7:14; John 21:15-19

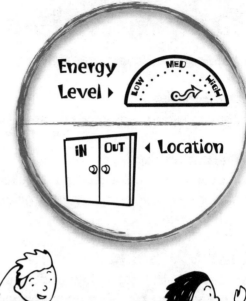

Energy Level ▸ LOW MED HIGH

IN OUT ◂ Location

Materials

Bibles.

Lead the Game

1. Read John 21:15-19 aloud. **Peter denied he knew Jesus three times. But Jesus forgave him and Peter turned into a great leader of the early church. When we do wrong things, it is like turning away from God. But God always forgives us and wants us to turn back toward Him. Let's play a game that reminds us of turning around to move in a new direction.**

2. Students stand shoulder-to-shoulder on one side of a playing area at least 40- feet (12-m) long. Stand at the other end of the playing area and call "run." Students run toward you. Call "freeze." Students must freeze. Shout, "Turn around." The students must turn away from you. Call "run." Students run in the opposite direction from you. Continue shouting any variation of these commands (slow motion, crawl, hop, etc.). When the first student reaches you, student becomes caller and a new round begins.

Options

1. Blow a whistle before you call each command, so students know to prepare for a change and you don't have to call as loudly.

2. The first student who tags you in each round leads the next round.

3. If you have a smaller playing area than suggested, students may walk, crawl or hop rather than run.

Discussion Questions

1. **When are some times kids your age might want to disobey God?**

2. Read 2 Chronicles 7:14 aloud. **What does God promise to do when we ask His forgiveness?**

3. **When was a time you decided you wanted to stop doing wrong things and asked God for forgiveness and help to obey His commands instead?** Give an age-appropriate example from your own life.

Two-by-Two Relay

Bible Focus ▸ Genesis 6:9—9:17

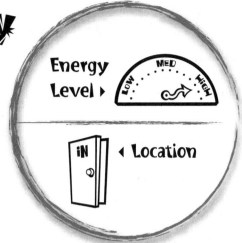

Energy Level ▸

iN ◂ Location

Materials

Bibles, index cards, marker.

Lead the Game

1. **Noah showed his love for God by obeying Him and building the ark. The animals even obeyed by getting on board! Let's play a game about the animals getting on board the ark.**

2. **What kinds of animals came on the ark with Noah?** Write each animal students suggest on a separate index card. (You may also prepare cards ahead of time.) Mix order of cards and place in a stack.

3. **Many of the animals that came onto the ark came in pairs.** Students line up in pairs. (If you have an uneven number of students, form one or more trios.) Each pair of students takes a card and quickly decides an action to imitate the animal on their card (arms down in front of face like the trunk of an elephant, hopping for a rabbit or frog, etc.). At your signal, each pair links arms and moves across the playing area in the manner chosen. When they get to the other side of the playing area, pair stands up and makes the noise of their animal and then returns to line in the same manner.

4. If you have time, shuffle the cards and play again so that each student gets a chance to imitate more than one kind of animal. Students change partners for each round of the game.

Discussion Questions

1. **What animal would you most like to be? Why?**

2. **What animal did you have the most fun acting like?**

3. **Noah obeyed God by building an ark. What are some ways a kid your age can obey God?** (Help people in need. Speak kind words to stop an argument.)

Whisk-Broom Relay

Bible Focus ▸ Joshua 3

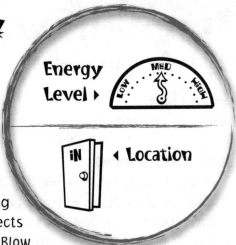

Energy Level ▸

LOW MED HIGH

iN ◂ Location

Materials

Bibles, masking tape, obstacles for course (table, chairs, books, etc.), balloons, two whisk brooms.

Preparation

Lay masking-tape lines at opposite ends of the playing area. Use tables, chairs, stacks of books or other objects to create two identical obstacle courses (see sketch). Blow up and tie two balloons.

Lead the Game

1. **Joshua obeyed God as he led the Israelites across the Jordan River. In our game, we will guide balloons through an obstacle course.**

2. Divide class into two teams. Teams line up behind masking-tape line. Give the first student in each line a whiskbroom and a balloon. Demonstrate the proper path through each obstacle course.

3. Students use whiskbrooms to move balloons through obstacle course and back to the starting line, touching the balloons only with brooms. After each student completes the course, he or she hands the whisk broom and balloon to the next student who repeats the course. Continue until all students have had a turn.

4. A volunteer from the first team to complete the course answers the Discussion Questions below. Repeat relay as time allows.

Option

If space is limited, prepare one obstacle course and then time how long it takes each team to complete it.

Game Tip

Have a few extra balloons inflated in case balloons pop during the game.

Discussion Questions

1. **You encouraged your teammates to try and win the game. Who are some people who could encourage you to obey God?** (Parents. Friends. Teachers.)

2. **How do you think God could help you obey Him?** (Help to remember a Bible verse. Give courage.)

Life Application Games

Praising God

Leaven Hunt

Bible Focus ▸ Exodus 12:12-42

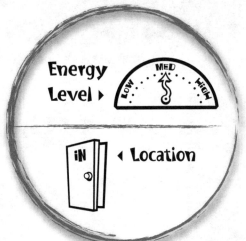

Materials

Bibles, scissors or paper cutter, construction paper in two colors, ruler, pencil, clock or watch with second hand; optional—bite-size candy or crackers.

Preparation

Cut construction paper into 1-inch (2.5-cm) squares, making approximately 40 squares of each color. Hide squares in your classroom.

Lead the Game

1. **Every day we see things that remind us to praise God for the great things He has done! During the Passover celebration, God's people remember the way He rescued them from slavery in Egypt. Today we are going to play a game that reminds us how fast the Hebrews left Egypt.**

2. **The Hebrews left Egypt in such a hurry that God told them to make their bread without yeast because it wouldn't have time to rise. Another name for yeast is "leaven." The yeast, or leaven, is what makes bread rise, or get bigger. To get ready to celebrate Passover, it's a custom to look all over your house to remove anything made with leaven.** Divide class into two teams and explain that each team will have 30 seconds to collect paper squares representing leaven. Assign each team one of the two colors.

3. At your signal, students begin looking for paper squares. Call time after 30 seconds. Each team counts the total number of squares they were able to find. (Optional: Give candy or crackers to the team who found the most squares.) If time permits, students close eyes or briefly leave room while you or older student hides squares again. Repeat activity.

Discussion Questions

1. **What are some of the great things God has done that you have read about in the Bible?** (Helped the Israelites escape from Pharaoh's army. Helped the Hebrew people get to the Promised Land. Healed people. Sent Jesus to die for our sins.)

2. **What are some of the great things God has done for you and your family?** Tell your own answer as well as inviting volunteers to respond.

3. **When can you praise God for the ways He helps you?**

Musical Cans

Bible Focus ▸ Acts 16:16-40

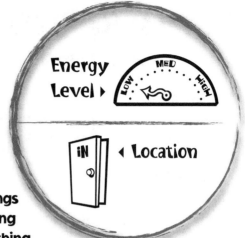

Energy Level ▸ LOW · MED · HIGH

iN ◂ Location

Materials

Bibles, children's music CD, empty soda can for each student.

Lead the Game

1. One of the ways to give thanks to God for all things and in all circumstances is by singing and making music to God. Paul and Silas were jailed for teaching about Jesus. While in jail, they prayed and sang hymns. We're going to play music in our game today and answer questions about thanking God.

2. Play a game like Musical Chairs with students. Students form a large circle, standing about 1 foot (30 cm) apart. Give each student a soda can to place at his or her feet. Ask one volunteer to put his or her can to the side of the playing area, away from the circle.

2. Start the music. Students begin to walk clockwise around the cans. When you stop the music, each student picks up the closest can. The student left without a can answers one of the Discussion Questions. Continue playing as time allows.

Option

Substitute index cards in a variety of colors for soda cans.

Discussion Questions

1. **When are some times it might be hard for a kid your age to thank God?** (When something scary, bad or sad is happening.)

2. **Why should we still give thanks to God in these hard times?** (Because we can trust that God will help us through the hard situations. He will always care for us, no matter what situation we are in.)

3. **What are some good things for which to thank God? How has God shown His goodness to you?**

Musical Verse

Bible Focus ▸ Ephesians 5:19-20

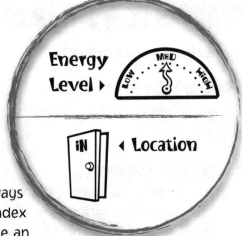

Energy Level ▸ LOW MED HIGH

iN ◂ Location

Materials

Bibles, children's music CD and player, one chair for each student, index cards, marker, Post-it Notes.

Preparation

Place chairs in a large circle facing inward. Print "always giving thanks to God the Father for everything" on index cards, one word on each card. Mix up the cards. Make an X on one Post-it Note. Stick a Post-it Note, including the one with the X, to the back of each chair.

Lead the Game

1. **God's gift of joy helps us do something very important in all situations. Let's play a game to learn what we are able to do when we have God's gift of joy.**

2. As you play music, students walk around the inside of the circle of chairs. Stop the music after a few moments. Each student sits in a chair.

3. Students look over the backs of their chairs to locate the chair with the X on it. Give student sitting in the marked chair a verse card. Student places card on the floor in the middle of the circle.

4. Move Post-it Notes to different chairs so that the note with an X is on the back of a different chair. Then repeat play. When music stops, students sit down and check for the X. Student in the marked chair gets a second verse card and decides whether it should be placed before or after the first card. Continue play until all verse cards are placed in the right order. Students refer to Ephesians 5:20 for correct order if needed. Ask Discussion Questions below.

Discussion Questions

1. **What is one thing we'll do when we have God's gift of joy?** Volunteer reads verse from completed cards aloud. (Give thanks to God for everything!) **What does Ephesians 5:19 say we'll do when we have joy?** (Sing and make music to the Lord.)

2. **What are some things for which you usually thank God?** (Food. Family. Friends. Health. Safety.)

3. **What could you give thanks for when you have a bad day at school?** (You can read. You have a school to attend.) **When you are sick?** (You have a bed to rest in.) **When you have to go to the dentist?** (You have teeth to clean. You have money for the dentist.)

Out of the Ark

Bible Focus ▸ Psalm 101:1

Materials

Bibles, index cards, marker, tape.

Preparation

Make two sets of cards printed with the names of animals (aardvark, armadillo, baboon, cheetah, elephant, gazelle, giraffe, horse, hyena, raven, tiger, warthog). Tape cards to floor as shown in sketch, making sure there is one card for each student minus one. (If you have an even number of students, join the game with your students.)

Energy Level ▸ LOW MED HIGH

iN ◂ **Location**

Lead the Game

1. Students read Psalm 101:1 in their Bibles. **What did the person who wrote this verse want to praise God for? We show that we want to praise God for His justice when we do what is right. We are going to play a game to talk about times when it is hard to do what is right.**

2. Lead students to play this game similar to Fruit Basket Upset. One student is selected to be "Noah" and stands in the middle of the room. Other students stand next to the cards (one student per card.) Noah calls out the name of one animal. Students standing behind cards with that animal's name try to change places before Noah can take one of the places.

3. The student left without a space becomes Noah. Student tells a situation in which doing what is right is made more difficult because others are doing wrong. Lead students to discuss situation by asking the Discussion Questions below. Then student calls out a name of a different animal.

4. Game continues until time is called or until everyone has had a chance to be Noah. When Noah says, "All animals out of the ark!" all students must change places.

Discussion Questions

1. **Why is it hard to do what is right in this situation?**

2. **What could you say or do to help a person in this situation do what is right?** (Pray for the person, asking for God's strength for him or her. Encourage this person with an e-mail or phone call.)

3. **How can you praise God in this situation?**

Pickup Praise

Bible Focus ▸ Acts 2:42-47

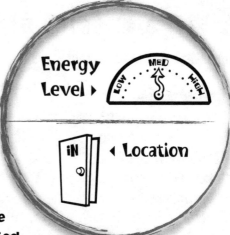

Energy Level ▸

Location ▸ iN

Materials

Bibles, 3-inch (7.5-cm) squares of construction paper (at least 10 squares for each student), markers, stopwatch or watch with second hand.

Lead the Game

1. **The first Christians spent time praising God as the church grew larger. When we worship and obey God, other people may learn about Him and come to love Him! Let's play a game to name reasons we have for praising and worshiping Him.**

2. Give each student 10 squares of paper and a marker. Students number squares 1 to 10 and then randomly place squares on floor, numbered side down, spreading out squares as much as possible throughout the playing area.

3. Divide group into two teams. Teams line up shoulder-to-shoulder on opposite sides of the playing area. Assign numbers to students as in the game Steal the Bacon (see sketch).

4. Call two numbers. Students with those numbers from each team have five seconds to collect as many construction-paper squares as possible. Call "Stop" when time is up; students return to teams with the squares they collected and add the numbers on the squares. Volunteer(s) from team with the highest number total tells a reason to praise God.

5. To play another round, volunteers return squares to playing area, numbered side down. Play as many rounds as time allows. (Replace crumpled squares as needed.)

Discussion Questions

1. **When is it hard for kids your age to obey God?** (When pressured by friends to do wrong. When sports crowd out time to worship God). **What could someone else do to help a kid obey God in that situation?**

2. **When do you like to worship God? What have we done to worship God today?**

3. **When have you seen someone else worship and obey God? How did that help you learn more about God? How could you help someone else learn about God?**

Praise Phrases

Bible Focus ▸ Luke 17:11-19

Energy Level ▸ LOW MED HIGH

◂ Location iN

Materials

Bibles, index cards, marker, a cardboard box for every group of four to six students, paper, pencils.

Preparation

On the index cards, print individual words that can be used in giving praise to God: "I," "we," "give," "thanks," "for," "God," "love," "gifts," "help," "sing," "joy," "your," "Son," "food," etc. Prepare at least three cards for each student, repeating words as needed. Place cardboard boxes around the playing area.

Lead the Game

1. **When Jesus healed and sent away 10 lepers, only one came back and praised God for His gift of healing. God's gifts to us bring us joy and cause our thankfulness to overflow! Let's play a game to give God thanks and praise for all His good gifts.**

2. Give each student at least three cards. Students form groups of four to six.

3. Each group stands around a cardboard box, 3 to 5 feet (.9 to 1.5 m) from the box. Students take turns tossing cards like Frisbees into the box, tossing each card only once.

4. When all students have finished tossing, students in each group collect cards that landed in their box and use the words to write sentences praising God. Encourage groups to tell their favorite praise sentences to the rest of the students. Continue discussion using questions below.

Discussion Questions

1. **What are some good gifts God gives us?** (People who love us. Food. Clothing. Forgiveness of sins. Talents.)

2. **What can you do to thank God for these gifts?** (Tell Him words of praise and thanks. Tell other people how great He is. Sing songs of thankfulness to Him. Use the gifts He has given us to praise Him.)

3. **When are some times you can thank God?** (Before bed. Walking to school. Riding bike. At church.)

Praise Shuffle

Bible Focus ▸ Mark 11:1-11; Philippians 2:10-11

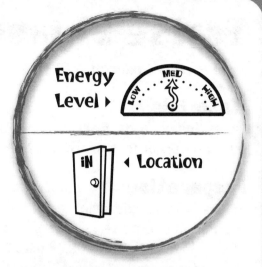

Energy Level ▸

iN ◂ Location

Materials

Bibles, 12x18-inch (30x45-cm) sheets of green construction paper, scissors, marker, jar lids, large sheet of paper, pencils, scratch paper.

Preparation

Cut large palm branches from green construction paper and divide them into sections to make game boards as shown. Make one for every four students. Label each one as shown.

Lead the Game

1. **When Jesus entered Jerusalem on a donkey, people lined the road and praised Him. Let's play a game about praising Jesus.**

2. Divide class into two groups to play a game like Shuffleboard. Place a game board on the table or floor. Invite volunteer from one group to place a jar lid upside down at one end of game board and flick it to the other end. If the lid lands in the "Reason" space, ask, **Why do you think people praise Jesus?** (He is the Savior. He loves us. He created the world. He cares for us, He answers our prayers.) List students' ideas on a large sheet of paper. If the lid lands in the "Worship" space, ask, **What are some ways people worship Jesus?** (Sing praise songs to Him. Spend time helping others, Give money to church and others who need it. Read and do what He says in the Bible.) Add ideas to paper. If lid lands on a number space, team earns that number of points. Record points on large sheet of paper. Repeat with a volunteer from the other team flicking the lid from the opposite end of the game board.

3. Continue game for several rounds. **Another way to praise Jesus is by reading Bible praises aloud to Him.** Team that scored the highest number of points reads Philippians 2:10-11 aloud together. **How do these verses describe worshiping Jesus?** Students respond.

Discussion Questions

1. **Many people bow before kings and other important people to show respect. Why does Philippians 2:10-11 tell us to worship Jesus in this way?** (He is Lord, or King, of all the earth. We should give glory to God.)

2. **What does it mean for our tongues to "confess" that Jesus is Lord?** (We say aloud that Jesus is the Lord.)

3. **How can you do what these verses say?** (Sing songs of praise to Jesus.)

Praise Squares

Bible Focus ▸ Daniel 2

Energy Level ▸ LOW MED HIGH

iN ◂ Location

Materials

Bibles, index cards, marker, masking tape, rubber ball or beach ball, whistle.

Preparation

Print one letter of the alphabet on each index card, excluding the letters Q, X and Z. Make one large masking-tape square on the floor of the playing area and then divide the square into four sections. Mix up the alphabet cards and place a stack of five or six cards near each section.

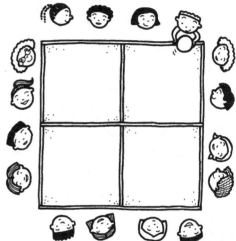

Lead the Game

1. **Daniel praised God for giving him the ability to interpret dreams for the king. Daniel prayed and praised God. When we pray to God, we can worship Him for how wise and powerful He is and what He has done. In our game today, let's talk about some of the things for which we can worship God.**

2. Lead students in a game like Four Square. Students stand around the outside edges of the square.

3. Give ball to any student who bounces the ball to any other student. Student catches the ball and bounces it to another student. Students continue bouncing the ball. After a short time, blow the whistle. Student holding the ball takes an index card from the nearest stack of cards. Student tells something God has done or made that begins with the letter on the card and then returns card to bottom of the stack.

4. Repeat play as time permits.

Discussion Questions

1. **Who are some people who often receive praise in our world today?** (Athletes. Movie stars.) **Why is it important to worship and praise God?** (Because God is greater than anyone else, He deserves our worship and praise. We want to tell God we love Him and how glad we are about all the things He has done for us.)

2. **When are some times we praise God at church? At home?**

3. **What do you want to praise God for today?** Tell your own answer to this question before inviting volunteers to answer.

Praise Toss

Bible Focus ▸ 2 Chronicles 5—7

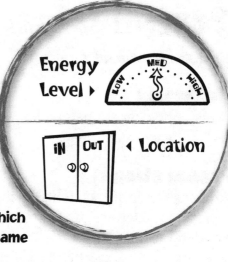

Energy Level ▸

Location ▸ iN OUT

Materials
Bibles, beach ball or other soft ball.

Lead the Game

1. After Solomon had built God's Temple, he prayed and praised God for giving the people a place to worship. God has done so many great things for which we can worship Him! Let's play a game to joyfully name some of the great things God has done.

2. Students stand in a large circle. Assign each student a number.

3. Stand in the center of the circle with the ball. Call out one of the numbers you assigned as you toss the ball into the air. Student whose number you called catches the ball and names one reason to thank God or one thing that God has done or made.

4. After naming reason or thing, student tosses ball into the air and calls out another number. Student whose number is called catches ball and names a reason to thank God or one thing that God has done or made. Game continues as time allows.

Options

1. During the game, list the reasons or things the students name. After playing the game for a while, gather together for a prayer time. Students thank God and celebrate the great things He has done, referring to list.

2. If you have more than 20 students, bring another ball and form two circles to play game.

3. To add variety, call out "Circle switch" several times during the game. At that signal, all students must move to new positions in the circle but keep their same numbers.

Discussion Questions

1. **What are your favorite parts of God's creation?**

2. **What are some things you have learned about God from the Bible? What are some of the great things God has done for you or people you know?** Share your own answer after students tell ideas.

3. **What are some ways you can worship God and thank Him for all these wonderful things?** (Sing to Him. Pray to Him. Write Him a letter or draw a picture to express your thanks. Make up a song to tell Him how much you love Him and appreciate what He has done.)

Search-abilities

Bible Focus ▸ 1 Thessalonians 5:18

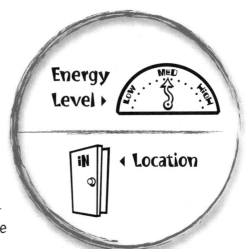

Energy Level ▸ LOW MED HIGH

iN ◂ Location

Materials

Bibles, construction paper in a variety of colors, marker, scissors.

Preparation

Print "Praise God" on different-colored sheets of construction paper, one paper for each team of no more than eight students. Cut each paper into eight or more puzzle pieces. Hide pieces around the room.

Lead the Game

1. **God has given each of us abilities—things we're good at or like to do. Let's play a game using different skills and abilities to find one great reason to use our abilities.**

2. Divide class into teams of no more than eight students. Teams line up on one side of the classroom. Assign each team a color.

3. Call out an ability (read books, play piano, kick soccer ball, etc.). First student in each line pantomimes the ability while he or she looks for a puzzle piece of the assigned color. When student finds a puzzle piece, he or she returns to his or her team, still pantomiming the ability. Second student in line takes a turn.

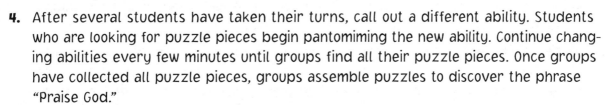

4. After several students have taken their turns, call out a different ability. Students who are looking for puzzle pieces begin pantomiming the new ability. Continue changing abilities every few minutes until groups find all their puzzle pieces. Once groups have collected all puzzle pieces, groups assemble puzzles to discover the phrase "Praise God."

Option

Ask an older student to help lead the activity by calling out different abilities every 20 seconds.

Discussion Questions

1. **What are some ways of praising God? How might a kid your age praise God in one of those ways?** (Play or sing a song of praise. Read aloud a Bible verse praising God.)

2. Read 1 Thessalonians 5:18 aloud. **In what ways have we used our abilities to praise and thank God today?**

3. **What are some ways you have seen people in your family use their abilities to praise God?**

Tic-Tac-Toe Praise

Bible Focus ▸ Exodus 12:12-42

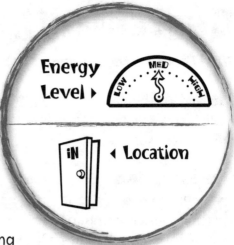

Energy Level ▸ LOW MED HIGH

iN ◂ Location

Materials
Bibles, construction paper, marker, masking tape.

Preparation
Print the following gifts from God on separate sheets of construction paper: forgiveness, family, prayer, love, courage, talents, salvation, Jesus, power. Use masking tape to make a life-sized Tic-Tac-Toe grid in the playing area. Place one paper, words facedown, in each section of the grid.

Lead the Game
1. **After David had the ark of God brought to Jerusalem, he wrote a psalm that praised God for all His gifts to His people. A great way to celebrate and praise God together as His family is to remember all the good gifts He has given us and praise God for them. Let's play Tic-Tac-Toe to help us remember God's gifts.**

2. Divide class into two equal teams. Assign one team X and one team O. Volunteers from each team take turns choosing sections of the Tic-Tac-Toe grid to stand in with arms in X or O shapes (see sketch). Teams continue taking turns until one team has three students standing in a row or until all sections of the grid are occupied.

3. Invite a volunteer from the winning team (or the team who had the last turn) to choose one of the papers on which a team member is standing. That team member turns the paper over and reads the words aloud. Then a volunteer tells a way in which God has given him or her that gift or a way he or she wants to praise God for that gift (sing a song, say a prayer, etc.).

4. Repeat game as time permits, volunteers turning over different cards at the end of each round.

Discussion Questions
1. **What has God given you to show His love for you?** Volunteers respond. **How has God given you courage? When has God forgiven you?**

2. **Why is it important to celebrate these gifts God gives us?** (To recognize God's constant goodness to His people. To remember the good gifts God gives us every day.)

3. **What are some ways to praise God together?** (Sing praise songs together. Take turns talking to God, thanking Him for His gifts.)

Life Application Games
Prayer

Practice, Practice!

Bible Focus ▸ Daniel 6

Energy Level ▸ LOW MED HIGH

iN ◂ Location

Materials

Bibles, masking tape, materials for one or more of the activities below.

Preparation

Set up one or more of the activities below.

Lead the Game

1. **Daniel prayed to God three times a day. Talking to God is so important that He wants us to pray every day so that praying becomes a habit. The more we pray, the more we get to know God and the ways in which we can love and obey Him. Let's practice doing some thing several times to see if we get better at it.**

2. Explain activities to the students. Students move around to the different activities as time allows. Make sure students try the chosen activity more than once so that they get to practice it.

Beanbag Toss

Set a large plastic bowl or tub about 5 feet (1.5 m) from a masking-tape line. Students stand behind line, face away from tub and toss beanbag over shoulder back toward the tub.

Ball Bounce

Place a trash can about 8 feet (2.4 m) away from a masking-tape line. Students stand behind line and throw the ball to bounce it into the trash can. The ball must bounce at least once before it enters the trash can.

Marshmallow Move

Set an open bag of marshmallows and a pair of chopsticks 4 feet (1.2 m) from a plastic bowl. Students use chopsticks to pick up a marshmallow and carry it to the plastic bowl without touching marshmallow with their hands.

Discussion Questions

1. **Which activity was the hardest? The easiest?**

2. **How did the activities become easier the more you practiced them?**

3. **What would help you remember to pray every day?** (A reminder from your parents. Making a sign to help you remember. An alarm clock ringing at the time you want to pray.)

Prayer Hop

Bible Focus ▸ Matthew 6:9-13

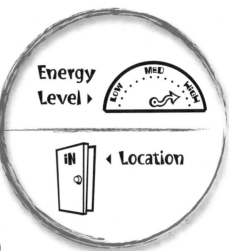

Energy Level ▸

Location ▸ iN

Materials
Bibles, index cards, marker, masking tape, four chairs.

Preparation
Divide the Lord's Prayer (Matthew 6:9-13) into 10 phrases. Print each phrase on a separate index card. Make a duplicate set of cards. Make a masking-tape line on one side of the classroom. Place chairs in two rows of two in center of the playing area, one row for each team. Place five cards on each chair, using one set for each team.

Lead the Game
1. **Jesus taught us how important it is to pray to God. Let's play a game to help us remember what Jesus said in the prayer He prayed as an example for us.**

2. Divide class into two teams of five students each. Teams line up behind masking-tape line. At your signal, first student in each line hops to each chair in his or her line, picking up top card on each stack. Student then returns to tag next student in line. Continue until all cards have been collected.

3. When team has collected all its cards, team members put the cards in order, referring to Matthew 6:9-13 in their Bibles as needed. First team to finish reads prayer aloud. Repeat relay as time permits.

Option
Bring a snack for the class. Before playing the game, draw a small star on one of the cards. Student who collects that card serves a snack to all students at the end of the game.

Discussion Questions
1. **What are some things Jesus prayed about? What did Jesus ask His Father in heaven to do?**

2. **What are some things you can talk to God about?** (Problems at school. Family members I'm thankful for. Things I need help with.)

3. **What are some things you can thank and praise God for? What are some things you need God to help you with?**

Prayer Phrases

Bible Focus ▸ Matthew 6:9-13

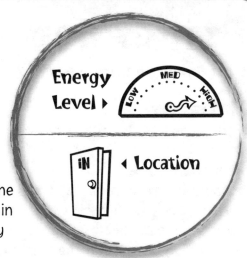

Energy Level ▸ LOW MED HIGH

iN ◂ Location

Materials

Bibles, two chairs, index cards, marker.

Preparation

Write true and false phrases of the Lord's prayer, one phrase per card (Our Father in heaven, Our Father in church, Give us today our daily bread, Give us today our daily pizza, etc.). Mix up the cards.

Lead the Game

1. **Jesus taught us a way to pray that we call the Lord's Prayer. Today we're going to play a game to help us learn this prayer.**

2. Divide the class into two equal teams. Have each team sit in a row on the ground so that the two teams are facing each other with about 4 feet (1.2 meters) between them. Place chairs as shown in sketch. Designate one chair to be the "yes" chair, and the other chair to be the "no" chair.

3. Assign a number to each student, assigning the same series of numbers to both teams so that there is a number one on each team, etc.

4. Explain to students how all of the phrases can be answered "yes" or "no." After reading the first phrase ask, True or false? and call out a number. Students with those numbers get up and try to be the first to sit in the chair that represents the correct answer. The student who sits in the correct chair first scores a point for his or her team.

Option

For mostly younger students, give each student his or her own number. When you ask a question, call out one of the assigned numbers. Student with that number sits in the appropriate chair to answer the question. Also, it may be easier to put the cards in verse order, alternating true and false cards.

Discussion Questions

1. Lead students in reading Matthew 6:9-13 aloud. **How does saying this prayer help you know God's love for you?** (God takes care of my important needs. God fogives us when we sin.)

2. **How does knowing this prayer help you at home? At school? With friends?** (Helps me forgive my sister. Helps me avoid a fight at school.)

Prayer Sentences

Bible Focus ▸ Nehemiah 2:1-5

Energy Level ▸ LOW MED HIGH

IN ◂ Location

Materials
Bibles, sheet of paper, markers, Post-it Notes; optional—masking tape.

Preparation
Print the sentence "God answers my prayer" on the sheet of paper.

Lead the Game
1. **Nehemiah prayed to God, asking Him for help in rebuild the torn-down walls of Jerusalem. When we pray, we can tell God good and bad things that have happened to us. Let's play a game to help us remember to pray and to know that God answers our prayers.**

2. Give each student a Post-it Note. Assign each student a word from the sentence "God answers my prayer," repeating words as needed. Students write assigned words on their Post-it Notes, referring as necessary to paper you prepared. Each student puts his or her Post-it Note on his or her back. (Optional: Use masking tape to attach notes securely.)

3. Students begin moving around the playing area. At your signal, students form groups and line up in order to spell out sentence. Students who form sentence first are the winners.

4. Repeat game as time permits. Vary the game by inviting students to suggest other information they know about prayer with which to play the game ("God wants everyone to pray to Him." "God is pleased when we pray.")

Options
1. Students attach Post-it Notes to legs, arms or feet.
2. If space is limited, students move around playing area by hopping, jumping or tiptoeing.

Discussion Questions
1. **Read Nehemiah 2:1-5. What did Nehemiah pray for?** (That the king would allow him to rebuild the city of Jersualem.)
2. **Why do you think praying helps us grow closer to God?**
3. **When can you pray?**

Watch Your Back!

Bible Focus ▸ Acts 12:1-17; Colossians 4:2

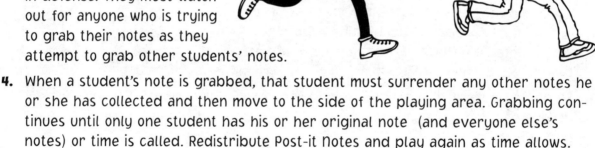

Energy Level ▸ LOW MED HIGH

iN ◂ Location

Materials

Bibles, large Post-it Notes.

Lead the Game

1. God provided an angel to free Peter from prison. God always answers our prayers, though sometimes He does it in ways we don't expect. That's why Colossians 4:2 tells us we need to be watching for the ways He answers. Let's play a game in which we need to be watchful, too!

2. Place a Post-it Note on the back of each student.

3. At your signal, students begin trying to grab Post-it Notes from each other. Students may not hold onto or touch their own Post-it Notes in defense. They must watch out for anyone who is trying to grab their notes as they attempt to grab other students' notes.

4. When a student's note is grabbed, that student must surrender any other notes he or she has collected and then move to the side of the playing area. Grabbing continues until only one student has his or her original note (and everyone else's notes) or time is called. Redistribute Post-it Notes and play again as time allows.

Option

Instead of Post-it Notes, play game with long, narrow fabric strips that students tuck into their clothes.

Discussion Questions

1. **What did you watch for while you played this game? What happened if you didn't watch?**

2. **Because we know God always answers prayer, what should we do after we pray for something?** (Be watching for how God is going to answer our prayer. Not worry about things we have prayed about, but trust God to take care of them.)

3. **What kinds of things should we talk to God about when we pray?** (Things we are thankful for. Reasons we love Him. Problems we or other people are having and need His help with.)

Life Application Games

Serving Others

Amazing Feet

Bible Focus ▸ John 13:1-17

Materials
Bibles, two large sheets of butcher paper, crayons.

Preparation
Place sheets of butcher paper and crayons on the floor in an open area of the room.

Energy Level ▸ LOW MED HIGH

iN ◂ Location

Lead the Game

1. **Jesus showed His love to His disciples and served them by washing their feet during the last meal He ate with them. Let's play a game where we serve each other, too.**

2. All students take off shoes and place them in a large pile on one side of the playing area. Group students into two equal teams. Assign each team a paper on the floor.

3. Students on each team line up in pairs. At your signal, the first pair in each line runs to his or her team's paper. Students trace each others' feet on the paper and return to their team. Continue until all students have had their feet traced.

4. When tracing is completed, pairs take turns running to the shoe pile. Students must find partner's shoes (with help from partner as needed) and put shoes on partner's feet. Game continues until all students have had their feet traced and are wearing their shoes.

Options

1. If you have more than 14 to 16 students, form more than two teams and limit each team to eight students.

2. If a team has an uneven number of students, play the relay with them.

Discussion Questions

1. **What are some ways Jesus loved and served people when He was here on Earth?** (Healed them. Fed them. Taught them the best way to live. Washed the disciples' feet.)

2. **How does Jesus show love for us today?** (Answers our prayers. Promises to always be with us.)

3. **What are some ways we can show Jesus' love to people today?** (Be patient with brothers or sisters. Help others at school. Play games fairly.)

Fishy Service

Bible Focus ▸ John 6:1-15; Romans 12:13

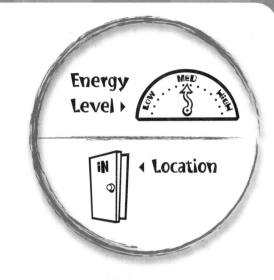

Energy Level ▸ LOW MED HIGH

iN ◂ Location

Materials
Bibles, goldfish crackers, large bowl, small paper cups.

Preparation
Fill bowl with crackers. Place bowl on one side of the playing area.

Lead the Game

1. **A boy shared his lunch with Jesus. Then He took that lunch and multiplied it to feed thousands of hungry people. Sharing what you have can show your love for God and bring kindness to many people. Let's share some fish crackers in our game today!**

2. Group students in teams of six. Each team lines up in a single-file line across the playing area from the cracker bowl. Give the first student in each line a small paper cup.

3. At your signal, the first student in each line walks quickly over to the bowl, scoops out approximately the same number of crackers as there are students on his or her team and returns to team. Student lets each team member take a cracker from the cup. If student did not get a cracker for each team member, student returns to bowl to get more crackers.

4. Next student in line repeats action, collecting crackers and serving one to each team member. Play continues until all students on each team have had a turn and have served each team member a cracker.

5. Ask one of the Discussion Questions below to a volunteer from the first team to be finished. Continue discussion with remaining questions.

Discussion Questions

1. **How do you usually feel when someone shares something with you?** (Thankful. Special. Loved.)

2. **Sharing what you have is one way to show kindness. What are some of the things you can share with others at home? At school?** Volunteers respond. **With whom can you share these things?**

3. **With whom does Romans 12:13 tell us to share?** Have a student read the verse aloud. (God's people who are in need.) Tell students a way your church shares resources with people who are in need.

Helpful Actions

Bible Focus ▸ Acts 11:19-30

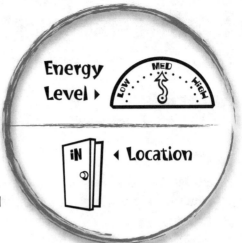

Energy Level ▸ LOW · MED · HIGH

iN ◂ Location

Materials

Bibles, slips of paper, marker, paper bags, paper plates.

Preparation

Print the following words on slips of paper, one word on each paper: "head," "shoulder," "hand," "elbow," "knees". Prepare two sets of papers and put each set in a separate paper bag.

Lead the Game

1. **The people of the early church were persecuted for believing in Jesus. But they did what they could to help one another. We can also show faithfulness by using what God gives us to help others. Let's help each other play a game using the bodies God has given us!**

2. Group students into teams of no more than eight. Students within teams form pairs. (If there is not an even number of students on each team, students repeat relay as necessary.) Teams line up in pairs on one side of the room.

3. Give one bag of papers and one paper plate to each team. Volunteer on each team chooses two slips of paper from his or her team's bag. Students read papers aloud. The first pair of students on each team places the paper plate between the two body parts listed on the chosen slips of paper (see sketch).

4. At your signal, the first pair of students on each team walks to the other side of the room and back, keeping the paper plate in position. As pairs return to teams, the next pairs position the plates in the same way and walk across the room. Relay continues until all pairs have had a turn with the plates in that position. Ask a volunteer from the team that finished first to answer one of the Discussion Questions below.

5. Begin a new round of the game with new pairs choosing slips of paper for their teams.

Discussion Questions

1. **What parts of your body can you use to help other people?** (Arms. Legs. Mouth. Mind.) What skills? (Skill at drawing. Skill at taking care of other kids.)

2. **What are some ways to help other people using (your arms)?** (Carry groceries into the house. Fold laundry. Hold a crying baby.) Repeat question with other gifts.

3. **What are some ways you can use the money or possessions God has given you and your family to help other people?** (Give money to organizations that help others.)

Secret Pass-Off

Bible Focus ▸ Acts 3:1-16

Energy Level ▸ LOW MED HIGH

iN ◂ Location

Materials

Bibles, marbles, paper clips or other small objects.

Lead the Game

1. **In the name of Jesus, Peter healed a man who couldn't walk since his birth. Jesus helps us share what we have to help other people. Let's play a game in which we are secretly trying to give something away.**

2. Choose at least one volunteer to become a "watcher." One watcher for every six or seven students will be needed. Watchers close eyes while you quietly give marbles or other small objects to no more than half of remaining students.

3. All students put hands behind backs and begin walking around the room, passing objects to each other while keeping hands behind backs. Watchers open eyes and try to detect who are holding the objects. To increase challenge, all students should pretend to pass objects.

4. Call time after a minute or so. Watchers name students they think are holding objects. If their guesses are correct, students holding objects give them to the Watchers. If their guesses are incorrect, begin a new round of play. After the second round, choose new Watchers whether or not all objects have been collected. Play as many rounds as time allows.

Discussion Questions

1. **Was it easier to be a watcher or a secret giver in this game?**

2. **Why does Jesus tell us it is important to give to each other?** (Giving or helping others show how we love them. We show our love for God by helping others.)

3. **Besides money, what else does Jesus help us give to others?** (Being a friend to someone who is lonely. Helping someone who can't do something on their own.)

Serving Charades

Bible Focus ▸ Matthew 25:14-30; Luke 19:12-27

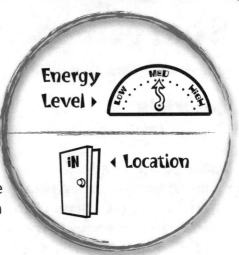

Energy Level ▸

Location ▸ iN

Materials
Bibles, large sheet of paper, marker.

Preparation
Write true and false phrases of the Lord's prayer, one phrase per card (Our Father in heaven, Our Father in church, Give us today our daily bread, Give us today our daily pizza, etc.). Mix the cards.

Lead the Game

1. Jesus told a story about people who did or did not use some gifts given to them. The skills you have, or the things you are good at doing, are sometimes called talents. **What are some of the talents you and other kids your age have?** (Playing the piano. Spelling words correctly. Reading books. Kicking a soccer ball.) List students' ideas on large sheet of paper.

2. When you have listed eight to 10 talents, play a game like Charades. **We can use the talents God gave us to serve others. Let's play a game to act out some of those talents God gave us.** Ask a volunteer to stand in front of group. Whisper to the volunteer one of the talents from the list. Volunteer pantomimes talent.

3. Students guess the talent the volunteer is pantomiming. When students guess correctly, ask **How can you serve others using this talent?** Extend discussion using questions below. Repeat with the other talents on the list as time allows or until all students have had a turn to pantomime a talent.

Option
Play team charades. Form two teams. Tell a volunteer from each team a talent. At your signal, volunteers pantomime talent. First team to correctly guess the talent wins. Repeat with different volunteers and talents.

Discussion Questions

1. **Why is it true that we can use any talent to serve others?** (Anything we do can be done in a way that shows care for others and love for God.)

2. **Why is it important to use the talents God has given you?** (God wants us to show His love to others. If we don't practice the skills and talents we have, we may lose them.)

3. **What are some ways to use your talents to serve others at church? At school?**

Snack Service

Bible Focus ▸ John 13:1-17; Galatians 5:13

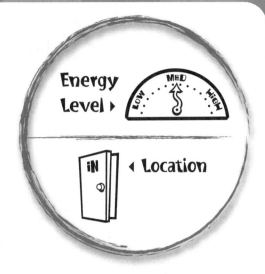

Energy Level ▸ LOW MED HIGH

iN ◂ Location

Materials

Bibles, individually wrapped snacks (at least one per student), paper plates.

Preparation

For each group of five to seven students, place five to seven snacks on a paper plate.

Lead the Game

1. **Jesus showed His love to His disciples by washing their feet, as a house servant would do. Because we love God, it's important to be ready to serve others with a gentle attitude. Let's play a game to practice serving others.**

2. Group students into teams of five to seven students each. Teams line up on one side of the classroom. Set an empty paper plate next to the first student on each team. Place a plate of snacks across the playing area from each team.

3. At your signal, the first student on each team walks quickly to the other side of the room, retrieves a snack from the team's plate and brings it back, placing it on the team's empty plate. The next student in line repeats the action, leaving as the first student places the snack on the plate. Play continues until all members of the team have collected a snack.

4. Each student takes a snack from the team's plate and gives it to someone else on the team. Students chew and swallow the snacks, and then begin to whistle. First team to have all its students whistle wins.

Discussion Questions

1. **How did we serve one another in this game?** (Gave each other snacks.)

2. **How can we serve others at school? At home? On the playground?**

3. **Read Galatians 5:13 aloud. What do you think it means to serve someone with love?** (Be kind and gentle when we help. Don't have a bossy or proud attitude. Pay attention to the needs of others.)

Toe Service

Bible Focus ▸ John 15:13

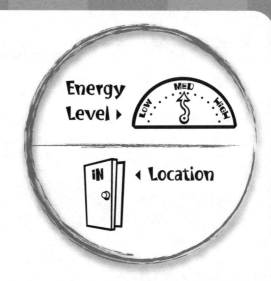

Energy Level ▸ LOW MED HIGH

iN ◂ Location

Materials

Bibles, index cards, marker.

Preparation

Print the words of John 15:13 on index cards, one word per card. Make one set of verse cards for every eight to 10 students.

Lead the Game

1. **One of the ways Jesus showed His love just before He suffered and died to take the punishment for our sins was to wash His disciples' feet. Washing feet was something a servant would usually do. Let's play a game that uses our feet!**

2. Group students in teams of eight to 10. Each team lines up single-file on one side of playing area. Students remove shoes and socks. Place a mixed-up set of verse cards across the playing area from each team.

3. At your signal, the first student from each team skips across playing area to cards, picks up one card and places it in between his or her first two toes. Student walks back to team with card held between toes. If card falls before he or she returns to the team, student must stop to replace card. Next student in line repeat action until all cards have been collected. Students on each team work together to order verse cards. First team finished reads verse aloud. Students check verse in Bible.

Option

If your class has fewer than 16 students, all students act as one team and race against the clock.

Discussion Questions

1. **Jesus showed us His love and laid down His life for us by dying on the cross. How might we do what John 15:13 says and show love to our friends?** (Help them even when we don't feel like it. Be friendly even if they aren't being very friendly to us. Think of a caring thing you can do and do it.)

2. **What can we do to thank Jesus for laying down His life for us?** (Accept His offer to take the punishment for our sins and believe in His death and forgiveness.)

Life Application Games

Showing Love to God

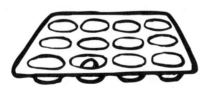

Ability Blast

Bible Focus ▸ Matthew 25:14-30

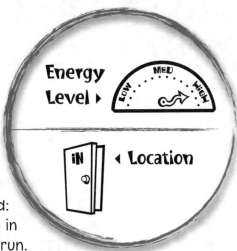

Energy Level ▸ LOW MED HIGH

iN ◂ Location

Materials
Bibles, index cards, marker, children's music CD and player, tape.

Preparation
Print one of the following abilities on each index card: play baseball, play piano, math skills, spell, compete in gymnastics, write, read, play soccer, draw, sing, act, run.

Lead the Game

1. **Jesus told a story about some people who used their abilties, and a person who didn't. We can show our love to God by using the abilities He has given us. Let's play a game to think of some of those abilities and how we can be faithful to use them!**

2. Play a music CD as students walk around the room. When you stop music, each student quickly moves to a corner of the room, making sure there is approximately the same number of students in each corner.

3. Tape an index card in each corner. Students in each corner read card and plan a way to pantomime the ability. Groups take turns pantomiming abilities for the other groups to guess. Ask a Discussion Question from below after abilities have been guessed.

4. At the end of each round of play, collect cards and repeat entire game as time allows, distributing a new set of ability cards each round.

Discussion Questions

1. **What does it mean to be faithful?** (To keep doing something you said you would do. To keep your promises.)

2. **How does Colossians 3:23 describe being faithful?** Ask an older student to read the verse aloud. (Doing something with your whole heart. Doing something to please God, not just to please the people around you.)

3. **What are some ways to be faithful to using the abilities God has given you?** (Practice using the abilities. Keep using them to help others. Have a good attitude while using your abilities. Use your abilities to please God, doing the best you can do.)

Add-a-Fruit Relay

Bible Focus ▸ Galatians 5:22-23

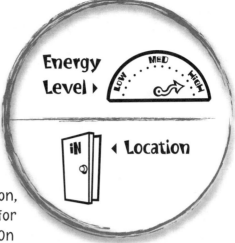

Energy Level ▸ LOW MED HIGH

iN ◂ Location

Materials
Bibles, white paper, marker, colored paper, butcher paper, masking tape, scissors, pencils.

Preparation
Draw a fruit shape (apple, banana, orange, pear, lemon, etc.) on white paper. Shape should be large enough for students to write on. Photocopy onto colored paper. On a sheet of butcher paper, draw the outline of a large leafy tree. Attach the paper to the wall or place it on the floor on one side of the playing area.

Lead the Game

1. **Growing the fruit of the Spirit in our lives begins with love for God. Let's play a game to learn more about the fruit of the Spirit!**

2. Divide group into equal teams. Each student cuts out a fruit shape. Read Galatians 5:22-23 aloud. Assign each student the name of one of the fruit of the Spirit to write on his or her shape, referring to verses in Bibles. Students then attach masking-tape loops to the backs of their shapes.

3. Teams line up in single-file lines across the room from the tree. At your signal, students on each team take turns running to the tree, attaching shape to it, returning to team and tagging the next student in line. Play continues until each student has attached a fruit shape. Have teams sit down as they finish.

4. Ask a volunteer from the first team that finished to answer one of the Discussion Questions below or to recite Galatians 5:22-23. Repeat relay and continue discussion as time allows.

Option
To simplify preparation, each student draws a fruit on a Post-it Note and writes name of a fruit of the Spirit on the note. Students use Post-it Notes instead of fruit shapes in relay.

Discussion Questions
1. **Which of the fruit of the Spirit in Galatians 5:22-23 are most needed by kids your age?**

2. **How has someone you know shown a fruit of the Spirit?**

3. **When might a kid your age show love? Patience? Joy?** Repeat with other fruit of the Spirit as time allows.

Balloon Trolley

Bible Focus ▸ Genesis 4:1-4; 1 Chronicles 16:29

Energy Level ▸

Location ▸ iN

Materials
Bibles, balloons, garbage bag, chairs.

Preparation
Inflate one balloon for every pair of students, plus several extras. Transport inflated balloons to class in garbage bag. Place several chairs about 3 feet (.9 m) from the edge of one side of the playing area, making sure chairs are at least 4 feet (1.2 m) from each other and that there are approximately two chairs for every eight students.

Lead the Game

1. **Abel offered a gift to God that was the best he could give. We can show thankfulness to God by offering Him our love, time, abilities and money. Let's play a game to think of ways to offer God those things!**

2. Students form pairs. Give each pair a balloon. Students in pairs decide the best way to hold balloon between themselves without touching it with their hands (between hips, between upper arms, between back and stomach). Pairs practice moving around room in manner chosen.

3. Invite pairs to stand opposite chairs. Pairs position balloon in manner chosen. At your signal, all pairs move toward chairs, walk around one chair and return to starting position without dropping balloons. First pair back to the starting side names one way to show thankfulness to God. Repeat play as time allows, with first pair finished telling a way to give God their time, a way to give God their money or answering one of the questions below.

Discussion Questions

1. **How can kids your age give their time as an offering to God?** (Play fairly with a brother or sister. Help clean up trash in their neighborhood.)

2. **When have you or your family given money or other things you own to show thankfulness to God?** (Given books to a missionary family. Given money to church to help other people learn about God.)

3. **Why is it important to give offerings to God?** (Helps us remember God's gifts to us.)

Bread, Basket, Fish

Bible Focus ▸ Mark 6:30-44; John 6:1-15

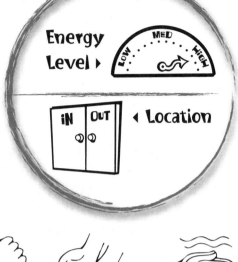

Energy Level ▸

Location

Materials

Bibles, large sheet of paper, marker.

Lead the Game

1. **When we give to God, He can do great things with our gifts to Him. A boy once gave his lunch to Jesus. Jesus used this small lunch to feed a huge crowd. Let's play a game to remind us of the gifts given by this boy.**

2. Students form two teams and stand in the center of a large playing area. Designate a safe zone (wall, door, etc.) for each team, one on each end of the playing area.

bread

basket

fish

3. Play a large-group version of Rock, Paper, Scissors using the words "bread," "basket" and "fish" and these signs: bread—fist, basket—two hands cupped together, fish—two palms pressed together swimming like a fish. Basket defeats bread because bread is put into the basket. Bread defeats fish because bread is wrapped around fish for eating. Fish defeats basket because live fish can flop out of the basket. Write signs and scoring system on large sheet of paper to which students can refer.

4. Each team huddles near its safe zone and chooses one sign. Then, after moving to the center of the playing area, all members of each team say "bread, basket, fish" aloud in unison and show their team's chosen sign. Winning team chases the losing team back toward the losing team's safe zone. Any student who is tagged joins the winning team. If both teams show the same sign, teams rehuddle and play again. Repeat game as time permits, with team members taking turns choosing their team's sign.

Option

Play game in pairs. After the first round, each winner plays another winner and each loser plays another loser. Game is over when one student has won five rounds. Play as many games as time and interest allow.

Discussion Questions

1. **What did Jesus do with the boy's bread and fish?**

2. **What can we give to God to show love for Him?** (Actions that show obedience to God. Time when we pray to Him or read His Word. Money to help others.)

3. **How might God use gifts like these?** (Kind action might help someone who is sad and remind the person of God's love.)

Faithfulness Toss

Bible Focus ▸ Daniel 3

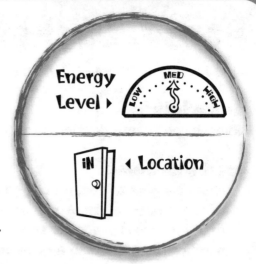

Energy Level ▸ LOW MED HIGH

iN ◂ Location

Materials

Bibles, two muffin tins, paper, pencil, coins.

Lead the Game

1. Daniel showed his love for God by refusing to pray to anyone other than God. Acting in ways that show belief in God demonstrates our faithfulness and love for God. Let's play a game to name some ways to show belief in God.

2. Have group line up in two equal teams. Place a muffin tin about 4 feet (1.2 m) from each team. Give one volunteer on each team a sheet of paper and a pencil to record points.

3. Give two coins to the first student in each team's line. Student tosses coins, one at a time, at his or her team's muffin tin. If coin goes into a cup, the team scorekeeper records one point. Continue until each student has had a turn, totaling points after each student's turn.

4. One or two times during the game call "Stop." A volunteer from the team with the most points tells one way to show belief in and faithfulness to God. (Pray to God. Read your Bible. Tell the truth. Tell others about God. Obey God by being kind to others, even when it is hard.) Repeat game as time allows.

Options

1. Instead of using muffin tins, use clean yogurt cups or draw circles on a large sheet of paper.

2. Label small, circular stickers from one to five. Attach a sticker to bottom of each muffin tin cup. Students earn the number of points on sticker.

3. Instead of tossing coins, students place marshmallows or gummy fruits onto plastic spoons and fling them at muffin tins. Score game as above.

Discussion Questions

1. **How does (praying) show you believe in God?** (You are trusting God to hear you and answer your prayers.) Repeat question with different actions that show belief in God.

2. **When are some times you have seen other people show their belief in God?** Briefly share your own answer before you ask for responses from students.

3. **How can you show faithfulness to God when you are with your friends? When you are with your family?**

Paper-Chain Relay

Bible Focus ▸ Hebrews 11—12:2

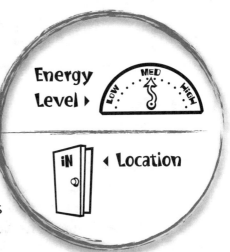

Energy Level ▸ LOW MED HIGH

iN ◂ Location

Materials

Bibles, paper, scissors, ruler, tape or staplers, markers.

Preparation

Cut paper into 1 1/2- to 2-inch-wide (3.75- to 5-cm wide) strips, making at least two for each student. Make piles of 12 to 16 strips each on one side of the playing area. Next to each pile, place roll of tape or a stapler.

Lead the Game

1. **When we remember the actions of the people in God's family, we are encouraged to show faith in God. Let's play a game to remember that we can all be part of that family and to help us think about ways others help us love and obey God.**

2. Group students in teams of no more than six to eight. Teams line up in single-file lines across the playing area from the piles of paper strips.

3. Give the first student in each line a marker. At your signal, the first student from each team runs to his or her team's pile and writes his or her name on a paper strip. Student bends strip and tapes or staples it into a loop. Student leaves loop and returns to his or her team and gives the marker to next student in line who repeats action, looping his or her strip through the first student's loop to create a paper chain. Teams continue until all students have had a turn.

4. Play another round of the relay, this time asking each student to write the name of a person who taught him or her about God.

5. Connect all paper chains and display in classroom as a visual reminder of people in God's family. Ask an older student to read Hebrews 12:1-2 aloud.

Discussion Questions

1. **What stories about Bible people help you want to love and obey God?**

2. **How can kids your age show faith in God?** (Do what God says in the Bible. Pray to God and ask His help in loving Him and others.)

3. **Who is someone you know who loves and obeys God? What can you learn about how to obey God from that person's example?** (Learn to tell the truth. Learn to thank God for forgiveness.)

Perpetual Motion

Bible Focus ▸ Daniel 1; 6; Mark 12:30

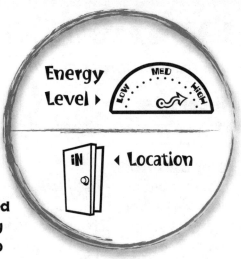

Energy Level ▸ LOW MED HIGH

iN ◀ Location

Materials

Bibles, two Frisbees.

Lead the Game

1. Loving and obeying God your whole life are the wisest things to do! Daniel always loved and obeyed God, even when it meant he would have to disobey the king. Let's play a game in which we try to keep something going on for a long time.

2. Divide group into two equal teams. Teams line up at one end of room. Place Frisbees at opposite end of the room in a direct line with each team.

3. At your signal, the first player in line high-fives the next player in line, who high-fives the next player and so on down the line. After receiving a high-five, the last player in line runs to his or her team's Frisbee and spins it on its edge. Player then runs to the front of the line and keeps the motion going by high-fiving the next player in line and so on. Players shift down one position in line as each runner returns. The first team to get its players back in their original position wins.

4. Volunteer from winning team answers this question: What is one way a kid your age can love and obey God? Repeat game as time permits, varying the ages used.

Options

1. Instead of Frisbees, students may spin two sturdy paper plates stapled face-to-face or empty soda cans.

2. Limit the number of students on each team to six or seven. Provide additional Frisbees if more teams are needed.

Discussion Questions

1. **Why are loving and obeying God our whole lives the wisest things we can do?** (God tells us the best ways to live. Loving and obeying God is what we were created to do.)

2. **How did Daniel show that he loved and obeyed God?** (Had the courage to ask for and eat vegetables rather than what the king commanded. Prayed to God even when another king outlawed it.)

3. **Read Mark 12:30 aloud. What can you do to show that you love and obey God?** (Praise Him with songs. Pray to God, telling God why you love Him. Obey God's commands in the Bible. Tell the truth. Care for others.)

Sharing Love

Bible Focus ▸ Mark 12:41-44; Luke 20:45-47; 21:1-4

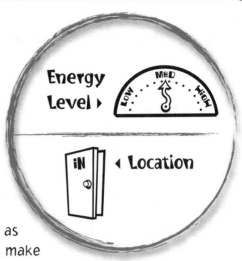

Energy Level ▸ LOW MED HIGH

iN ◂ **Location**

Materials

Bibles, two coins for each student, one or more of each of the following containers: paper plates, paper cups, coffee cans, plastic bowls.

Preparation

Set out containers and make a masking-tape square as shown in sketch. (If you have more than 16 students, make additional squares with additional containers in them.)

Lead the Game

1. **In the Bible we read a story about a poor woman who showed she loved God by generously giving her last two coins. We are going to play a game with coins and think about how we can give generously to God as a way of thanking Him for His love.**

2. Give each student two coins. Students stand around the square. Students take turns tossing coins, trying to get coins into containers. When a student's coin lands in a container, he or she tells a way to give to God or to others (donate food to needy people, treat others kindly, pray for others, etc.). After each student has had a turn, collect coins and redistribute. Students trade places around the square and play again. Repeat game as time permits.

Options

1. Set up the containers on one end of a table. Students line up and toss coins from the opposite end of the table.

2. Place candy or stickers on some of the plates and in the bottom of some of the cans, bowls and cups. When a student's coin lands in one of these containers, student gets candy or stickers.

Discussion Questions

1. **What does it mean to give generously?** (Give more than what is required or expected.)

2. **What are some ways you can give generously at school?** (Share your lunch. Help others with what you are learning if they don't understand. Help your teachers.) **At home?** (Offer to do chores that you don't usually do. Share toys with your brothers and sisters. Share a computer game.)

3. **How can you give generously to God to show your thankfulness for His love?** (Give my time by reading the Bible and praying. Care for others to show God's love.)

Tunnel Ball

Bible Focus ▸ Genesis 12:1-9; 15:1-6; 18:1-15; 21:1-7

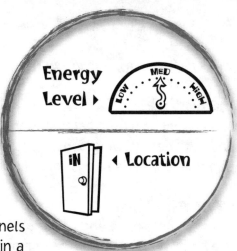

Energy Level ▸

iN ◂ Location

Materials
Bibles, at least three shoe boxes or other cardboard boxes, scissors, measuring stick, marker, masking tape, foam balls or tennis balls.

Preparation
Cut both ends out of boxes to form tunnels. Set up tunnels at least 7 feet (2.1 m) from each other, arranging them in a circular course (see sketch). Number each tunnel. Use masking tape to make a start/finish line.

Lead the Game
1. **In the Bible Abraham had to wait a long time for God to keep His promise to send Abraham a son. We can wait patiently and depend on God to keep His promises. Let's play a game that might take some patience.**

2. Group students into two teams. Give each team a ball.

3. Students on each team take turns rolling the ball cooperatively around the course from start to finish, with each student allowed one roll at a time. Each student begins his or her turn from where the ball stopped rolling. The ball must pass through each tunnel in order. Volunteer from team that finishes first answers one of the Discussion Questions below.

Options
1. Print each of the following verse references on three index cards, one reference per card: Joshua 1:9; Psalm 29:11; 136:26. Tape one index card on each tunnel. As students roll the balls through the tunnels, a team member finds the verse and reads God's promise aloud.

2. Instead of rolling the balls, each student taps the balls with a toy plastic golf club or a mallet made by taping a dry kitchen sponge to one end of a yardstick.

Discussion Questions
1. **What are some of the promises God has given us in the Bible?** (He will always love us. He will always be with us. He will answer our prayers.)

2. **When might you need to wait patiently for God to keep a promise?** (When praying about a problem. When you need God's help to know what to do.)

3. **What might help us wait patiently for God to keep His promises?** (Remember the times He has helped us in the past. Thank Him for His love for us. Pray and ask Him for patience.)

Life Application Games

Showing Love to Others

"After You"

Bible Focus ▸ Luke 18:9-14; Philippians 2:3

Materials

Bibles, one tube sock for each pair of students.

Energy Level ▸ LOW · MED · HIGH

◂ Location — iN OUT

Lead the Game

1. Jesus told a story about a person who humbly asked God for mercy. When we care about others, we remember God's love for them, and our humble and gentle attitudes help us not look down on them. Let's each practice a humble attitude by putting others first in our game today.

2. Students form pairs. Pairs stand on one side of the playing area.

3. Give each pair a tube sock. Partners hold sock between them, each with one hand on the sock. Pairs practice stepping over the sock, one foot at a time, without letting go of the sock.

4. To begin game, students stand at one side of the playing area. At your signal, one student in the pair says "After you," and his or her partner takes a step, putting one foot and then the other over the sock. Then the partner who stepped says "After you," and the other partner takes a turn. Students continue in this manner, moving across the playing area and back.

5. After all pairs have returned to the starting area, ask the pair who finished first to answer one of the Discussion Questions below, or play several more rounds and then lead the discussion.

Discussion Questions

1. **What are some examples of a humble and gentle attitude?** (Letting others go first. Not thinking you are better than anyone else. Listening carefully when others speak.)

2. Ask an older student to read Philippians 2:3 aloud. **What does this verse say about having a humble attitude?** (Don't do things because you are trying to get something for yourself or because you think you are better than other people. Don't spend too much time thinking about yourself.)

3. **When we have humble attitudes, we don't spend our time comparing ourselves to others. What should we think about instead?** (Ways to love God and others. How we can help others.)

All Strung Up

Bible Focus ▸ Acts 10

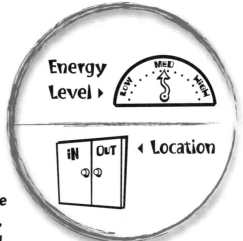

Energy Level ▸

Location ▸

Materials

Bibles, ball of yarn of the same size for every 4 to 6 students.

Lead the Game

1. **God showed Peter how His love was for everyone in the world. Because God's love is for everyone, not just for people like us, we need to accept all kinds of people. Let's play a game in which we work together with people who might be different from us in some ways.**

2. Students number off to form teams of four to six players. Teams form single-file lines in center of the playing area, leaving plenty of space between teams.

3. Give the first student in each line a ball of yarn. The first student holds the end of the yarn to his or her stomach with one hand and then passes the rest to the next student in line. Students continue passing yarn to student at end of line who wraps it around his or her back and passes it back to the front of the line. Passing continues until students have wrapped themselves (from the waist down) with the entire ball of yarn. (Note: Students should stand as close together as possible to speed up the wrapping process.) The first team to finish names a way to accept other people who are different from them or a way to share God's love with people who are different.

Discussion Questions

1. **What are some ways the people on your team are different from each other?** (Hair color. Places we live in. Names. Interests. Ages.)

2. **What kinds of things do all people have in common?** (Need air, water, food and shelter. Loved by God. Jesus died for our sins.)

3. **How are we to treat all people, even if they seem different from us?** (Love them in the same way we want to be loved.)

4. **What can we do to help all people learn about God's love?** (Pray for them. Tell them about God's love. Invite them to church.)

Call the Ball

Bible Focus ▸ Acts 4:32—5:11

Energy Level ▸ LOW MED HIGH

Location ▸ iN OuT

Materials

Bibles, bounceable ball best suited for your playing area (playground ball, tennis ball, Ping-Pong ball or small rubber ball).

Preparation

Depending on the type of ball with which you are playing and the ability of your students, choose three actions from the Action List below.

Lead the Game

1. **A couple in the Early Church chose to lie about a gift they were giving to God. They said one thing but did another. One way to show our love for God is by making sure our words and actions match. Let's practice matching our words and actions.**

2. Group students into two even teams. (Join one team yourself if needed to even up teams.) Teams line up in single-file lines across the playing area from each other, leaving a wide space between the first player of each team (see sketch).

3. Demonstrate the three actions you chose, identifying each action by name. Give the ball to the first student in one line. Student with ball calls out one of the actions listed below and bounces the ball in that manner to the first student on the other team. First student on the other team catches ball and calls out another action, moving the ball in that manner back to the other team. If the ball does not move in the manner called, student tries again. Game continues until all students have had at least one turn to call out an action and move the ball.

Action List

Single bounce, double bounce or triple bounce: bounce ball the appropriate number of times; **dribble and toss:** dribble ball halfway across playing area and then toss ball; **left-hand bounce or right-hand bounce:** bounce ball with left or right hand; **no bounce:** toss ball with no bounce; **grand slam:** bounce ball very high and hard; **baby bounce:** bounce ball low to the ground.

Discussion Questions

1. **What does it mean to make your words and your actions match?** (Do what you say you are going to do. If you tell someone a good way to act, act that way yourself.)

2. **What are some ways your words and action can match at home? At school?**

3. **Making our words match our actions is one way to show goodness. How does God help us have the fruit of goodness?** (Gives the Bible to help us understand right ways to act. Reminds us of ways to speak and act to show goodness.)

Compassion Check!

Bible Focus ▸ Luke 7:11-17; 1 Peter 3:8

Energy Level ▸ LOW MED HIGH

iN ◂ Location

Materials
Bibles, soft object (a beanbag, rolled-up socks, crumpled-newspaper ball, foam ball, etc.), large sheet of paper, marker.

Lead the Game

1. **Who are some people who might feel sad or lonely?** (Single parent, new kid at school, friend whose parents just got a divorce, younger kid who is lost, kid whose best friend moved away, older neighbor who lives alone, person in the hospital, older person in a nursing home, someone whose husband or wife died, etc.) Invite volunteers to name additional people who might feel sad or lonely. List ideas on a large sheet of paper. **How does 1 Peter 3:8 tell us to act toward others?** Students read verse in their Bibles and respond. **Jesus showed compassion to a widow by raising her dead son to life. What are some ways a kid your age can show compassion to someone who is sad or lonely?** (Give flowers, send a card, invite the person to have lunch with you, spend time talking with the person, pray for the person, etc.) List these ideas on large sheet of paper, too.

2. Give a volunteer the soft object. Other students stand scattered around the area behind the volunteer. Without looking at other students, volunteer describes a person who might be sad or lonely, referring to large sheet of paper, and then throws soft object up over his head toward the other students. Student who catches object hides it behind his or her back or passes it off to another student who passes or hides it behind his or her back (object may be passed as many as three times). Then all students hide hands behind their backs and shout together, "Compassion Check!"

3. Volunteer who threw the object turns around and has two guesses to name the player holding the object. If volunteer is correct, the person with the object tells a way to show compassion to the person named, using ideas listed. If volunteer is not correct in guessing player with object, volunteer tells a way to show compassion. Repeat activity as time permits, choosing a new volunteer to throw the object each round.

Discussion Questions

1. **Which of the commands in 1 Peter 3:8 is hardest for kids your age to obey? Why?**

2. **To whom can kids your age show compassion?**

3. **What are some ways to show compassion?**

Compassion Corners

Bible Focus ▸ Luke 10:25-37

Energy Level ▸ (LOW MED HIGH)

Location ▸ iN

Materials

Bibles, four sheets of paper, index cards, marker, masking tape, small paper bag.

Preparation

Print the words "heart," "soul," "mind" and "strength" on four sheets of paper and four index cards, one word per paper and card. Post each paper in a separate corner of the room. Place index cards in bag.

Lead the Game

1. **Because we have experienced God's great love for us, we can show His love and compassion to others. In our game today, we'll describe ways to show love and compassion every day.**

2. Volunteer reads Luke 10:27 aloud. **What does this verse describe?** (How we are to love God.) Volunteers read aloud the words on the papers in the corners of the room.

3. Students stand in a circle. Ask a volunteer to be "It." "It" stands in the middle of the circle. Students walk around the circle. After a few moments, "It" calls "Stop." Students move quickly to the nearest corners. "It" picks an index card from bag and reads card aloud before returning card to bag. Volunteer from the corner named on the index card tells one way to show love for God or compassion to others (obey God's Word, be kind to others, pray to God, be friends with people who speak a different language, etc.), recites Luke 10:27 or answers a Discussion Question below. Student who answered becomes the new "It" and game continues as time allows.

Discussion Questions

1. **How has God shown His love and compassion for you?** (He sent His Son, Jesus, to die on the cross to forgive my sins. He answers my prayers. He helps me do right.) **How can you show your love for God?** (Tell Him. Follow His commands. Pray to Him. Read the Bible. Tell others about Him.)

2. **What are some other words or phrases that describe ways of showing love?** (Help. Care. Encourage. Pray for. Share with.)

3. **What are some things you could do to show your love for others at home? At a park? At school?**

Courage Collection

Bible Focus ▸ 1 Samuel 24; Luke 6:27

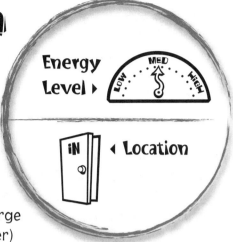

Energy Level ▸

iN ◂ Location

Materials

Bibles, large sheet of colored butcher paper, marker, newspaper, masking tape, two bowls, flour, marshmallows, pencils, paper.

Preparation

Draw lines to divide butcher paper into at least 12 large sections. In each section print a number (five or lower) and a word from Luke 6:27, including the reference. Tape paper to wall. Spread newspaper on the floor under the paper and out about 4 feet (1.2 m) from wall. Fill bowls ⅓ full with flour and place at edge of newspaper.

Lead the Game

1. **In the Old Testament David demonstrates love for an enemy who was trying to kill him. We think of our enemies as people we don't like, but God can give us the courage to love our enemies! Let's play a game to find out what Jesus said about loving enemies.**

2. Divide group into two teams. Teams line up single file at edge of newspaper.

3. Each student takes a turn to dip a marshmallow into the flour, and then toss it at the paper. Teams attempt to hit all sections to collect each word of the verse and earn as many points as possible. Have an older student on each team write on a sheet of paper which words of the verse have been collected and the number of points earned. Student refers to Bible for verse order. Students take turns tossing marshmallows until both teams have collected all the words of the verse. A volunteer from the first team to finish reads Luke 6:27 aloud or answers one of the Discussion Questions below.

Discussion Questions

1. **What are some ways to show love and do good things for people you might think of as enemies?** (Don't be mean back to them. Don't say mean things about them to others. Smile and be friendly to them.)

2. **What can you do when it seems too hard to show God's love to an enemy?** (Ask God for courage to do what's right. Ask a parent or teacher for advice on how to show love.)

Crazy Fruit

Bible Focus ▸ Galatians 5:22-23

Materials

Bibles.

Energy Level ▸ LOW MED HIGH

iN ◂ Location

Lead the Game

1. **The fruit of the Spirit is shown through love for God and others. Let's play a game to think about ways to show God's love.**

2. Students sit in a circle. One volunteer is selected to be the Farmer and stands in the middle of the circle. Assign each student a fruit (banana, strawberry, peach, grape, pineapple, orange, etc.), making sure to assign each fruit to more than one student.

3. The Farmer calls out the name of a fruit. Students with that fruit jump up to trade places in the circle before the Farmer can take one of the places. If the Farmer calls out "Crazy Fruit!" all students must change places.

4. The student left without a place becomes the new Farmer. Before calling out a fruit name, the Farmer tells one way to show love for God or others. Ask Discussion Questions below to guide student as needed. Repeat play as above. Game continues as time allows or until all students have had a chance to be the Farmer.

Blueberries

Options

Play another round of the game using the names of the fruit of the Spirit from Galatians 5:22-23 instead of using the names of actual fruits. Ask students to name the fruit of the Spirit as a review before assigning them to each student. You may want to list the fruit of the Spirit on a large sheet of paper for students to refer to during the game and discussion.

Discussion Questions

1. **What can you do to show (patience) to someone you know?** Repeat question with other fruit of the Spirit. **Practicing the fruit of the Spirit is a way to show love for others.**

2. **What are some ways to show love for God?** (Obey Him. Sing songs of praise to Him. Thank Him in your prayers. Tell others about Him.) **How can you show your (faithfulness) to God? How does showing (self-control) demonstrate love for God?**

3. **Who is someone you know who shows love for God and others? How does he or she show that love? What can you do to show love for God or others in that way?**

Encourage Cards

Bible Focus ▸ Hebrews 10:24

Materials

Bibles, masking tape, measuring tape, index cards in at least two colors, marker.

Energy Level ▸ LOW · MED · HIGH

iN ◂ Location

Preparation

On the floor, use masking tape to mark off a 3-foot (.9-m) square for each team (see sketch). On one color of index cards, print Hebrews 10:24, one word or the reference on each card. Use a different color of cards to make an identical set for each team.

Lead the Game

1. **When you've been away from home, what did you miss the most?** Volunteers respond. **At the Olympics, each team has a house that is named for the country they came from, such as U.S.A. House or Canada House. If athletes or other visitors feel homesick, they can gather at their country's house with people from their own country.** Indicate masking-tape squares on the floor. **These squares are your Houses. To play this game, your team needs to collect all its cards and put the verse in order. You can leave your House, but only if you stay connected to someone! Everyone outside of the box has to be connected to someone who is inside the box.**

2. Divide class into teams. Each team stands inside a House. Assign each team one color of index cards. Scatter index cards on the floor at varying distances from the boxes. At your signal, teams collect their index cards by forming an unbroken chain with at least one team member remaining in the House (see sketch). Students may sit or lie on the floor if necessary to stretch farther, as long as they are connected at all times by hand or foot. As cards are gathered, they are passed back to the House with team members remaining connected. When all cards have been gathered, the team places the cards on the floor of the House in correct verse order.

Discussion Questions

1. **This verse is talking about encouraging others to do good things. Sometimes it's hard to do what you know is right. When are times when you know a good thing you can do, but it's hard to really do it?** Volunteers respond.

2. **God gives us other people on His team to encourage us to do good things. What are some things you can do to encourage your friends?** (Pray for them. Offer to help. Help them learn what the Bible says to do.)

Frisbee Frenzy

Bible Focus ▶ 2 Kings 4:8-37; 1 John 3:18

Energy Level ▶ LOW MED HIGH

iN ◀ Location

Materials

Bibles, paper plates, markers.

Preparation

Divide the playing area in half with a masking-tape line.

Lead the Game

1. **God sent the prophet Elisha to help a poor widow who had a very sick son.**

2. Give each student a paper plate and a marker. **What are things that some people need?** (Food, water, friends, family, help with homework, help with a job or chore, etc.) Each student writes something that people need on his or her plate. Divide class into two groups. Groups stand on opposite sides of the room. At your signal, all students toss paper plates Frisbee-style across the room.

3. Each student catches or picks up one plate. Student writes an example of a way to show God's love to someone with the need on plate he or she caught.

4. Students toss and catch plates again. Several volunteers read the needs and responses on plates. Lead students to discuss words and actions that can be used to show God's love by asking one of the Discussion Questions below.

Option

After students have written needs and responses on plates, students take turns tossing plates into a box or wastebasket. When a plate lands in the box or basket, student answers a question.

Discussion Questions

1. Read 1 John 3:18. **Why do you think it is important to show God's love instead of just talking about it?**

2. **What are some words that describe the way people who show God's love act?** (Joyful, peaceful, patient, kind, good, faithful, gentle, etc.)

3. **What are some ways you can show God's love to someone this week?**

Frozen Poses

Bible Focus ▸ Luke 6:27-28; 7:1-10

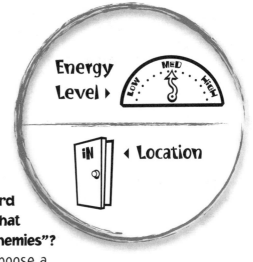

Energy Level ▸ LOW MED HIGH

iN ◂ Location

Materials

Bibles, children's music CD and player; optional—large sheet of paper, marker.

Lead the Game

1. **What kind of motion would remind you of the word "friends"?** (Shaking hands, giving a high-five.) **What kind of motion would remind you of the word "enemies"?** (Clenched fist, crossed arms.) Lead students to choose a motion for each word.

2. **The Jews of Bible times called the Romans enemies because they were under Roman rule. But one time Jesus healed a Roman ruler's sick servant. Let's talk about some ways we can help people become our friends instead of enemies.** As you play the CD, students move randomly around the room. After playing a song for 30 to 60 seconds, stop the music. Call out either "friends" or "enemies." All students must freeze in the appropriate pose. If you called out "friends," ask a volunteer to tell a way to show God's love and friendship to someone others dislike (Smile at the person. Don't make fun of the person. Talk to him or her.). (Optional: List students' responses on large sheet of paper.) If you called out "enemies," ask a volunteer to tell a way to show God's love and friendship to someone who has been mean to him or her (Forgive. Ignore the person's actions. Pray. Be kind instead of mean.). Play game as time permits. Ask the Discussion Questions during the music pauses.

3. After playing the game, invite volunteers to each tell one of the ways of showing friendship he or she can do this week. Tell students what you plan to do also. (Optional: Refer to the ideas for showing friendship listed on the paper.)

Discussion Questions

1. Read Luke 6:27-28. **Why do you think God wants us to love our enemies?**

2. **How can you love your enemies?**

3. **What would happen if kids your age prayed for their enemies?** Tell an answer before asking kids to respond.

Good Sam Relay

Bible Focus ▶ Luke 10:25-37

Energy Level ▶ LOW MED HIGH

Location ▶ iN OuT

Materials

Bibles, masking tape, adhesive bandages, basket, 10 coins.

Preparation

Make a starting line on the floor with masking tape. For each team, make an X on the ground with masking tape about 5 feet (1.5 m) from the starting line. About 5 feet (1.5 m) on the ground beyond the X, place a bandage for each player. Near the wall opposite the starting line, place the basket. Set coins a few feet in front of the basket.

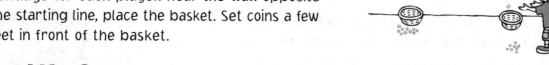

Lead the Game

1. **Let's play a game to help us remember the story that Jesus told about someone who was traveling to Jericho.**

2. Divide class into teams. Students form pairs within teams. Ask a pair to help you demonstrate how to complete the relay. Partners run to X on ground. One player lies on X and is the Hurt Man. The other player runs around player twice. Then partners switch roles. Next, partners run to bandages, place one bandage on each other and then run to basket. Each partner tosses a coin into basket. Partners run back to team and then the next pair begins relay.

3. At your signal, the first pairs run the relay. The first team to complete the course wins. Ask the winning team one or more of the Discussion Questions and repeat game as time allows.

Discussion Questions

1. **Who helped the hurt man?** (A Samaritan.) **Why was it unusual for the Samaritan to be kind to a Jewish man?** (Jews and Samaritans had been enemies for many years.)

2. **What did the Samaritan do that was kind?** (He bandaged the man's wounds, took him to an inn and paid the innkeeper to take care of the man.)

3. **Why did Jesus tell this story?** (To explain whom our neighbor is. To show that we should be kind to anyone in need.)

Human Pretzel

Bible Focus ▸ Acts 17:16-34; 2 Timothy 2:24-25

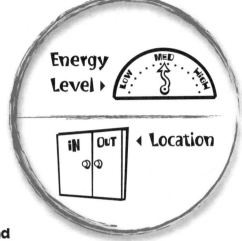

Energy Level ▸

iN OUT ◂ Location

Materials

Bibles.

Lead the Game

1. **When Paul preached the truth of Jesus to the people of Athens, he showed respect for their culture and customs. We can show God's love through attitudes and words that are gentle and respectful. Let's try to use gentle and respectful words to help each other out of a tangled situation!**

2. Divide class into groups of six to eight students each. Each group stands shoulder-to-shoulder in a circle, facing inward.

3. Students hold hands and then tangle the circle without letting go of each other's hands. Students may step over hands, move under raised arms, etc.

4. **Now see if you can get untangled without letting go of each other's hands!** Remember to work together and use gentle, kind and respectful words while you are untangling! Students gently untangle themselves. (Note: Students do not need to be facing the same direction after being untangled.)

Options

1. Model conversation by using a kind tone as you walk between the groups and suggest ways for students to get untangled. (For example, "Sam, what if you lift your hand up and over Jill's head?")

2. After older students have completed the activity once, they may regroup and race against each other in the untangling process. Remind students to use gentle and respectful ways of talking about what to do.

Discussion Questions

1. **What are some gentle and kind words you like to hear?** ("Thank you." "Sorry." "You can have the first turn." Words that are encouraging instead of bossy. Words that show we care about the other person.) **When is it hard to use kind and gentle words?**

2. **Why is it important to have gentle and respectful attitudes when we are trying to show God's love to others?** (Love is gentle and kind. Arguing with people doesn't help them to know about God's love.) Ask an older student to read 2 Timothy 2:24-25 aloud.

3. **Think of one person you would like to have a more gentle and respectful attitude toward. What is a way you can show gentleness to that person this week?**

Kindness Circle

Bible Focus ▸ Acts 3:1-10

Materials

Bibles, large sheet of paper, marker, playground ball or tennis ball.

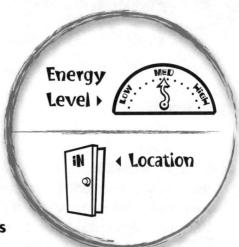

Energy Level ▸

iN ◂ Location

Lead the Game

1. Peter showed kind actions by healing a man who couldn't walk. Our kind actions demonstrate God's love. In our game we'll show some kind actions.

2. **What are some kind actions we can do?** (Listen to someone who is upset. Give someone flowers. Call someone who is sick. Sweep floor for a grandparent.) List students' ideas on large sheet of paper.

3. Choose one volunteer. Other students stand in a large circle, spreading their legs so that each student's right foot is touching the left foot of the student next to him or her. Volunteer stands in the middle of the circle. Give ball to the volunteer.

4. Volunteer rolls the ball toward a student in the circle, trying to get the ball between the student's legs. Students in circle may use hands to bat away the ball, but they cannot move their feet. If volunteer gets the ball past a student, that student goes to the middle of the circle and pantomimes a kind action from the list on the large sheet of paper. Students guess kind action being pantomimed. First student to guess pantomimed action takes a turn rolling the ball. If volunteer does not get the ball past any student, volunteer rolls ball again. After three unsuccessful tries, volunteer pantomimes a kind action before a new student is chosen to roll the ball. Continue playing game as time allows.

Discussion Questions

1. **What are some kind actions you can do at home? At school? In your neighborhood?** (Let your brother or sister choose which video to watch. Help your parents empty the dishwasher. Invite a new kid to play a game at school. Carry groceries for a neighbor.)

2. **Why do your kind actions help other people learn about God's love?** (They can see some of the ways God cares for them. They might ask why you are being kind, and you can tell them about God's love.)

3. **What is one kind action you can do this week? For whom?**

Kindness Toss

Bible Focus ▸ 2 Kings 4:8-37; Matthew 5:7

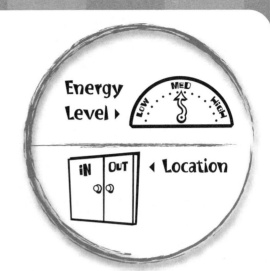

Energy Level ▸ LOW MED HIGH

iN OUT ◂ **Location**

Materials
Bibles, large container, index cards, soft balls or beanbags, marker.

Preparation
Place the container on the floor on one side of the playing area.

Lead the Game

1. **God's prophet Elisha showed kindness to a woman whose son had died. God will help us look for ways to be kind to others and care for them. Let's try doing that during our game today!**

2. Group the students into teams of six to eight. Teams line up single file about 5 feet (1.5 m) from the container. Give each student an index card. Give the first student on each team a ball or beanbag.

3. Stand near the container with the marker in your hand. Students from each team take turns tossing the ball or beanbag into the container. Each time a student gets the ball or beanbag into the container, print one letter of the word "kindness" on his or her index card.

4. When a student gets all the letters for the word, he or she continues taking turns, giving any letters scored to the next person in line. Continue until all students have "kindness" written on their cards.

Discussion Questions

1. **How did we show kindness in this game?** (Gave letters to other people.)

2. **What are some other ways to be kind to and care for others?** (Include everyone in your games. Ask someone to play with you if he or she is looking lonely. Share with others. Help someone or get help for someone who needs it. Use kind words when you speak to others.)

3. Read Matthew 5:7 aloud. **Jesus taught that it is good to show mercy to others. What can you do to discover ways to be kind to others?** (Pray and ask God to help you think of kind things to do. Take more time to notice the people around you instead of just doing your own thing.)

Listen Up!

Bible Focus ▸ Zechariah 7:9

Energy Level ▸ LOW MED HIGH

iN ◂ Location

Materials

Bibles, large sheet of paper, marker, masking tape.

Preparation

Print the words of Zechariah 7:9 on a large sheet of paper. Display the paper in your playing area.

Lead the Game

1. **Listening to others and treating them fairly show God's goodness. Let's play a game to practice listening to others.**

2. Students form two equal teams. Whisper a number to each student on each team (for example, whisper the numbers one through eight if there are eight students in the team). Do not give out the numbers in order.

3. Students walk around the playing area and clap the number you whispered to them. They may not talk to each other; they must listen to the number of claps to figure out what number each student was given. Students line up in their teams in numerical order.

4. The first team to line up correctly says Zechariah 7:9 in order, each student saying one word at a time, referring to the paper as needed.

5. Begin a new round of the game, whispering a different number to each student. Students play again as above.

Discussion Questions

1. **How does listening to other people help you show God's goodness to them?** (God listens to and cares for us, so we are showing other people what He is like when we listen to and care for them.)

2. **What does Zechariah 7:9 tell us to do? How might listening to someone be a way to show mercy and compassion for them?** (When you listen to people, you can find out what they need or how they are feeling, and then you will know how to best help them.)

3. **When is it hard for kids your age to treat other people fairly? What can you do in those situations to treat people fairly and show them God's goodness?**

Memory Moves

Bible Focus ▸ John 15:12

Energy Level ▸ LOW MED HIGH

iN ◀ Location

Materials

Bibles, large sheet of paper, marker, tape.

Preparation

Print John 15:12 on large sheet of paper and display paper where students can read it.

Lead the Game

1. **We can follow Jesus' example by showing love to people others ignore. Let's play a game that reminds us to show love to others.**

2. Ask a volunteer to read John 15:12 aloud. **Jesus spoke these words. What did Jesus command in this verse?** (To love others like Jesus has loved us.) Students say verse together.

3. Students stand in a circle. In order around the circle, assign each student a word of the verse for which to create a motion. Each student thinks of and practices a simple motion for his or her word.

4. To begin, the student with the first word of the verse says word while doing motion. The next student says the first word while doing the first student's motion and then says his or her own word while doing his or her motion. Continue around the circle, each student saying and doing the previous words and motions and adding his or her own word and motion until the entire verse is recited with motions. Invite volunteers to try saying the entire verse with motions.

Discussion Questions

1. **What kinds of people does Jesus love?** (All people, even people whom others ignore.)

2. **In what ways did Jesus show love to people when He was on Earth?** (Talked to them. Helped them with their problems. Cared for them. Fed them.) **What can we do to follow Jesus' examples of loving people?**

3. **When are some times kids your age get ignored?** (At school on the playground. At a friend's house.) **What are some ways to show love to these kids?** (Talk to them. Invite them to play a game with you. Share school supplies with them.)

Name Game

Bible Focus ▸ Genesis 1:26-27; 2:7,15-23

Materials
Bibles.

Game Tip
Print "Vowel = Jump" and "Consonant = Squat" on a chalkboard or a large sheet of paper for students to refer to during the game.

Energy Level ▸

LOW MED HIGH

iN ◂ Location

Lead the Game

1. **God created us to know Him and love each other. One way to care for others is to learn their names. Let's play a fun game with everyone's name.**

2. Group students into teams of six to eight students each. Teams line up in single-file lines leaving at least 4 feet (1.2 m) between each team.

3. **In our game today, each person will take a turn to call out to his or her team the letters of his or her name. When a vowel (A, E, I, O or U) is said, team members jump up in the air. When a consonant (any of the other letters) is said, team members squat down. Let's practice with my first name.** Call out the letters of your first name; all students jump up and squat down according to the letters called.

4. At your signal, the first student on each team begins calling out the letters of his or her first name while the other students on the team jump up or squat down according to the letter called. When the first student is done, the second team member calls out the letters of his or her name with teammates responding as above. Each team continues the process as quickly as possible, sitting down as soon as all members of the team have spelled out their names. Ask a volunteer from the first team to finish to answer one of the Discussion Questions below. Students form new teams and play again as time allows.

Discussion Questions

1. **What are some ways we can get to know God?** (Read the Bible. Listen to older people who love God talk about Him. Ask your parents, pastor or teacher questions about God.)

2. **What are some of the things you already know about God?** Volunteers respond.

3. **Why should we show love to other people?** (To show God's love. Jesus tells us that loving God and loving others are the most important things to do.) **What are some ways to show love to other people?**

Overflowing Love

Bible Focus ▸ 1 Thessalonians 3:12

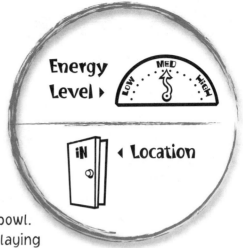

Energy Level ▸

iN ◂ Location

Materials

Bibles, dried beans, measuring cup, two of each of the following: large plastic bowls, spoons, large paper cups, shallow baking pans or boxes.

Preparation

Pour at least three cups of beans into each plastic bowl. Place plastic bowls and spoons on one side of the playing area. Put paper cups in shallow pans or boxes and place them on the opposite side of the playing area.

Lead the Game

1. **Being kind means doing good things for others without expecting anything in return. Let's play a game about a Bible verse that tells us how God helps us to be kind.**

2. Divide class into two teams. Teams line up in single-file lines next to spoons. Read 1 Thessalonians 3:12 aloud. **What does this verse ask God to do?** ("Make your love increase and overflow.") **You'll know your love is over-flowing when you show love and kindness to others without even thinking about what they might give you in return.**

3. **In this game, see how long it takes to make your team's cup overflow with beans.** At your signal, the first student on each team takes a spoonful of beans, walks quickly to his or her team's cup, drops in the beans, returns to his or her team and hands the spoon to the next player. Any spilled beans need to be picked up. Next student in line repeats action. Relay continues until both teams have made their cups overflow with beans, and the beans spill into the pan or box. Repeat as time allows, asking the Discussion Questions below between rounds.

Discussion Questions

1. **When are some times it's easy to show kindness to others?** (When others have been kind to us.) **When might it be hard?** (When we're angry.)

2. **What can we do when we don't feel like being kind?** (Ask God's help. Remember God's kindness to us.)

3. **What are some ways you could let kindness overflow with your family? Your friends at school? Someone you dislike?** Students respond. **What good things might happen?**

Paper-Airplane Fun

Bible Focus ▸ Luke 6:36

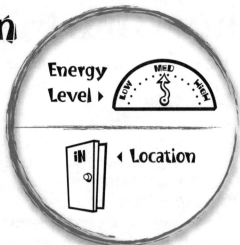

Energy Level ▸

Location

Materials

Bibles, paper, markers.

Preparation

Practice making a paper airplane following sketches below. Print "share food with friend" on a sheet of paper and then fold paper to make airplane.

Lead the Game

1. Fly prepared airplane to a student. Student unfolds airplane and reads aloud what is written on it. **To share food with a friend is something we can do during lunch at school or when a friend comes to our house to play. What is a way you might share food that is not expected?** (Share food with a homeless person or cook a meal for a needy family.) Student writes idea on paper airplane, refolds it and flies it back to you. Discuss the idea of showing mercy to others in unexpected ways, asking the discussion questions below.

2. Each student writes on separate papers two or three situations in which they could show mercy to other people (someone got hurt on the playground, parent had a hard day at work, kid is sitting all alone in the lunch room, etc.). Students make paper airplanes from papers on which they wrote.

3. Students form two teams. Teams stand against opposite walls of the room. Volunteer from each team throws one airplane to the opposite team. Team unfolds airplane and reads situation aloud and then works together to think of a way to show mercy in that same situation. Team writes idea on airplane, refolds it and flies plane back. Continue with new volunteers from each team as time permits, discussing situations and responses.

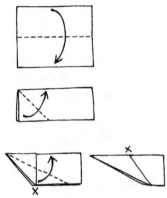

Discussion Questions

1. **How does Luke 6:36 tell us we should act?** (Merciful.) **What does it mean to be merciful?** (To show kindness or love beyond what is expected.)

2. **How can we show mercy in an unexpected way at school? In our neighborhood? To people living in other countries?**

3. **What are examples of showing mercy and helping someone who is hurting on the outside?** (Get help for someone if they are injured.) **On the inside?** (Choose the new kid at school for your baseball team if he or she is lonely.)

Red Carpet Crossing

Bible Focus ▸ Genesis 13:1-9; Romans 12:18

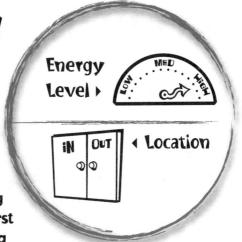

Energy Level ▸ LOW MED HIGH

iN OUT ◂ Location

Materials
Bibles, two sheets of red construction paper for every pair of students.

Lead the Game

1. **Abram made peace with his nephew Lot by letting him choose which land to live in. Putting others first can help us be peacemakers. Let's practice putting others first by playing a game where we must help others.**

2. **Red carpets are often laid down for important people to walk on as they enter buildings. When we treat someone as being important or special, we say we are giving him or her the "red-carpet treatment." In this game, we'll practice putting each other first by giving each other the red-carpet treatment with these papers.**

3. Students form pairs on one side of the classroom and decide which student in each pair will be the helper. Give each pair two sheets of red construction paper. At your signal, each helper lays down a sheet of paper for his or her partner to step on. Helper places the next paper one step away and partner moves to that sheet. Helper picks up first sheet and places it in front of his or her partner. Pairs move in this manner to the opposite side of the playing area and then race back to their starting positions. Winning pair answers one of the Discussion Questions below.

4. Students switch roles and repeat game. (Replace paper that has torn.)

Option
If there is not enough room for all pairs to play at one time, have them form teams of up to six pairs each. Teams complete game in relay fashion, one pair from each team going at a time.

Discussion Questions

1. **How did you put others first in this game?** (Moved the paper for them, so they could get across the floor and finish the game.)

2. Say Romans 12:18 aloud. **What are some ways to put others first at home? At school?** (Stop what you are doing to help your mom when she asks. Let your sister have the last cookie. Let your classmate have the first turn at the computer.)

3. **How does putting others first help us make peace?** (Keeps fights from starting. We show we care for the other person.)

Relaying Love

Bible Focus ▸ Luke 10:25-37

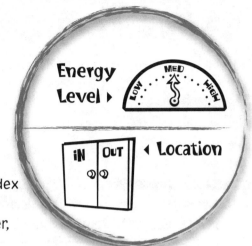

Energy Level ▸ LOW MED HIGH

iN OUT ◂ Location

Materials

Bibles, index cards, marker.

Preparation

Print each of these kinds of people on separate index cards: baby, old person, basketball player, soccer player, toddler, movie star, teenager, race car driver, juggler.

Lead the Game

1. **In Bible times, Jewish and Samaritan people didn't get along. So Jesus told a story about a Samaritan who helped a Jewish man who had been robbed and beaten. Loving God means loving all kinds of people. We're going to play a game in which we need different kinds of people to play.**

2. Group students into two equal teams. Teams line up on one side of an open area in your classroom. Stand between the two teams.

3. At your signal, the first student in each team runs to you. Show him or her one of the cards you prepared. Student returns to his or her team and then moves across the room and back as though he or she is a (basketball player). Students continue taking turns until all students on the team have had a turn. Play as many rounds of the game as time permits.

Options

1. Make additional cards to use in the relay: tiptoe, walk backwards, jump, hop, slide, etc.

2. Place a chair or cone on the opposite side of the room from each team. Students must move around the chair or cone to complete the relay.

Discussion Questions

1. **What kinds of people were needed to play this game?** (Toddler. Basketball player.)

2. **One way to love God is to show His love to all kinds of people. How can you show love to people who are different from you?** (Play with or talk to kids you don't usually play with. Ask a new person to sit with you and your friends at lunch. Don't join in with others who are making fun of someone else.)

3. **Why does God want us to love others?** (Because God made and loves all people. Each person is important to God.)

Shout It Out

Bible Focus ▸ Galatians 6:2

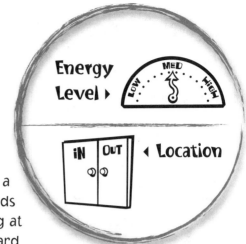

Energy Level ▸

iN | OuT ◂ Location

Materials
Bibles, blindfold.

Lead the Game

1. Students play a game like Marco Polo. Blindfold a volunteer. Volunteer begins calling out "Who needs help?" Students respond "I know," while moving at random around the room. Volunteer moves toward students by listening to their voices. Volunteer continues asking question and students respond until volunteer has tagged a student.

2. Tagged student names a type of disability (blindness, deafness, etc.), and then volunteer tells a way to show God's love to person who has the named disability. Ask some of the following questions to help students think of ways to show God's love to people with different kinds of disabilities: **What are some other kinds of disabilities people might have?** (Cannot see or hear. Have difficulty moving or talking. See words or pictures differently.) **What are some ways people with these disabilities might need help?** A blind person might need to be told when someone else comes in or out of the room. A person in a wheelchair might need a door opened or something carried for him or her. A deaf person might need to see your mouth to be able to read your lips when you talk.)

3. Repeat activity with new blindfolded volunteers and discussing different types of disabilities as time allows. Ask the Discussion Questions between rounds.

Game Tip
If blindfolded volunteers are not able to tag students quickly enough, students stand frozen while they respond to volunteer.

Discussion Questions

1. Read Galatians 6:2. **How does this verse say to treat others?**

2. **How can you help carry the burden of a friend who can't see? Can't hear? Can't move easily? Is in a wheelchair?**

3. **What are more ways to show God's love to people with disabilities?**

Three-Legged Race

Bible Focus ▸ 2 Kings 5

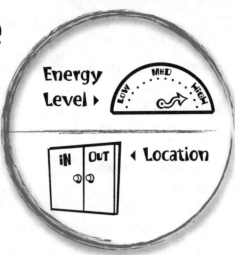

Energy Level ▸ LOW MED HIGH

Location ▸ iN OuT

Materials

Bibles, scarves or fabric strips at least 21 inches (52.5 cm) in length.

Lead the Game

1. The prophet Elisha helped a king's leader to be healed of leprosy. Helping others is something we can do to show God's love to others. Let's play a game in which you have to help your partner.

2. Group students into pairs. Guide pairs to tie inside legs together with a scarf or fabric strip (see sketch). Allow students time to experiment walking around an open playing area in your classroom or outdoors. **What makes it hard to move quickly? What can you do to make it easier?**

3. Pairs stand on one side of open playing area in your classroom or outdoors. At your signal, pairs race to the other side of the playing area. Repeat race several times or as time and interest permit.

Discussion Questions

1. **What are some other games in which the players need to help their teammates?** (Soccer. Volleyball.) **How do players in these games help each other?**

2. **What are some ways in which others have helped you?**

3. **What are some ways in which you can help someone younger than you? Older than you?**

Verse Bowl

Bible Focus ▶ 1 Corinthians 13:7

Energy Level ▶ LOW · MED · HIGH

◀ Location iN

Materials

Bibles, Post-it Notes, marker, 10 empty plastic soda or water bottles, pencils, tennis ball.

Preparation

Print the words and reference of 1 Corinthians 13:7 on Post-it Notes, one word on each note. Stick each note on a plastic bottle. Also print the words and reference of 1 Corinthians 13:7 on a sheet of paper. Photocopy one verse paper for each student. Set plastic bottles in a bowling-pin formation on one side of the playing area.

Lead the Game

1. **God's patience with us shows us how to be patient with others. Let's play a game to find out a little more about patience.**

2. Give each student a verse paper and a pencil. Ask a volunteer to read the verse aloud. Students line up about 7 feet (2.1 m) from the verse bottles.

3. The first student in line rolls the tennis ball at the bottles. Student takes verse paper and pencil over to bottles and reads words on the knocked-over bottles. Student crosses off those words on the verse paper, returns bottles to original positions and goes to the end of the line. Next student in line repeats action. Play continues until all students have crossed off all words on their papers. The students who finish first may assist the other students by reading words on bottles and setting them back in place.

Discussion Questions

1. **When did you have to be patient in this game?** (Waiting for your turn. Waiting for others to finish crossing off words.) **Which word in our verse is most like the word "patience"?** ("Perseveres.") **Perseverance means continuing to do something even when it is hard and patience means waiting without complaining.**

2. **How does God show patience toward us?** (He forgives us when we're sorry. He takes care of us, even when we don't thank Him.)

3. **When are some times you can be patient with your family? With your classmates?**

Wall-Building Relay

Bible Focus ▸ Nehemiah 1—4; 6:15,16;
1 Thessalonians 5:11

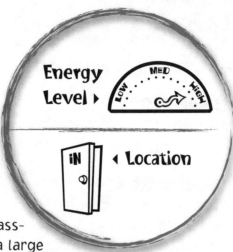

Energy Level ▸ LOW MED HIGH

iN ◂ Location

Materials

Bibles, large sheets of paper, masking tape, Post-it Notes, stopwatch or watch with second hand.

Preparation

Tape two large sheets of paper on one wall of the classroom, leaving space between the two papers. Place a large stack of Post-it Notes next to each paper.

Lead the Game

1. The good news about being in God's family is that we can encourage one another to love and obey God and to do His work! That's what happened when Nehemiah and some others in Israel worked together to rebuild the wall around Jerusalem. Let's work together to build our own wall.

2. Group students into two teams. Teams line up on opposite side of the playing area from the sheets of paper.

3. At your signal, start your stopwatch and send the first student on each team to his or her team's paper. Student sticks a Post-it Note onto the bottom part of the paper and then returns to line. Next student in line runs to wall and repeats action. Students on each team continue taking turns building their team's wall.

4. After several minutes, call time. Compare the walls built and ask a volunteer from the team with the largest wall to answer one of the questions below. Then ask students to answer the other Discussion Questions. If time allows, turn papers over for students to play the game again.

Option

Instead of using Post-it Notes, students build walls by taping newspapers to long lengths of butcher paper.

Discussion Questions

1. **Why is it important to encourage other people?** (It is a way to follow God's command to love one another.) Have an older student read 1 Thessalonians 5:11 aloud.

2. **What are some things that we could call God's work?** (Caring for needy people. Praying for others. Telling others about Jesus.)

3. **What are some things you could do or say to encourage others to do God's work?** (Pray for them. Offer to help them.)

Life Application Games

Telling Others About Jesus

Fast Phrase

Bible Focus ▸ Matthew 3; John 1:29-34

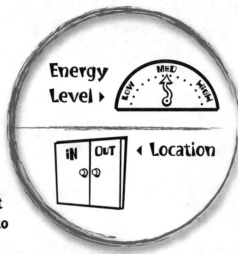

Energy Level ▸ LOW MED HIGH

Location ◂ iN OUT

Materials

Bibles.

Lead the Game

1. **John the Baptist's announcement about Jesus helped everyone know—even people today—that Jesus is the Savior. We're going to play a game to announce that great news, too!**

2. Choose a volunteer to be the "announcer." At your signal, students begin walking around the room at random. When the announcer says "Hear this! Hear this!" students stop walking, spin around where they stand and sit down on the floor as quickly as they can. The first student to sit down tells something he or she knows about Jesus or answers one of the questions below and becomes the new announcer. Repeat play as time and interest allow. (If the first student to be seated has already been the announcer, he or she chooses someone who hasn't yet had a turn to be the announcer.)

Option

Invite the announcer to say "Hear this! Hear this!" in an attention-grabbing way: loudly, clapping on each syllable, etc.

Game Tip

If it is difficult to determine who is the first student seated, call out another criteria (student wearing the most blue, whose birthday is closest, most letters in last name, etc.).

Discussion Questions

1. **Some people learned that Jesus is the Savior by hearing John's announcement or by seeing Jesus being baptized. What are some ways you have learned that Jesus is God's Son, the Savior?**

2. **What does it mean to say that Jesus is the Savior?** (Jesus saves us from the punishment we deserve for our sins.)

3. **How might a kid announce that Jesus is God's Son, the Savior?** (Tell a friend what he or she knows about Jesus. Ask a friend to come to church.)

He's Alive! Relay

Bible Focus ▸ Matthew 28:1-10; Mark 16:1-11; Luke 24:1-12; John 20

Materials

Bibles, large sheets of brown or gray paper, scissors, black markers; optional—Post-it Notes, pencils.

Preparation

Cut paper into rock shapes, creating one "rock" for every four to six students. Place paper rocks on one side of the playing area. Place a black marker next to each paper rock.

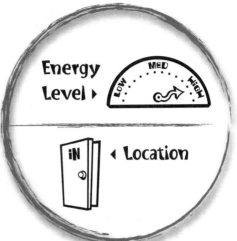

Energy Level ▸

◂ Location

He is risen! hallelujah Jesus is alive!

Lead the Game

1. **John the Baptist's announcement about Jesus helped everyone know—even people today—that Jesus is the Savior. We're going to play a game to announce that great news, too! When Mary Magdalene went to Jesus' tomb on Easter morning, what did she find?** (The stone had been rolled back and the tomb was empty.) **Mary, Peter and John discovered that the tomb was empty because Jesus had risen from the dead and was alive! What did they all do next?** (Told everyone that Jesus had risen!)

2. **What are some things we can say to share the good news about Jesus' resurrection?** ("Jesus is alive!" "He is risen!" "Christ conquered death!" "Hallelujah!" "Jesus rose!") List students' responses on a large sheet of paper. (Optional: Each student writes one phrase on a Post-it Note.)

3. Group students into teams of four to six, creating at least two teams. Teams line up across the playing area from the paper rocks. At your signal, the first student from each team runs to his or her team's paper rock, writes one good news phrase on the rock, calls out the phrase and returns to his or her line, tagging the next student, who repeats the action. (Optional: Student sticks Post-it Note phrase on rock.) Students refer to list of responses during relay if necessary. Relay continues until all students have had a turn. Repeat relay as time permits.

Discussion Questions

1. **What does Jesus' death and resurrection mean for us?** (Our sins can be forgiven when we believe in His death and resurrection. Jesus has the power to forgive our sins.)

2. **What do you want to do when you hear the good news about eternal life through Jesus' death and resurrection?** (Tell others. Thank God. Celebrate.)

3. **With whom can you share this good news?**

Hop and Tell

Bible Focus ▸ Acts 14:8-20

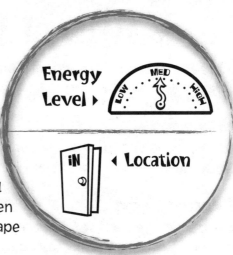

Energy Level ▸ LOW MED HIGH

iN ◂ Location

Materials

Bibles, markers, butcher paper, masking tape.

Preparation

On butcher paper, draw one large snail-shaped spiral for every five students. Divide each spiral into a dozen spaces, marking the center circle "REST" (see sketch). Tape each paper spiral to the floor.

Lead the Game

1. **The Apostles Paul and Barnabas healed people and preached Jesus wherever they went. To help others learn about God, we can tell them about the great and wonderful things He has done. In our game today, we are going to practice telling some of those great and wonderful things!**

2. Gather students into groups of five, instructing each group to stand at one of the snail-shaped spirals.

3. The first student in each group hops on one foot all the way around the spiral to the "REST" circle where he or she can rest on both feet before turning and hopping back on one foot. If he or she hops back and forth without hopping on any lines or putting both feet down (except in the "REST" circle), student writes a great and wonderful thing God has done in any one of the spaces. Next student repeats action and if he or she is successful, student writes a great and wonderful thing God has done in another space. Continue game until all students have written something or as time allows.

Option

Rather than preparing snail-shaped spirals ahead of time, allow groups to create their own game paths in class. Suggest curved or zig-zag path options.

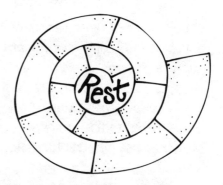

Rest

Discussion Questions

1. **What are some of the great and wonderful things God has done that you wrote down?**

2. **What are some more great things God has done that you have read about or heard about in the Bible?** (Created the world. Saved Noah and the animals from the flood. Sent Jesus to us. Pushed back the waters of the Red Sea, so the Israelites could escape the Pharaoh of Egypt.)

3. **What are some great things God has done for you or other people you know?** (Took the punishment for sins. Answered prayers. Showed His love to us.)

Secret Pass-Off

Bible Focus ▸ Matthew 3:13-17; Mark 1:4-11; John 1:29-34

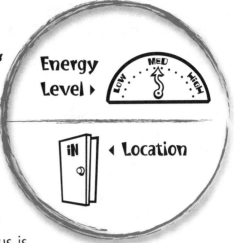

Energy Level ▸

Location ▸ iN

Materials

Bibles, small index cards, marker.

Lead the Game

1. **When Jesus was baptized, God announced from heaven that Jesus is His Son. Let's play a game to make some other announcements about Jesus.**

2. **What are some true sentences about Jesus?** (Jesus is God's Son. Jesus died and rose again. Jesus came to earth and was born as a baby. Jesus healed blind people. Jesus made the sea calm.) List sentences on separate small index cards.

3. Students stand in a circle (shoulder-to-shoulder if possible) to play a game similar to Button, Button, Who's Got the Button? Choose one student to be "It." "It" stands in the middle of the circle and closes eyes.

4. Give one of the index cards to a student in the circle. "It" opens eyes. At your signal, students pass card around the circle behind their backs, trying to keep "It" from seeing who has the card. After 20 to 30 seconds, signal students to stop passing card. "It" tries to identify who has the card. After "It" guesses or after two tries, student holding the card reads aloud the announcement about Jesus. (Give help with reading as needed.) Choose a new volunteer and repeat play with a different index card as time allows.

Options

1. Play music from a children's music CD while students pass cards.

2. If you have a large group of students, students pass more than one index card at a time.

Discussion Questions

1. **God spoke from heaven to tell everyone that Jesus is His Son. What are some ways people make announcements today?** (By e-mail or on a web page. Send a letter or flier. Tell the news on the radio or TV. Send announcement.)

2. **What did Jesus do as God's Son?** (Died to save all people from their sins. Healed people. Cared for the sick and the poor. Taught people how to love others.)

3. **How can we help people today learn that Jesus is God's Son?** (Invite them to church. Tell them stories about Jesus.)

Sprint to Share Jesus

Bible Focus ▸ Acts 26; 1 Peter 3:15

Energy Level ▸ LOW MED HIGH

◂ Location iN OUT

Materials

Bibles, masking tape, one spoon for every 6 to 8 students, dry beans.

Preparation

Make a masking-tape line on one side of an open playing area.

Lead the Game

1. **The Apostle Paul told about Jesus to everyone he could. He often was thrown in prisons and had opportunity to speak to important leaders. Just like Paul, it is important for us to keep on telling people about God our whole life, looking for ways to share God's love with others in every situation. In our game today, we are going to discuss different ways to share God's love.**

2. Group students into teams of six to eight. Teams line up single file opposite the masking-tape line. Hand a spoon to the first student on each team. Place five or six beans in each spoon.

3. At your signal, the first student from each team moves across the playing area to the masking-tape line. Students may use only one hand to hold the spoon, trying not to drop any of the beans and putting spilled beans back in spoons before continuing. Once they have crossed the line, students turn around and return to their teams. Then, students pass the spoons to the next players who continue in the same manner until all team members have had a turn.

4. Volunteer from the first team to finish tells a situation when kids could tell others about God and share His love.

Discussion Questions

1. **What are some ways to share God's love at home? In your neighborhood?**

2. Read 1 Peter 3:15 aloud. **Why is it important that when you tell someone about God's love, you also treat them and other people around them with love and kindness?**

3. **What are some things you could tell others if they asked you about God?** (How Jesus loves me always. How God answers prayers.)

W·I·T·N·E·S·S

Bible Focus ▸ Acts 1:8

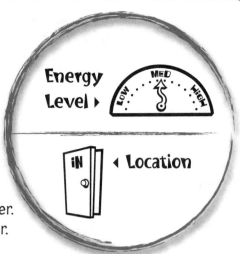

Energy Level ▸

iN ◂ Location

Materials
Bibles, large sheet of paper, marker, masking tape, soft ball, large container.

Preparation
Draw a line down the center of a large sheet of paper. Print "Team 1" on one side and "Team 2" on the other. Display in classroom.

Lead the Game

1. **Jesus' disciples witnessed, or saw, the miracles Jesus did. The miracles showed everyone Jesus is God's Son. So when the disciples went out and "witnessed," they were telling others about Jesus.** Divide class into two teams. Play a basketball-type game similar to H-O-R-S-E. Teams take turns attempting to toss ball into a container. Each time ball lands in container, team writes a letter of the word "witness" on its side of the paper.

2. When one team completes the word, a volunteer from that team answers one of the discussion questions below.

3. The first team to finish tells a situation when they could tell others about God and share His love.

Option
Divide the group into teams by a new method for each round. Try one or more of the following: Students line up in alphabetical order according to the first letter of first names. Divide line evenly. Students group themselves by a color on their clothes or the kind of shoes they are wearing. Combine groups to make two even teams. Students line up in order of the last digit of their phone numbers. Divide the line into teams.

Discussion Questions

1. **Why do you want to be part of God's family?** (Tell your own reasons for becoming a Christian before asking students to tell reasons. Also be careful to not push students who are not comfortable answering the question.)

2. Read Acts 1:8 aloud. **What does God give us to be able to witness Jesus to others?** (The Holy Spirit).

3. **What are some ways you can tell others about Jesus?**

Witness Walkabout

Bible Focus ▸ Acts 28:17-31

Energy Level ▸ LOW MED HIGH

iN ◂ Location

Materials

Bibles, children's music CD and player, construction paper, markers, stopwatch or watch with second hand.

Lead the Game

1. **Paul wanted to go to Rome so he could tell the Romans about Jesus. The Book of Acts tells us Paul spent two years in Rome writing and telling others about Jesus.** Distribute construction paper to students. **What kinds of people could you talk to about Jesus?** (Parents. Brothers. Sisters. Older neighbors. Younger kids. Grandparents. Grocery store workers.) As students name specific people, students take turns writing people on separate sheets of paper. Make a list on a single paper for your own reference. Continue printing specific people on papers until there is a paper for each student. **What are some of the ways we can tell others about Jesus?** (Show a video about Jesus. Answer their questions about Jesus. Tell what you have learned from reading the Bible or from Sunday School. Give them a book about a Bible story. Write a letter about when you chose to believe in Jesus.)

2. Play a game like a Cakewalk with students. Place people papers in a circle on the floor. Play song for 20 to 30 seconds as students move around the circle. When music stops, each student stands on the paper closest to him or her. Name one of the people from your list. Student standing on that paper says something about Jesus he or she can tell that person. If student needs help thinking of things to tell others, ask the Discussion Questions below.

Discussion Questions

1. **Who is Jesus? What did He do for all people? Why is that important? What is the most important thing you know about Jesus?**

2. **When did you first learn about Jesus? Who talked to you about Jesus?**

3. **What are some things you could tell others if they asked you about God?** (Jesus loves me. God forgives me. God loves everyone and wants everyone to believe in Jesus.)

Recreational Games

All Together Now

Materials
Chalk, masking tape or rope, several balloons.

Preparation
Make a start and finish line with chalk, masking tape or rope on the ground approximately 20 yards (9m) apart. Inflate balloons.

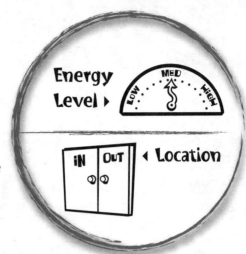

Energy Level ▶ LOW MED HIGH

iN OUT ◀ Location

Lead the Game

1. Divide group into two teams. Each team stands behind the starting line and makes a tight circle with their hands extended into the middle. Each team member grabs a hand of two other team members. The teacher places a balloon on the top of each team's grasped hands (see sketch).

2. When the teacher says "Go!" each team runs to the finish line and back keeping the balloon on top of their grasped hands. It is against the rules to wedge the balloon between arms. If a team lets the balloon drop, they must start over. The first team to complete the race wins.

Option
For a greater challenge, increase the number of balloons for each relay run.

A-MAZE-ing Art

Materials

Outdoor area with asphalt or concrete surface, sidewalk chalk in various colors.

Preparation

Secure the outside area before the game.

Lead the Game

1. Divide group into teams of three or four players. Give each team a variety of chalk.

2. Each team uses chalk to draw a complicated maze on the ground. First, players draw a simple outline of the path. Then they fill in the outline with details such as dead-ends and obstacles. When the mazes are complete, teams take turns trying to walk through each other's mazes.

Option

Team can draw mazes on paper with pencils or colored pens if outdoor space is not available. Teams trade papers and try to solve each other's mazes.

Back to Balloons

Materials

Chalk, masking tape or rope, chair, several inflated balloons.

Preparation

Make a starting line with chalk, masking tape or rope. Place a chair at the opposite side of the playing area.

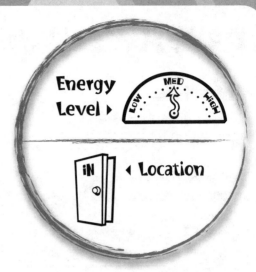

Energy Level ▸ LOW MED HIGH

iN ◂ Location

Lead the Game

1. Divide group into teams. Children in each team group themselves into trios. (One or two may need to participate twice to even out the trios.) Both teams stand behind the starting line. The first trio on each team must stand back-to-back and lock arms. The teacher places a balloon between their backs (see sketch).

2. When the teacher says "Launch!" the first trio on each team must go around the chair at the opposite side of the playing area and back to the starting line without dropping the balloon. Then the balloon is given to the next trio, who runs the relay following the same procedure as the first trio. The relay continues until each team member has participated. If a trio drops their balloon, they must start their leg of the relay again. The first team to finish wins.

Option

To play an outdoor version of this game, use small beach balls instead of balloons.

Bail Out!

Materials

Inflatable two- or three-man raft or small wading pool, water, two or three empty plastic one-gallon milk jugs, craft knife, sidewalk chalk or rope.

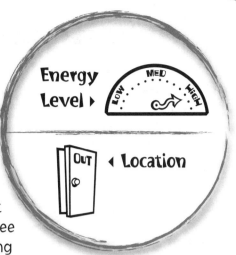

Preparation

In outdoor area, fill raft or wading pool with water. Cut off the neck of each milk jug to enlarge the opening (see sketch a). Use sidewalk chalk or rope to make a starting line about 20 feet (6 m) from raft. Make a finish line about 10 feet (3 m) beyond raft.

Lead the Game

Does anyone know what SOS means? (Save Our Ship.) **Our "ship" is full of water! To save it, we'll have to bail it out.** Divide class into two or three evenly numbered teams. Teams line up behind starting line. Give the first player on each team a milk jug. At your signal, first player on each team carries milk jug to raft, fills jug with water and runs to finish line. Player then flings water out past finish line and runs back to give jug to next player. The first team to have all players complete the relay wins.

Game Tip

Explain how it's become common for us to connect SOS to the phrase "Save Our Ship," but actually SOS doesn't stand for anything! It was adopted in 1906 as an international distress signal because Morse code for SOS (• • • — — — • • •) is easy to send by telegraph and unlikely to be misinterpreted.

a. Cut.

b.

Balloon Kisses

Materials

One balloon for every two children plus a few extras, chalk or masking tape, measuring tape.

Preparation

Use chalk or masking tape to mark off two lines 30 to 40 feet (9 to 12 m) apart. Inflate balloons.

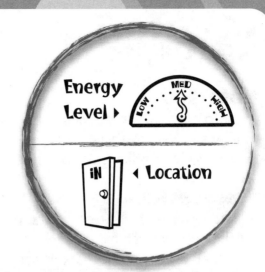

Energy Level ▶ LOW MED HIGH

iN ◀ Location

Lead the Game

1. **At a hot air balloon rally, one of the races involves one balloon "kissing" another balloon. This is done when one balloon flies close enough to touch another balloon. Today we will play a game that imitates this balloonist trick.**

2. Divide group into teams of four players. Members of each team then divide into pairs. Give each pair a balloon. One pair in each team stands at one starting line and the other pair stands opposite their teammates on the other starting line. Partners stand side-by-side and link arms.

3. When the teacher says "Launch!" all the partners on both sides gently hit their balloons into the air with their free hands, trying to keep balloons up as they run toward their teammates. If the balloon drops to the ground they may pick it up, but must keep their arms linked. If the balloon pops, teacher provides a replacement. When each pair reaches their teammates, they continue to hit their balloons into the air to make their balloons touch. When the balloons touch, team shouts "Balloon Kiss." Pairs hold onto their balloons and run back to their starting places. Each pair then repeats process to accomplish two more balloon kisses, then they return to their starting positions and sit down. The first team with all members sitting wins.

Option

For a wet—and more difficult—version of this game, use water balloons.

Batty Tag

Materials

Masking tape or rope.

Preparation

Use masking tape or rope to mark two boundary lines about 40 to 50 feet (12 to 15 m) apart.

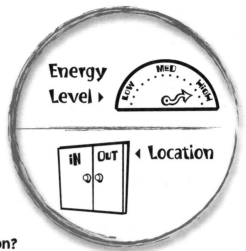

Energy Level ▸ LOW MED HIGH

iN OUT ◂ Location

Lead the Game

1. **What are some animals you might see in a canyon?**
(Cougars, deer, eagles, otters, beaver, rabbits, etc.)
What is one animal you might see flying at night or in a cave? (A bat.) **Bats aren't dangerous animals. In fact, they can be good to have around your camp. Why are bats good to have around?** (They eat insects.) **One bat can eat 600 mosquitoes in an hour! In this game, see how many mosquitoes our bat can catch.**

2. Choose a volunteer to be the Bat. The Bat stands in the center of playing area. The rest of the players are Mosquitoes and stand behind either boundary line. At leader's signal, the Mosquitoes run back and forth between boundary lines, whilethe Bat attempts to tag them. When they cross the boundary line, they are "safe." Tagged players join hands with the Bat to become the Bat's wings. The Bat continues to chase Mosquitoes, with players on each end of the chain tagging Mosquitoes. Once the Bat has six players, call out **Split!** and have the chain become two Bats. Play continues until only one Mosquito remains. The remaining Mosquito becomes the first Bat for the next round.

B-Ball Tag

Materials

Masking tape, chalk or rope, measuring tape, one or more basketballs or playground balls; optional—four sports cones.

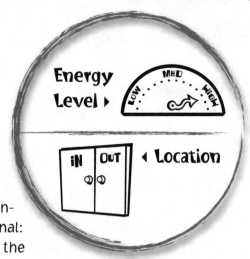

Energy Level ▶ LOW MED HIGH

iN OUT ◀ Location

Preparation

Using masking tape, chalk or rope, mark off a rectangular playing area 10x20-feet (3x6-m) in size. (Optional: Use four sports cones to define the four corners of the playing area. Or play game on a basketball court.)

Lead the Game

Choose one or more students to be Dribblers. Hand each Dribbler a ball. All other players position themselves within the playing area. On your signal, Dribblers begin dribbling as they attempt to tag another player. Players move to avoid being tagged, but stay inside the playing area. If a player is tagged, he or she takes the Dribbler's place and tries to tag other players.

Option

For younger children, adapt the game as follows: Dribblers carry the ball. At teacher's signal, Dribblers stop to bounce and catch the ball once before continuing to tag other children.

Beach Bowling

Materials

Several bags of sand, chalk or rope, measuring stick, two buckets, water, two softballs, two pieces of paper, two pencils, four 16-oz. plastic drinking cups; optional—two plastic trash bags.

Energy Level ▸ LOW MED HIGH

◂ Location OUT

Preparation

Pour two piles of moistened sand on pavement or grass. (Optonal: Pour sand on top of plastic trash bags for easy clean up.) Set buckets filled with additional water close to sand piles for additional dampening if needed. Use chalk or rope to make a line about 10 feet (3 m) from each pile of sand (see sketch a).

Lead the Game

1. Divide group into two equal teams. With plastic cups, two members of each team mold sand into six sand bowling pins (see sketch b). They act as ball retrievers and "pin setters" and stand near bowling pins.

2. The other members of each team line up behind lines. Player number one on each team rolls softball, trying to knock down as many sand pins as he or she can. Teams write down number of sand pins knocked down, then the "pin setters" rebuild pins. The first player then replaces one "pin setter," who goes to the end of the team line. Then second player of each team bowls and then replaces the other "pin setter." This continues until each player has had a turn to bowl or until time is up. Teams total their points. Team with the highest score wins.

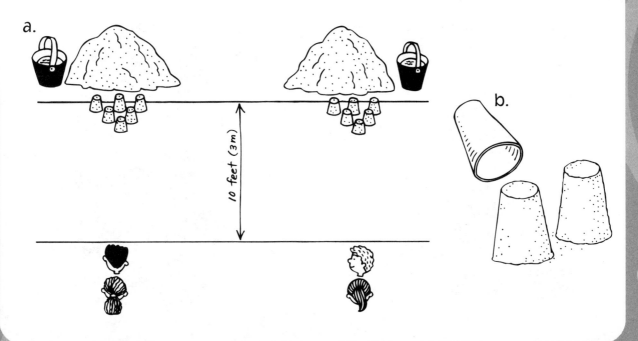

a.

10 feet (3m)

b.

Beach Fun Relay

Materials

Four laundry baskets or boxes, water, chalk or rope, beach equipment (boogie board, kick board, sand shovel, snorkeling mask, swim fins, etc.), measuring stick; for each child—at least one water balloon.

Energy Level ▶ LOW MED HIGH

OUT ◀ Location

Preparation

Place water balloons in two baskets or boxes—an equal number in each basket or box. Mark a starting line with chalk or rope. Place an empty basket or box for each team on starting line. Approximately 15 feet (4.5 m) away, place a water balloon basket or box for each team (see sketch).

Lead the Game

1. Divide group into two equal teams. Pass out beach equipment. Each player selects one item of beach equipment to use in transporting the water balloons.

2. At your signal, the first player on each team races to his or her team's basket of balloons. The player selects a water balloon, and then transports balloon back to his or her team's empty box using the beach equipment. (Examples: Carry balloon on kick board. Carry balloon while wearing swim fins. Carry balloon with sand shovel.) If a water balloon breaks in transit, the player may go back to the balloon box, select another water balloon and try again. (You may wish to set a limit of two tries for each player.) Once the team member returns, the next player races to retrieve a balloon. The team with the most balloons in their box wins.

Crab Balloon Ball

Materials

5 balloons (or more), water, chalk or rope, pitcher, large cardboard box, measuring tape.

Preparation

Pour approximately two tablespoons of water from pitcher into each balloon. (The water helps stabilize the balloons when they're being hit in the air.) Inflate balloons, tie them and put them in the box. Make a line down the middle of the playing area.

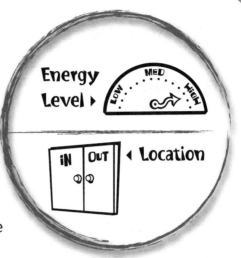

Energy Level ▸ LOW MED HIGH

iN OUT ◂ Location

Lead the Game

1. Divide group into two teams. Team A plays on one side of the line and team B plays on the other side. Team members spread out and get into crab positions (on hands and feet, backs to the ground, see sketch). If crab position is too difficult for children, they may play on their hands and knees.

2. Teacher tosses a balloon to Team A. A player on Team A, while staying in the crab position, uses a hand or foot to volley the balloon over the line to Team B. Teams volley the balloon back and forth as long as possible, using hands or feet. Players can move around, but they must stay in the crab position. When the balloon hits the ground, the teacher throws it back to the team that last hit the balloon. If the balloon pops, the teacher replaces it with one of the balloons in the box. (Keeping score as in volleyball is optional.)

Option

Give a balloon to each team and see how many times they can hit the balloon before it touches the ground.

20 feet (6 m)

Crab Walk

Materials
Rope, measuring tape.

Preparation
On grassy area, use rope to mark off two lines 30-feet (9-m) long and 15-feet (4.5-m) apart.

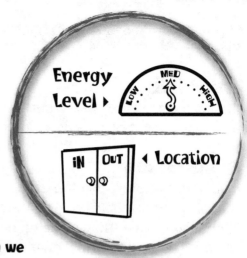

Energy Level ▸

iN OUT ◂ Location

Lead the Game

1. **Crabs have eight legs and walk sideways. Today we are going to have a crab race.** Divide group into teams of four players. Each team will work together to move as a crab. Each team sits down along the start line (see sketch a).

2. First team member sits cross-legged and rests hands on the ground. The second team member wraps his or her legs around the waist of the first team member (see sketch). The third and fourth team members wrap their legs around the waist of the team members ahead of them (see sketch b).

3. When the teacher says "Go!" each "crab" begins to move sideways, using hands to propel themselves to the finish line. The first "crab" to reach the finish line wins. If a "crab" breaks apart, it must stop until all players are reattached.

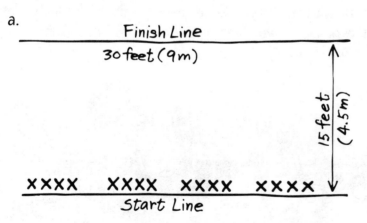

a.

Finish Line

30 feet (9m)

15 feet (4.5m)

XXXX XXXX XXXX XXXX

Start Line

b.

Crazy Beach Ball

Materials

Chalk or masking tape, measuring stick, rope or volleyball net, two poles secured in ground or in stands, large inflated beach ball.

Preparation

Use chalk or tape to mark a volleyball court (20x30 feet [6x9 m]) on floor, pavement or grass area. Stretch rope or volleyball net between poles, approximately 4 feet (1.2 m) from the ground (see sketch).

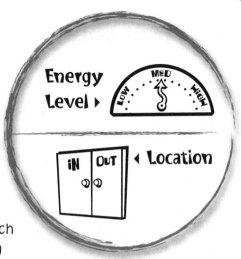

Lead the Game

Game is played similar to volleyball. Each team may have up to nine players (three rows of three players). To start each set, the server tosses the ball over the net from the front row. The ball may be hit with any part of the body above the waist. The ball is allowed to hit the ground once on each side before it is returned over the net. If the ball hits the ground twice before being returned, the opposing team scores a point regardless of which side served. The ball may be hit up to five times before it must go over the net. The ball may not be held. If a team hits the ball out of bounds, the opposite team scores one point. The first team to get 15 points wins.

Cybersharks

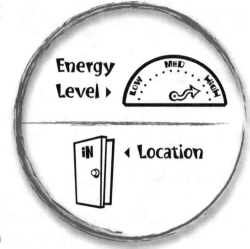

Energy Level ▸

iN ◂ Location

Materials

Large dark-colored tarp or plastic sheeting in a nearly 10-foot (3-m) square shape for every 20 children.

Lead the Game

Children sit around the edge of the tarp or plastic sheeting with their legs underneath it. Choose two children to be the "Cybersharks" and four children to be the "Rescuers." The rest of the class holds onto the edge of the tarp and waves it up and down. The two Cybersharks crawl underneath the tarp and randomly grab players' legs to try to "suck" them into their cyberspace under the tarp. The Rescuers try to pull players from the grasp of the Cybersharks. Cybersharks must stay on their hands and knees at all times. If a player is pulled under the tarp, he or she becomes another Cybershark. When only a few players remain holding the tarp, choose new Cybersharks and Rescuers to play another game.

Game Tip

Though this game appears rough, with adequate supervision it is great fun and works well.

cybershark

rescuer

Hares and Hounds

Materials
Several colors of chalk, balloons, masking tape.

Preparation
Make a starting line with chalk or masking tape. This game must be played on an open paved area such as a parking lot.

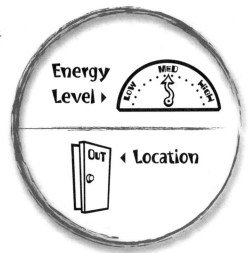

Energy Level ▶ LOW · MED · HIGH

OUT ◀ Location

Lead the Game

1. Divide group into teams of five players. Each team lines up behind the starting line. Each team chooses a member to be a hare. Each hare is given a different color of chalk and a balloon. The hares inflate their balloons without tying them off. The rest of the team members are hounds. Give each hound a balloon to inflate and tie.

2. When the teacher says "Launch," the hares let their balloons go. Wherever each hare's balloon lands, he or she marks a number one on the pavement. The hares continue inflating and releasing their balloons until they each have four numbers in their own color of chalk on the pavement. Then the hare runs back to his or her team and tags the first hound.

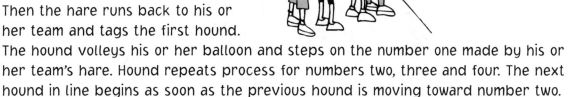

The hound volleys his or her balloon and steps on the number one made by his or her team's hare. Hound repeats process for numbers two, three and four. The next hound in line begins as soon as the previous hound is moving toward number two.

3. The teacher watches carefully to make sure each hound steps on the correct numbers. (A hound must keep volleying balloon in the air as he or she moves toward a number.) When each team member has completed this task he or she returns to the starting point and sits down. The first team to be sitting together wins.

Game Tip
This game works best with older children. For younger children, randomly mark numbers on ground before the game and have kids simply touch each number as they keep the balloon in the air, running as a relay team.

Hold the Ropes

Materials

Eight chairs, one inflated balloon for each team, plus a few extras, one 6-foot (1.8-m) rope for each team.

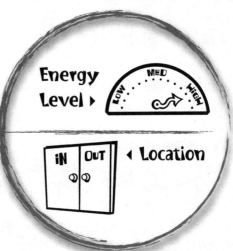

Energy Level ▸ LOW MED HIGH

iN OuT ◂ Location

Preparation

Place four chairs in a line along one end of the playing area and four chairs in a line on the opposite side at least 40 feet (6 m) apart.

Lead the Game

1. Divide group into four teams. Each team forms a line behind a chair. First player in each line is given a balloon and a rope. When the teacher shouts "Hold the ropes!" the first player on each team holds the balloon and the rope and runs around a chair at the opposite side, returning to his or her team. The first player hands the balloon to the second player. Then the first and second players, both holding the rope, run around the chair and back (see sketch).

2. The relay continues until the whole team is holding the rope, with the last player holding the balloon, as they run around the chair and back. If a player lets go of the rope or drops the balloon, the team has to return to the starting place and begin again. The first team to complete the relay wins.

Hoop Crash Race

Materials

Obstacles to get in the way of the hoops (chairs, books, boxes, etc.), masking tape, sidewalk chalk, or rope, two hula hoops.

Preparation

Create two similar obstacle courses that will provide a challenge rolling a hoop through. Mark a starting line for two teams to play side-by-side.

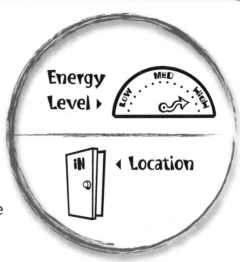

Energy Level ▸ LOW MED HIGH

iN ◂ Location

Lead the Game

Divide class into two teams. Each team lines up behind starting line. First player from each team places the hoop upright and rolls it through the obstacle course and returns to tag the next player. If the hoop falls over, the player rights it and continues on. First team to have all its players complete the relay wins.

Option

For an additional challenge, players use rulers to push the hoop through the course.

Human Foosball

Materials

Masking tape, chairs, tennis ball or soft foam ball.

Preparation

Tear off masking-tape strips (two for each student). Position chairs as shown in sketch.

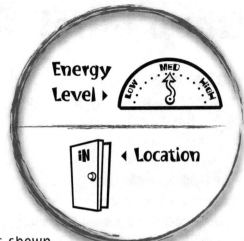

Energy Level ▸

LOW · MED · HIGH

iN ◂ Location

Lead the Game

1. Divide group into two teams. Position students as shown in sketch, both teams facing away from their respective goalie. Students should stand at least an arm's length from each other. Give each student two strips of masking tape. Students on one team make masking-tape Xs on floor to mark their positions. Students on other team make masking-tape Ls on floor.

2. Gently roll the ball toward the middle of the playing area. Students try to kick the ball toward their team's goal, each student keeping at least one foot on his or her masking-tape mark at all times and not touching the ball with his or her hands.

3. Students continue kicking ball until a goal is scored. (Note: Goalies only use their feet to defend goal.) Begin again by giving ball to a player from the team that did not score.

Options

1. Play outside with a soccer or playground ball, and use chalk to mark students' positions.

2. Players may be seated on chairs instead of standing on masking-tape marks.

3. If you have an uneven number of students, ask a volunteer to help you retrieve balls that roll out of the playing area. Rotate volunteer into the game after each goal is scored.

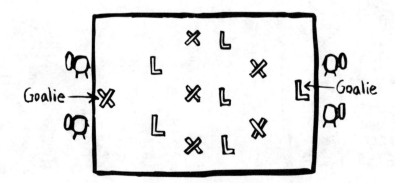

Goalie →

Goalie

Kings and Queens

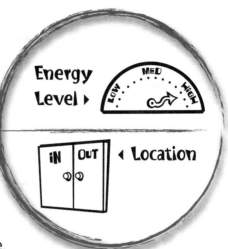

Energy Level ▸ LOW MED HIGH

iN OUT ◂ Location

Materials

Chalk, cones, rope or tape, 4 paper crowns, 4 paper collars (see sketch a), tape measure.

Preparation

Use chalk, cones, ropes or masking tape to mark two starting lines and two finish lines 30 feet (9 m) apart. Prepare paper crowns and collars (see sketch a) and place two crowns and two collars at each starting line.

Lead the Game

Children form two teams. Each team lines up behind their starting line. At teacher's signal, the first and second players on each team put on the crowns and cloaks. The first player takes the hand of the second player and races to the finish line. The first player removes his or her cloak and crown and stays at the finish line. The second player takes the first player's items and runs back to the starting line to give them to the third player to wear. Then the second player takes the third player's hand and runs to the finish line. The second player removes his or her cloak and crown and stays at the finish line while the third player and fourth players continue the game. The first team with all their players at their finish line wins.

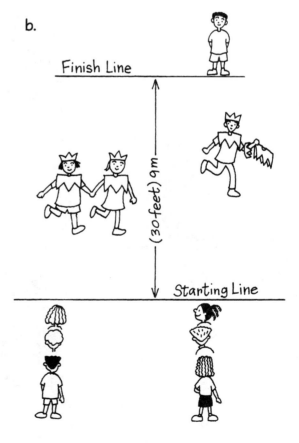

a.

fold↓   cut neck hole

18"

b.

Finish Line

(30 feet) 9m

Starting Line

Mass Transit

Materials

Chalk, 4 large appliance boxes, craft knife, whistle.

Preparation

With chalk, draw four starting lines on opposite sides of an open area at least 20 yards (18 m) square. Cut out two sides of each box (see sketch).

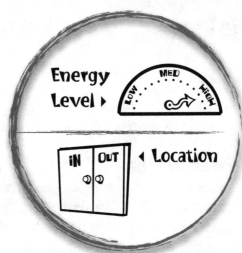

Lead the Game

1. Divide group into four teams. Each team chooses a name for their box for the race. Each team gathers at a starting line. Place a box by each starting line. Teacher acts as the leader of the race. When teacher blows the whistle, all team members get inside their box, lift the box and run to the opposite side of the playing area.

2. At the opposite side all team members must disembark from their box, run around it five times, give a high-five to each team member and get back in their gondola. Then the team runs back to its place. The first box to reach its starting place wins.

Newspaper Search

Materials

Identical newpapers or newspaper sections for each small group; optional—highlighter markers.

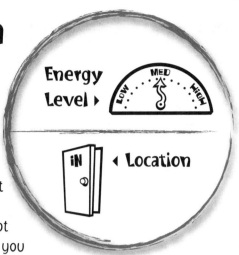

Energy Level ▶

iN ◀ Location

Preparation

Scan the newspapers ahead of time and choose about 10 items that the teams will have to find. Make a list of specific pictures, headlines, advertisements, etc. Jot down the page numbers in case you stump them and you need to show that the item is really there.

Lead the Game

1. Form a small group for each identical copy of newspaper.

2. Teams spread apart from each other (four teams may each use one of the four corners of the playing area). Give each team a newspaper. Call out the items one at a time. When a team finds the called item, they must rip it out and bring it to you or another designated leader. Optional: teams circle item with a highlighter marker and call out "Found it!" Check answer and if correct, move to next item.

3. Teams receive 50 points for correct answer. Only first team with correct answers receive points. Call out remaining items and keep score. Highest-scoring team wins.

Game Tips

1. This is a good game to build teamwork in small groups.

2. Ask church members to donate old newspapers so you have a supply on hand. Or get used newspapers at the end of the day from large hotels.

3. You could download pages from online newspapers and pass out identical copies to students.

Occupational Hazard

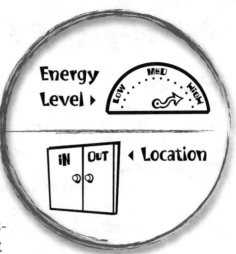

Materials

Large paper cups or cones, index cards, felt pen, props for occupations (see below).

Preparation

Arrange large paper cups or cones in a line to create a slalom course—one course for each team. Write the name of one occupation and the corresponding instructions on each index card (see ideas below). Make a set of cards for each team. At the beginning of each course, place cards and props for the occupations you choose.

Lead the Game

1. Instructions for each occupation:

   Baker: Carry a cracker on a spatula.

   Bricklayer: Take bucket of Legos to end of the course and build a wall using at least 20 Legos.

   Candlemaker: Carry candle in a candleholder through course.

   Carpenter: Carry five stacked blocks through course.

   Jester: Toss a tennis ball in the air while running through the course.

   Painter: Take a jar of mud or paint and a sheet of paper through course and then use fingers to paint a stick figure on the paper.

   Shepherd: Blindfold another member of your team. Without touching the team member, direct him or her through the course. Take off blindfold at the end of the course.

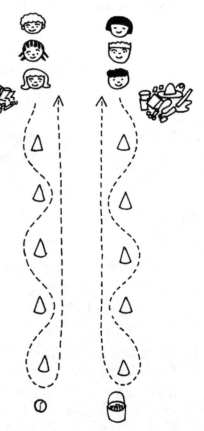

2. Teams line up behind index cards and objects. (Note: Cards do not have to be in same order for each team.) First player chooses an index card, takes the supplies he or she needs for that occupation and follows the instructions on the card for running the course. If player drops an item, he or she must stop and pick it up before continuing. Players leave supplies at the other end of the course and run straight back to tag the next player in line. First team to use all index cards is the winner.

Oops! Water Ball

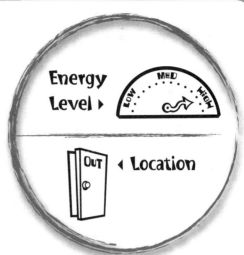

Energy Level ▶ LOW MED HIGH

◀ Location OUT

Materials

Volleyball net or rope and posts; sheets, blankets or plastic sheeting; clothespins; water balloons; water.

Preparation

Set up volleyball net in large outdoor area. Use clothespins to attach sheets, blankets or plastic sheeting across the entire width of the net. Teams should not be able to see each other (except for feet). Fill balloons with a small amount of water and tie to secure.

Lead the Game

Divide class into two equal teams. Begin play with only one water balloon. Teams toss the balloon back and forth across the net, trying to catch it and return it without breaking it. When the balloon breaks, the team who failed to catch it must shout "Oops Ball!" and the other team scores a point. Replace the broken balloon with two balloons (one for each side) and continue play. Add two balloons for each one that breaks. For added fun, poke a pinhole in some of the balloons so that players are squirted as they play.

Option

For a drier or indoor version, use Nerf-type balls instead of water balloons.

Reverse Baseball

Materials

Four bases, traffic cones or other large markers; rubber kickball; measuring tape.

Preparation

Set up bases, traffic cones or markers in a diamond shape as in regular kickball. Bases should be about 20 feet (6 m) apart.

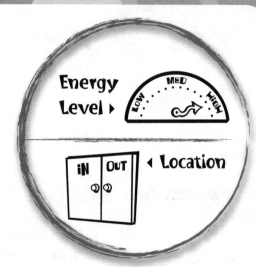

Energy Level ▸ LOW MED HIGH

iN OuT ◂ Location

Lead the Game

Divide class into two teams. Explain that the game is played like regular kickball; but in this "reverse universe," players must run around the bases backwards (going to third base first). Runners must be tagged with the ball to be out. If a runner reaches home base without being tagged, his or her team gets one point. Teams take turns after three outs.

Option

Increase the challenge by having players run the bases facing backwards as well.

home base

Robot Action

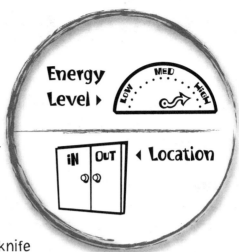

Energy Level ▸ LOW MED HIGH

iN OUT ◂ Location

Materials

Chalk or rope, two medium-sized boxes large enough to fit over children's heads, craft knife, markers and/or paint, old newspaper or recycled paper, two wastepaper baskets or cans, measuring tape, two sets of knee and elbow guards, two brooms.

Preparation

Use chalk or rope to mark a starting line. Use craft knife to cut two large eye circles out of each box. Use markers and/or paint to decorate each box to look like a robot's head. Crumple newspaper to make medium-sized trash balls—one for each player. Place trash balls in one big pile near the starting line. Place wastepaper baskets about 20 to 30 feet (6 to 9 m) from starting line. Wastebaskets will serve as the finish line.

Lead the Game

Divide class into two teams and have them line up behind starting line. First player on each team puts guards on knees and elbows and robot box over his or her head. Give both players a broom. Each "robot" sweeps one trash ball to the finish line, bends over to place the ball in the wastepaper basket and races back to tag the next player. The next player in line puts on the robot gear and continues the race in relay fashion. The first team to have all players dispose of a trash ball and return to the starting line wins.

shin guards

Robot-Wash Relay

Materials

Rope or chalk, one clothing item (sock, shirt) per child, two laundry baskets, four large wrapping-paper tubes, four shoeboxes without lids.

Preparation

Use chalk or rope to mark a starting line. Divide clothes evenly between the laundry baskets. Place baskets about 20 to 30 feet (6 to 9 m) from starting line.

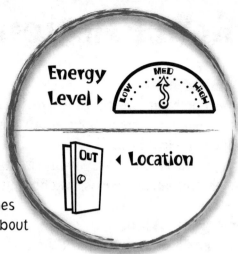

Energy Level ▸

LOW MED HIGH

OUT ◂ Location

Lead the Game

Divide class into two teams and have them line up behind starting line. First player on each team puts his or her feet in shoe boxes and arms in paper tubes. At teacher's signal, "robots" shuffle to their team's laundry basket and pick up one item of clothing with their tube arms. Holding clothing, the "robots" shuffle back to the starting line to tag the next players. Each player in line puts on the "robot" gear and continues the race in relay fashion. The first team to "wash" (retrieve) all their laundry and return to the starting line wins.

Rocket Launch

Materials

Volleyball net or rope, two sturdy chairs, water balloons, water, four small blankets or sheets.

Preparation

Tie volleyball net or rope across two chairs. Fill several water balloons with water and tie to secure.

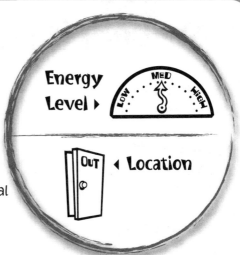

Energy Level ▸ LOW MED HIGH

OUT ◂ Location

Lead the Game

Divide class into four teams—two teams on each side of the net. Give a blanket or sheet to each team. Team members stretch the blanket or sheet taut. Choose one side of the net to make the first launch. Place water balloons in the center of both teams' blankets or sheets. Team members work together to "rocket" their balloons over the net. To improve teamwork, encourage teams to count backwards to launch saying, "3-2-1, launch!" Receiving teams try to catch the "rockets" on their blankets. Play continues back and forth across the net. (Note: Diagonal shots are allowed and will add greatly to the fun.) Teams score one point every time the receiving team fails to catch the "rocket" on their blanket or sheet. Replace broken "rockets" with new ones. For fun, poke a pinhole in one of the water balloons, so children get squirted as they play.

Option

For an indoor version of this game, use beanbags instead of water balloons.

Rowboat Race

Materials

Rope, tape measure.

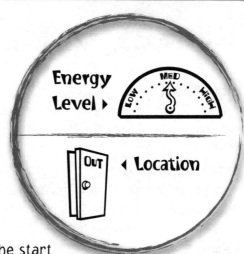

Energy Level ▶ LOW · MED · HIGH

OUT ◀ Location

Preparation

On grassy area, use rope to make a start and finish line about 15 feet (4.5 m) apart.

Lead the Game

1. Divide group into pairs. Each partner A sits on the start line with legs extended straight out and knees together. Each partner B sits facing partner A with soles of shoes touching. Partner B has knees bent and clasps hands of partner A (see sketch a).

2. To move, partner B pulls partner A until knees are in a bent position (see sketch b). then partner B pushes back to straighten his or her legs and pushes partner B's legs back into a bent position (see sketch d). This pushing and pulling motion "rows" players along, about a yard at a time. Give each pair a few minutes to practice "rowing." Then say, "Rowing positions!" Partners position themselves behind start line. On the command "Go!" the pairs begin rowing to the finish line. The pair that reaches the finish line first wins. If a pair breaks apart, they must stop and retake this rowing position before they begin rowing again.

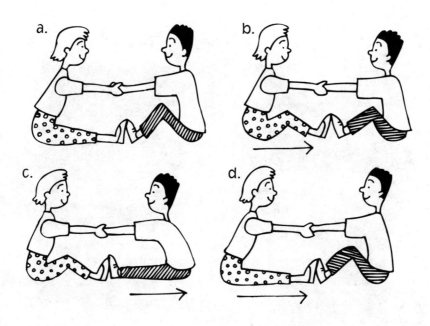

Shoot the Rapids

Materials

Two Slip'n Slides (or two 4x20-foot [1.2x6-m] lengths of heavy plastic sheeting), garden hose and faucet, two 5-foot (1.5-m) lengths of rope, two inner tubes or small inflatable rafts, several towels.

Energy Level ▸ LOW MED HIGH

▸ Location OUT

Preparation

Set up Slip'n Slides or plastic sheeting lengths on grassy area, parallel to each other. Attach hose to Slip'n Slide or have a helper hold hose over plastic during the game. Tie a rope to each innertube or raft and place at one end of each water slide.

Lead the Game

1. Children take off shoes and socks. Divide class into two teams. Each team forms pairs and lines up next to a water slide. **Some parts of a river are called rapids because the water moves very fast over the rocks. When people ride through the rapids on rafts, we call it shooting the rapids. Your partner will pull your raft through these wild river rapids, so hold on tight!**

2. Turn on water faucet. First player on each team sits on innertube or raft while partner walks alongside of water slide and pulls raft down slide. Partners switch places on their return trip. Then the next pair of players "shoots the rapids." Continue until everyone has played. (Note: Children's clothing will get wet. At end of game, have them use towels to dry off as much as possible.)

Option

For a dry version of this game, set sports cones in a grassy area to make two obstacle courses. Make "rafts" by tying ropes around innertubes, putting them inside plastic bags and knotting bags to close around ropes. One player from each team sits on raft while a partner pulls raft through obstacle course. Partners switch places for the return trip. Primary children may need to play this version without pulling another child in the raft. Either they may pull rafts empty through a slalom course or have a youth or adult volunteer pull them one way and then children pull raft back to start themselves.

Sports Switch

Materials

Sports cones, soft rubber or foam ball.

Preparation

Use cones to define the boundaries of a playing area about 30-foot (9-m) square.

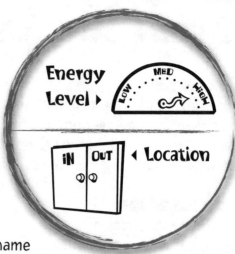

Energy Level ▸ LOW MED HIGH

iN OUT ◂ Location

Lead the Game

1. Divide class into four teams. Give each team the name of a major sport (baseball, football, basketball, hockey). Teams line up in four corners of playing area. One player is selected to be the Referee and stands in the middle.

2. The Referee calls out the names of two different sports teams. Teams with those names run to exchange places. The Referee tries to tag out one of the players by throwing ball at him or her. The hit player becomes the Referee for the next round. If the Referee calls out "Sports Switch!" all players must change places. Game continues as time allows.

Baseball
Hockey
Football
Basketball

Super Soccer

Materials
Two large heavy-duty trash bags; newspaper; duct tape; masking tape, chalk, or rope.

Energy Level ▸ LOW MED HIGH

◂ Location iN | OuT

Preparation
To make a giant ball, place one trash bag inside the other. Crumple sheets of newspaper into balls to stuff trash bags. When bags are full of newspaper balls, tie into a knot and secure with a length of duct tape. Wrap entire stuffed bag twice with tape, making a crisscross pattern (see sketch). Use masking tape, chalk or rope to mark goal lines at opposite sides of the playing area, approximately 20 feet (6 m) apart.

Lead the Game
1. **Raise your hand if you've ever joined a soccer team.** Students respond. **Soccer is played by teams all over the world; but in many countries, it's called football!** Students play soccer using the ball you prepared. As in regular soccer, only the goalies can use their hands.

2. Divide class into two teams of six to eight students. Each team chooses a goalie to stand on the far side of his or her team's goal line. Students kick the ball down the field, to another teammate or across the goal line. A point is awarded each time the ball crosses a team's goal line.

Option
Try these alternate Ideas:

- Backwards Ball—While playing game, students walk, run and kick backwards.

- Three-Legged Soccer—Each team divides into pairs. Using a bandana or other fabric scrap, students tie ankles together and move as a unit to play game.

- Fabric Fun—Each team divides into pairs. Each student in each pair holds one end of a bandana or other fabric scrap as the game is played.

- Foosball—Students keep one foot frozen in place at all times as they play the game. Only the goalie has free movement. You may wish to use a regular soccer ball with this option.

Game Tip
This game is great for extra-large groups!

Switch-a-Towel

Materials

Sports cones, for every three or four players—large beach towel.

Preparation

Use cones to define the boundaries of a playing area about 30-foot (9-m) square. Spread out towels on ground inside playing area, leaving an open space in the middle (see sketch).

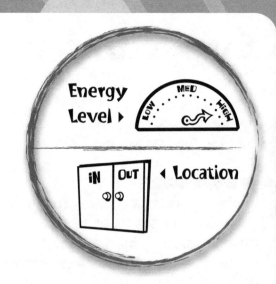

Energy Level ▸ LOW MED HIGH

iN OUT ◂ Location

Lead the Game

1. Select one player to be the Lifeguard. Lifeguard stands in the middle of the playing area while other players divide themselves out to stand on different towels.

2. Lifeguard points to two towels and calls out "Switch!" Players on each of the two towels run to the other towel while the lifeguard tries to tag them. Tagged players stand outside the playing-area boundaries; in succeeding rounds they may try to tag players without re-entering the playing area. If a Lifeguard calls out "All switch!" then all players must run to another towel.

Play continues until only one player remains untagged. That player becomes the Lifeguard for the next game.

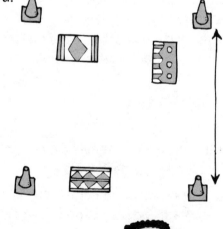

a.

Option

For older children, increase the challenge as follows: Lifeguard throws a soft foam ball to tag players. If the ball goes out of bounds, players who have been tagged out may pick up the ball and throw it back to the Lifeguard.

b.

Tower Tag

Materials

Rope, cones, tape or chalk; beanbags or handkerchiefs, two baskets.

Energy Level ▸ LOW MED HIGH

◂ Location IN OUT

Preparation

Using rope, cones, chalk or tape, mark two team lines approximately 50 feet (15m) apart. Mark another line to divide that area in half. Also, mark off a "tower area" in opposite corners of each team's play area. Place half of the beanbags or handkerchiefs on each team line. Place a basket behind each team line (see sketch). (Optional: Color-code the beanbags or use different items for each team.)

Lead the Game

1. Divide group into two equal teams. Each team stands on their half of the playing area. At the teacher's signal, players try to grab a beanbag from the opposing team's line and return it to their own basket without being tagged. Once a player has crossed the center line with an opposing team's item, he or she is "safe" and cannot be tagged. If a player is tagged by an opposing team member, he or she must forfeit the beanbag and stand in the opposing team's tower. An "imprisoned" player can be released only when a fellow teammate reaches the tower without being tagged and frees him or her. Both players then receive safe passage back to their teams.

2. The first team to collect all the beanbags from the other side or capture all the players on the opposite team wins.

Option

For a wet-game option, use water balloons instead of beanbags. Each team can have one or two colors of balloons for this game (team 1: yellow, red; team 2: blue, orange). For older students, tagging must be done with the water balloon (without it breaking—so no throwing).

Game Tip

This is an active game that will require refereeing.

Tower

Tower

25 feet (7.5m)

25 feet (7.5m)

Triangle Bowling

Materials

Rope, chalk, or masking tape; rubber kickball.

Preparation

Use rope, chalk or tape to outline a large triangle on the ground (the bowling-pin area) in the center of your playing area, large enough for up to 15 students to stand inside the triangle area comfortably. Make one setup for each group of 9 to 16 students. Approximately 25 feet (8 m) from each point of the triangle, draw or mark a foul line (see sketch).

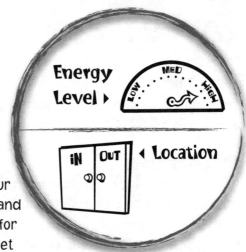

Energy Level ▸

Location ◂

Lead the Game

1. Choose one player as the Bowler and one as the Ball Return. All other players are Bowling Pins.

2. Pins stand inside the triangle area. They choose which foot they will pivot on. The Bowler stands behind the foul line and rolls the ball toward the Pins, attempting to hit the players. Pins can pivot on a foot in order to avoid being hit, but they must keep one foot on the ground. The Ball Return stands near the Pins and retrieves the ball each time and returns it to the Bowler. The Bowler gets two rolls. Teacher keeps score of Pins that Bowler hits.

3. After the Bowler is finished, the Bowler and Ball Return choose two new players and game begins again with all other players being the Pins. Game continues until all players have had a turn at being the Bowler and Ball Return. Announce the top-scoring winners.

Pins

Ball Return

Option

For younger kids, shorten the distance and have them jump with both feet to avoid being hit.

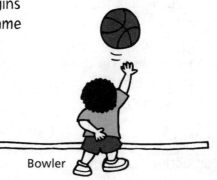

Bowler

Volleyball Relay

Materials

Masking tape, chalk, or rope; four sports cones; for every team of eight players—eight large Post-it Notes in one color (a different color for each team); one volleyball or beach ball.

Energy Level ▸ LOW MED HIGH

iN OuT ◂ Location

Preparation

Using masking tape, chalk or rope, make a large oval track on the playing area. Set out the sports cones on the track to mark quarter distances. Make a start/finish line next to one of the sports cones (see sketch).

Lead the Game

1. Students form teams of eight. Give each team eight Post-it Notes of the same color. (Optional: Students print their favorite numbers or their name on Post-it Notes.) Team members place notes on each other's backs. **At track events, the different team members wear tags made of large fabric squares. Numbers, names and sometimes the participant's country are written on the tags so spectators can identify who the runners are and to which team they belong.**

2. Two members of each team stand at each sports cone. At start/finish line, hand a ball to one player from each team. On your signal, the first players on each team toss their balls in the air and catch them as they run to the next sports cone. Students may not carry the balls. When each player reaches the next sports cone, he or she yells "Team Up!" and tosses the ball to one of his or her teammates, who then continues relay to the next sports cone.

3. Teams continue relay around the track twice so that all eight players run. The first team to have the last player cross the start/finish line wins.

Option

For younger children, have them carry the balls in their hands and only toss them to the next players.

Game Tip

This relay can be run with any number of students, provided the teams are even. Teammates simply distribute themselves evenly between the four sports cones. For instance, if you have six students on each team, two sports cones will have two players from each team and two sports cones will have one player from each team. The relay ends when the last runner on each team reaches the next sports cone.

Volunteer Hoops

Materials
Index cards in two (or more) different colors, two (or more) hula hoops.

Preparation
Mix up the index-card colors and randomly scatter them in your game-playing area.

Energy Level ▸ LOW MED HIGH

iN OUT ◂ Location

Lead the Game
1. Divide group into teams of three or four. Each team is assigned one of the colors of the index cards. Give each team a hula hoop. Teams spread out around the edges of your game-playing area.

2. Teams place hoop on ground and then all team members step into the hoop. Each team member holds the hoop with one hand. Teams will quickly move through the area, using their free hand to pick up their team's color of index card.

3. You can set a time limit or allow all the cards to be picked up by one team, to determine a winner. Mix up teams and play additional rounds.

Options
1. For older students, make a rule that no hoops can touch, causing the game to slow down and focus on team strategy to collect cards. Or you could assess penalty times for hoop touching. Simply make teams freeze for 10 seconds, while other teams continue to collect cards. You could also allow students to make up rules for the game.

2. Assign point values to cards, such as 100, 500, 1,000 points. Place the cards facedown so teams won't know the value until the card is picked up. You could also make wild cards that could give the team an advantage in the game, or even an instant-win card. The possibilities are endless!

Water Baseball

Materials

Masking tape, chalk or rope; measuring tape; baseball tee or sports cones; three sports cones, large trash can; water; baseball bat; large foam ball.

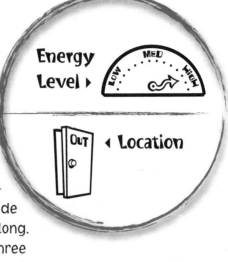

Energy Level ▸ LOW MED HIGH

OuT ◂ Location

Preparation

Using masking tape, chalk or rope, mark off a diamond-shaped playing area such as used in baseball. Each side of the diamond should be approximately 20 feet (6 m) long. Place baseball tee or sports cone at home plate and three sports cones at the points of the diamond. Place large trash can to the left of home plate and fill with water.

Lead the Game

1. Divide class into two teams. One team spreads out on the playing field with one player standing next to the trash can at home plate. The other team lines up near home plate. The first player in line stands at home plate with the baseball bat. Dunk ball in water in trash can until saturated and then place on tee or sports cone.

2. On your signal, the first player hits ball with bat and then runs around the diamond, touching the sports cones as he or she passes them. While batter runs, the players on the other team retrieve the ball and try to get it to the player at the trash can as quickly as possible. However, the players in the field cannot run. They can only throw the ball to each other. Player at home plate dunks the ball in the water in the can, ending the running player's turn. (Note: If this takes awhile, runner can run the bases two or more times.) If the ball is dropped, the nearest player runs to pick up the ball, and then returns to his or her position before throwing the ball to a teammate.

3. When the ball is in the can, the running player returns to home plate. His or her team is awarded one point for each sports cone that he or she touched while running. The next player in line takes a turn as described above. After three players have had a turn, teams switch positions. Continue until every student has had a turn at bat or as time permits.

Water Well Relay

Materials

Wading pool or large plastic bin; water; for each team of six to eight players—large coffee can and large car-washing sponge.

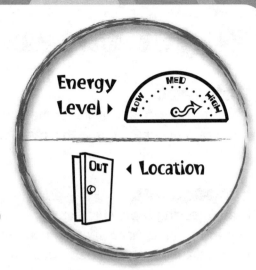

Energy Level ▶ LOW MED HIGH

OUT ◀ Location

Preparation

Fill wading pool or plastic bin with water. Place each team's coffee can and sponge about 20 feet (6 m) from the wading pool or plastic bin.

Lead the Game

1. **Many people in the world don't have running water to drink. To get clean water, they go to a well in the morning and gather water for that day's use. Let's play a game to carry water from the well** (indicate wading pool or plastic bin) **back to your water storage cans** (indicate coffee cans). **To give you an idea of how gathering water is hard work, we're going to use sponges to fill your cans!**

2. Divide class into teams of six to eight players each. Teams line up next to their coffee cans. At your signal, first player on each team carries the sponge to the well and fills it with water. Player runs back to team and empties cup into coffee can and passes cup to next player in line. Game continues as time allows or until each player has had a turn. The team with the most water in their can at the end of the game wins.

Option

For older players, choose a variety of ways to transport the sponge (hop, run backwards, etc.)

Game Tips

1. Show younger players how to hold a sponge under water to fill it.

2. You may want to use this game to introduce a foreign mission project.

Wheelbarrow Relay

Materials

Masking tape, index cards, clothespins, two baskets.

Preparation

Use masking tape to make a starting line and finish line at least 20 feet (6 m) apart on the floor. Place baskets on finish line.

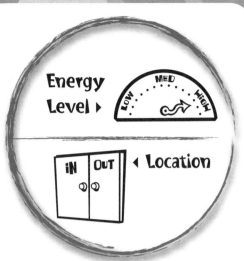

Energy Level ▶ LOW MED HIGH

iN OuT ◀ Location

Lead the Game

Divide class into two teams. Each team lines up behind starting line next to its cards. At your signal, the first student on each team clips an index card to his or her clothing and pretends to be the Wheelbarrow steered by the next player in line. The Wheelbarrow walks on hands toward the basket while the partner steers by holding the Wheelbarrow's feet (see sketch). At the basket, the Wheelbarrow stands up, drops card into basket, gives the clothespin to the partner and runs to the back of the line. The partner returns to the front of the line and is the next Wheelbarrow. Game continues in relay fashion until each student has had a chance to be a Wheelbarrow.

Option

Write words of a Bible verse on the index cards. Students place cards in order at end of game.

Game Tip

If you play this outside, have a pair of utility gloves for the Wheelbarrows to wear, especially if playing on asphalt. Wheelbarrows will hand off gloves during the game.

X Marks the Spot

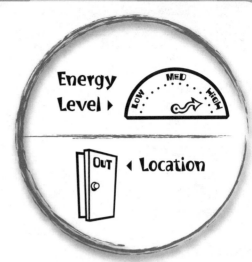

Energy Level ▶ LOW MED HIGH

◀ Location OUT

Materials

Chalk, several balloons.

Preparation

Use chalk to draw two large circles about 15 feet (3.5 m) in diameter. Make a large X in the middle of each circle. Inflate and tie balloons.

Lead the Game

1. Divide group into two teams. Each team sits inside one circle. Each team selects a helper who stands outside the circle. Give helper a balloon and a piece of chalk. When the teacher says "Launch," each helper throws a balloon into team's circle. Team members shout "warm air" and, without standing up, use their feet and hands to keep the balloon in the air. When the balloon is over the X, team members shout "cool air" and let it fall.

2. If the balloon touches the X, the helper gives the team a point by making a chalk mark on the pavement. If the balloon falls anywhere else, the helper retrieves the balloon and throws it into the circle again. When the teacher says "stop," the team with the most points wins.

Option

For older players, use several balloons in the circle at the same time.

15 feet (3.5 m)

Index of Games

Bible Index

Index of Games

Index of Games

Index of Games

Index of Games

Index of Games

Index of Games

Index of Games

Index of Games

Energy Level Index

Low

Medium

Index of Games

Index of Games

Index of Games

How to Use the CD-ROM

Getting Started:

- Insert the CD-ROM into the CD-ROM drive.

- Double-click on *The Really Big Book of Bible Games* pdf icon located on the CD-ROM.

- Once the file is opened you can manually scroll through the pages (using the scroll bar on the right of the Acrobat window), or you can access any game by clicking on the game title in the table of contents. At the bottom of each page the Return to Main Menu link will take you back to the game index.

- You can print single or multiple pages. In the Adobe Acrobat Reader print dialogue box select the appropriate button in the print range field. (Before printing please read "How to Make Clean Copies from This Book" on page 2.)

Problems?

If you have any problems that you can't solve by reading the printed or online manuals that came with your software, please contact the technical support department for the software manufacturer. (Sorry, but Gospel Light cannot provide software support.)

More Great Resources from Gospel Light

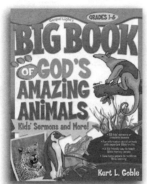

The Big Book of God's Amazing Animals

This book includes 52 lessons about a variety of animals that will intrigue kids, such as dolphins, penguins, koala bears, whales and condors. Each lesson relates facts about the featured animal to a particular Bible verse. As kids learn about fascinating animals that God created, they'll also learn about Him and how He wants them to live.

ISBN 08307.37146

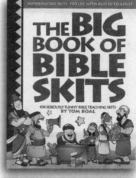

The Big Book of Bible Skits

Tom Boal

104 seriously funny Bible-teaching skits. Each skit comes with Bible background, performance tips, prop suggestions, discussion questions and more. Ages 10 to adult. Reproducible.

ISBN 08307.19164

The Really Big Book of Kids' Sermons and Object Talks with CD-ROM

This reproducible resource for children's pastors is packed with 156 sermons (one a week for three years) that are organized by topics such as friendship, prayer, salvation and more. Each sermon includes an object talk using a household object, discussion questions, prayer and optional information for older children. Reproducible.

ISBN 08307.36573

The Big Book of Volunteer Appreciation Ideas

Joyce Tepfer

This reproducible book is packed with 100 great thank-you ideas for teachers, volunteers and helpers in any children's ministry program. An invaluable resource for showing your gratitude!

ISBN 08307.33094

The Big Book of Christian Growth

Discipling made easy! 306 discussion cards based on Bible passages, and 75 games and activities for preteens. Reproducible.

ISBN 08307.25865

The Big Book of Bible Skills

Active games that teach a variety of Bible skills (book order, major divisions of the Bible, location references, key themes). Ages 8 to 12. Reproducible.

ISBN 08307.23463

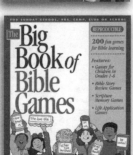

The Big Book of Bible Games

200 fun, active games to review Bible stories and verses and to apply Bible truths to everyday life. For ages 6 to 12. Reproducible.

ISBN 08307.18214

The Big Book of Bible Games #2

150 active games—balloon games, creative team relays, human bowling, and more—that combine physical activity with Bible learning. Games are arranged by Bible theme and include discussion questions. For grades 1 to 6. Reproducible.

ISBN 08307.30532

To order, visit your local Christian bookstore or www.gospellight.com

Gospel Light
God's Word for a Kid's World!™